Captive Market

Studies in Postwar American Political Development

Steven Teles, *Series Editor*

Series Board Members
Jennifer Hochschild
Desmond King
Sanford Levinson
Taeku Lee
Shep Melnick
Paul Pierson
John Skrentny
Adam Sheingate
Reva Siegel
Thomas Sugrue

Captive Market

Accountability and State Prison Privatization

ANNA GUNDERSON

OXFORD
UNIVERSITY PRESS

Oxford University Press is a department of the University of Oxford. It furthers
the University's objective of excellence in research, scholarship, and education
by publishing worldwide. Oxford is a registered trade mark of Oxford University
Press in the UK and certain other countries.

Published in the United States of America by Oxford University Press
198 Madison Avenue, New York, NY 10016, United States of America.

CIP data is on file at the Library of Congress
ISBN 978-0-19-762414-2 (pbk.)
ISBN 978-0-19-762413-5 (hbk.)

DOI: 10.1093/oso/9780197624135.001.0001

1 3 5 7 9 8 6 4 2

Paperback printed by LSC Communications, United States of America
Hardback printed by Bridgeport National Bindery, Inc., United States of America

Contents

Acknowledgments

It is difficult to remember a time in my adult life when I was not writing this book or thinking about private prisons. My interest in this phenomenon began as an intern at the *Arizona Capitol Times* as a college sophomore, when I read the paper's coverage of Arizona's use of private prisons. I was curious and surprised by this practice and wondered to myself, why does our state use it? What explains this odd policy choice? Much of my adult life thereafter helped to provide (some) answers to the questions my young, 19-year-old self posed. Little did I know that curiosity would lead me here!

Dozens of people have supported and encouraged me on this journey since I began grad school. Of course, much gratitude (and credit) goes to my dissertation committee at Emory University: Tom Clark, Michael Leo Owens, and Zachary Peskowitz. Tom's honest and consistent feedback, which most of all helped to calm me down so that I could keep doing what I was doing, was invaluable. He has taught me how to think critically, always keep trying, and perhaps most of all not to take myself too seriously. MiLO's commitment to the subject matter and to me as a scholar has been a constant source of support and very encouraging in times of stress. I remember thinking in my first year of graduate school after I met MiLO that he was the kind of political scientist I dreamed of being—I still have that dream. Zac's careful and patient readings of this manuscript (beginning with when I started this project as a second-year in his course!) have made all the difference in the final product. Thanks for taking a chance on me. These men are all models of good scholars, and I only hope to live up to their expectations.

Outside of the dissertation committee, though, plenty of other people have read many, *many* versions of this work (either as a dissertation, paper, or book). Jeff Staton and the Blender folks, the entire law and courts working group at Emory University (we save lives!), Michael Giles, Alex Bolton, Hannah Walker, the faculty at Emory for their feedback during talks, and the many audiences at the conferences where I presented. The help of the data wizards Rob O'Reilly and Chris Palazzolo in collecting the data set at the heart of this project was invaluable. I have received much encouraging support from other scholars in the discipline, and their public support of me and this work has been very humbling.

The support of my department at Louisiana State University (LSU) is also a gift, a department that took a chance on a young scholar with lots of ideas and enthusiasm for unconventional research topics. To the many scholars in the department who have encouraged me on this and other research projects, my most sincere thanks. And thanks to the Board of Regents Awards to Louisiana Artists and Scholars program for funding this project in my second year at LSU, which let me take a year off of teaching to finish this book. This invaluable institutional support has made all the difference in the final product.

Support from Oxford University Press (OUP) has been invaluable. To Steven Teles, who reached out and talked to me extensively as I finished the initial draft of the book and patiently answered my questions as a newcomer to book publishing, I so appreciate his great enthusiasm and interest in the project. To Dave McBride and all the others at OUP who have supported me and this project, I am very grateful. Also many thanks to the editors and reviewers of *Perspectives on Politics*, for their excellent feedback and suggestions on a paper published using part of the data and arguments presented here (see Gunderson, 2020c).

To the impressive group of women I am proud to call colleagues and friends: Laura Huber, Kirsten Widner, Dani Villa, Abbey Heller, Lauren Mattioli, Nancy Arrington, Bethany Morrison, Maggie Macdonald, Lizzy Weiner, and so many others. To Kirsten in particular, your patient discussions with me about the dynamics I describe in the book helped shape and make clearer my argument and its contribution. All of you inspire me to do and be a better scholar and friend and are a source of endless inspiration and support. You all are more than friends or colleagues; you are family and community. I would absolutely not be the person or scholar I am today without you all.

Thanks also go to my family. To my mom for an endless curiosity and desire to learn; to my sister, Kristin, for always keeping me grounded; to my dad, Leigh, Heather, Scott, and Kasey, for their support. To the entire Berens clan, many thanks for always being interested in my research and for accepting me as your own.

And finally, to Andrew. It is difficult to put into words the impact you have had on my life and on this book. Your unwavering support and willingness to move first to Atlanta and then to Baton Rouge for me and my career is a true gift. Without it (and you) I would not be the person and scholar I am today. You inspire me and push me and are the best sounding board for my ideas on this book and other projects. There is no one I would rather share this achievement with as it would not have been possible without you. Onto our next adventure. Nothing can stop us now.

AMG

1

Just Like Selling Cars, Real Estate, or Hamburgers

> . . . certainly the bloom is off the privatization rose in a significant number of states. Obviously some states have never privatized, but even those who have, I think it's fair to say that in a number of them, the experiment did not work out quite the way the state was hoping.
>
> —*State bureaucrat interview, 2020*

In the early 1980s, the incarceration rate had been steadily increasing for about a decade, straining state and federal resources as governments scrambled to find solutions to vast prison overcrowding. By 1984, one of the largest private prison operators in the contemporary United States, the Corrections Corporation of America (now CoreCivic), won its first contract to house detainees for the Immigration and Naturalization Service (INS) in Houston, Texas. When INS told two of the company's cofounders, Terrell Don Hutto and Tom Beasley, it needed the space three months earlier than expected, the men hastily looked for a replacement and found one: Houston's Olympic Motel. The motel was refurbished to be a secure facility, and Hutto ventured to Walmart to buy toiletries for the 86 men who arrived on Super Bowl Sunday in 1984.[1] Eventually, the permanent facility, the Houston Processing Center, opened; and detainees were then transferred to the permanent location, which is still in operation today. What is now a multibillion-dollar company began its operations in a Houston hotel, highlighting the humble beginnings of an industry that is now a key, albeit controversial, figure in American criminal justice.

Today, states across the country continue contracts with private companies to manage and operate correctional facilities. In some, states are enthusiastic about their "great partnerships" with private companies, as one state bureaucrat suggested in an interview. In others, the situation is not so sanguine. Mississippi is one example, contracting with the Management and Training Corporation (MTC) to operate Wilkinson County Correctional Facility. This facility, called the "killing field" by the inmates there, is just one Mississippi facility operated by MTC (Neff and Santo, 2019). Another, the East Mississippi Correctional Facility, was the subject of a federal civil rights lawsuit after neglect and violence ran rampant at the prison (Williams, 2018). States experienced a variety of outcomes in their experiments with prison privatization since the early 1980s, but nearly all have turned to the private sector for the operation of their state facilities at some point in that time period. Why? What incentivizes states to partner with private companies to incarcerate and detain their residents?

Private Prisons Enter the Market

This book investigates this seemingly straightforward question: why do states privatize their prisons? Though this question appears simple at first glance, it is much more complex than it appears. The literature primarily focuses on four explanations for this policy: partisanship, economics, unionization, and campaign contributions (e.g., Kim and Price, 2014; Nicholson-Crotty, 2004; Page, 2011; Schneider, 1999). Upon closer inspection, though, these explanations fall short of explicating the patterns in adoption of prison privatization.

First, partisanship does not seem to explain prison privatization as politicians of all stripes turned to this policy since the early 1980s, indicative of the broader neoliberal movement in American politics (Wacquant, 2009, 287–314). Second, it is also unclear whether and to what degree privatization saves money (Selman and Leighton, 2010, chap. 5), casting doubt on the economics explanation. Third, even the strongest corrections officers' unions have been unable to prevent privatization (Page, 2011, chap. 6). Finally, though campaign contributions and lobbying are often cited as the primary drivers of prison privatization, it is unclear whether these relationships drive new privatization or merely maintenance of existing public–private partnerships. And, as one interviewee suggested, he was unaware that private prison companies had donated to his campaign, providing some evidence that campaign contributions alone are likely not driving prison privatization.

Complicating each of these explanations is a general lack of data on prison privatization over time. Given that these explanations do not map onto the adoption of this policy, why do states privatize? This question is especially important in the face of tough normative questions about the appropriate role (if any) of profit in corrections and the exploitative nature of private prisons (Austin and Coventry, 2001; Bauer, 2019).

Enterprising business persons saw an opportunity to monopolize a previously undiscovered market as governments at all levels—state, local, and federal—scrambled to find solutions to their overflowing prisons and jails (Selman and Leighton, 2010, chap. 1). Private prisons were thus a solution to a complex policy problem, a solution which was eventually adopted by Democratic and Republican states alike (Gunderson, 2020c). Private prisons encouraged the development of an "iron triangle," a complex relationship between the bureaucracy, the legislature, and lobbyists to govern penal institutions (Lilly and Knepper, 1993). Beyond that, despite significant public attention to this policy, we know relatively little about consistent patterns of private prisons and the precise details of how they operate. We know even less about the additional forms of privatization in American corrections, from probation to private healthcare and prisoner transport. The focus on private prisons, as one interviewee suggested, is primarily driven by the severity of consequences for different forms of privatization: "the risk of catastrophically life ending or life altering outcomes is obviously much less with laundry than with medical care." Nevertheless, we do not devote much public or scholarly attention to these other forms of privatization. Prisons themselves are heavily privatized in individual sectors, like healthcare, laundry, or food services. Private companies are therefore at the heart of much of the American carceral machine. And yet, even the most public and scrutinized facet of this process—private prisons—is extraordinarily opaque, for scholars and the public alike. This book examines private prisons as an entry point to understand the role and motivations behind privatization in American corrections. I seek to demystify the private prison industry in a few ways. First, I describe patterns of private prison adoption and growth in the states since the mid-1980s; and second, I describe a theory that emphasizes the role of inmate litigation in conditioning states' responses to poor prison conditions. This theory claims that there are important incentives to reduce *accountability* for poor prison conditions in the decision to privatize, an important overlooked incentive in previous studies of privatization.

Incentives to Privatize: Accountability and Inmate Lawsuits

The central theoretical claim at the heart of this book is that an important incentive to privatize not currently emphasized in the literature is *accountability*. States' responses to inmate litigation condition the likelihood of privatizing. As the number of people incarcerated grew, so too did the volume of inmate lawsuits facing state governments. Inmates filed lawsuits at ever increasing rates because of growing legal and political concerns, and states were facing a mountain of prison litigation that they had previously never had to handle. Privatizing limits states' legal and political accountability for poor prison conditions. It is in this environment that the modern private prison industry was born.

I study two facets of litigation here. First, I argue that a higher number of inmate lawsuits, regardless of outcome, will make a state more likely to privatize its prisons. The state has an incentive to privatize to limit its legal and political accountability for these lawsuits. Legal uncertainty about who is responsible for the violations that occur within private prisons allows states to effectively (at least partially, if not completely) shift legal liability for these lawsuits onto private companies. Additionally, the layer of bureaucracy added when a state privatizes ensures it is difficult, if not impossible, to know *who* to hold responsible for poor prison conditions. Taken together, privatization helps states limit their legal and political accountability for lawsuits and prison conditions more broadly.

Second, I examine successful lawsuits specifically and argue that these court orders make it *less* likely for a state to privatize its prisons. Successful lawsuits are incredibly uncommon, 12% by generous estimates and 1.6% by other estimates (Ostrom, Hanson, and Cheesman, 2003; Schlanger, 2015). I argue that these cases prompt states to reevaluate their substandard prison rules and procedures and force corrections' bureaucracies to professionalize. These court orders thus remove the incentive to privatize to avoid accountability and make it less likely that a state will turn to a for-profit company to manage and operate their prisons.

These two expectations suggest that accountability and transparency are at the root of states' decisions to privatize their correctional facilities. Indeed, the opaque nature of private prisons helps states avoid accountability or, if they are beholden to judicial decrees, removes the incentive to privatize at all.

Continuing Controversies

The advent of private prisons in the 1980s, and the growing number of private facilities in the decades following, has done little to quell the controversy surrounding their use. Private prisons and the role of the market in government service provision has attracted considerable controversy in the scholarly, legal, and public communities (e.g., Austin and Coventry, 2001; Bauer, 2019). Though there is a surprising dearth of information regarding the public's opinion on privatization (see Ramirez, 2021 for one exception), the little evidence that does exist indicates that while citizens support market intervention into benign service areas such as garbage collection and janitorial services, they balk at private companies operating prisons of any kind (Thompson and Elling, 2002). Additionally, most Americans seem to agree that the government should not privatize prisons (Enns and Ramirez, 2018; Frost, Trapassi, and Heinz, 2019). The public at large is still therefore grappling with the consequences of adopting this policy.

It is not only citizens who are concerned about the normative implications of private prisons. The House of Representatives' Subcommittee on Courts, Civil Liberties, and the Administration of Justice held a hearing in 1985 specifically regarding the privatization of corrections and the feasibility of implementing that policy at the federal level. Robert Kastenmeier, the chair of the subcommittee, posed several questions at the beginning of the session about cost savings and inmate rights but ended his questions with this normative concern: "And the ultimate question: Can and should governments delegate this power to deprive persons of liberty?" (US Congress House Committee on the Judiciary, Subcommittee on Courts, and the Administration of Justice, 1986). Similarly, as the Tennessee government was considering a proposal from CoreCivic to take over the entire state's prison system, the state attorney general, W. J. Michael Cody, strenuously objected to delegating a responsibility like corrections to a private company. He argued "[t]he idea of a transfer or delegation thereof, [is] in direct opposition to the design and ends of their creation" (quoted in Cody and Bennett, 1987). And one Republican state legislator interviewed for this book emphasized the profit incentive of private prisons as concerning: "If you're going to make it about making money or losing money, you're losing track of what the scales of justice are asking us to do." An advocacy director echoed this sentiment: "I can't say I've observed that this company is better and this company is worse. The fundamental problem is the model. The problem is not this company or that company, it's a model that prioritizes private profit over the rights and interests of incarcerated people." These concerns are relevant not only to public opinion but also to policymakers at the national and state levels who explicitly considered these questions of accountability and the role of the government when deciding whether to privatize prisons.

Questions surrounding whether the government is able to delegate such broad authority to a private company or how this delegation squares with the constitution remain at the forefront of debates on prison privatization (Austin and Coventry, 2001). These concerns are largely normative as the federal government has dismissed these challenges as legally inconsequential. A presidential commission released a report on privatization in 1988 and did not consider these accountability concerns to be impediments to prison privatization—the report cites the federal statutes that permit prison privatization and notes no state had yet passed legislation[2] expressly prohibiting privatization of prisons (Linowes, 1988). Since then, most states have enacted legislation that expressly authorizes the full-scale privatization of prisons,[3] while others simply asserted that existing statutes were broad enough to provide legal authority for contracts to be awarded to private prison companies (Quinlan, Thomas, and Gautreaux, 2004). Despite the statutory approvals of this practice, however, questions of accountability and appropriateness remain.

An outstanding question centers around the accountability of for-profit corrections companies. Namely, while public managers of prisons are responsible to citizens through the legislative and executive branches, private managers are primarily responsible to their shareholders (Inman, 2012). A public manager is an employee of the state and can be removed from his post easily. A private manager, however, is beholden to both the government who contracted with them to provide the service and the shareholders of the company by which they are employed. As Laffont and Tirole (1991) point out, employees of private companies suffer from a conflict of interest between the government and their shareholders. Private companies then have competing incentives to perform the job for which they contracted with the government or to make money for their shareholders, which could result in those companies cutting corners to save money.

Proponents of prison privatization argue that these concerns can be incorporated into the construction of robust contracts to prevent companies from abusing their informational advantages. Indeed, several government representatives interviewed for this book cited the construction of a clear and specific contract as key to the success of prison privatization (see Chapter 2 for more details). Despite this strategy, it is practically impossible to write a contract comprehensive enough to govern every component of the service provided (Hart, Shleifer, and Vishny, 1997; Laffont and Tirole, 1991). Thus, the contract is incomplete by its nature since the government cannot fully specify the full spectrum of what must be done in every situation. Additionally, prison contracts can be ineffective at reining in irresponsible behavior on behalf of the companies themselves. Under such conditions, we might expect incentives for the private company to engage in cost-cutting at the expense of quality, whereas a manager of an equivalent public facility cooperates with the government to increase both quality and cost savings (Hart, Shleifer, and Vishny, 1997). This dilemma could be solved by a bureaucracy that effectively constrains private companies from taking advantage of incomplete contracts by appointing an on-site government monitor to ensure compliance with state standards, though the monitors face constraints as well (Selman and Leighton, 2010, 118–119). Both incomplete contracts and varying incentives can prompt a private company to renege on their contracts and start cutting corners, presenting both principal-agent and moral hazard problems. Private prison corporations receive information about the facility that may not be shared with the government, and the company's actions are not easily verifiable, an example of a moral hazard problem. The company has private information because it operates the prison on a day-to-day basis and can thus purposefully hide certain information if necessary. Though some contracts specifically require the presence of a facility monitor to prevent this from occurring, the inspections can be spotty and scheduled, making it easy for prison managers to anticipate the presence and concerns of government monitors. There is also some theoretical reason to believe that contract monitors who live in the same communities as the prisons they inspect may have a difficult time critiquing the operations there (e.g., Eisen, 2018; Selman and Leighton, 2010). Those private companies have a natural incentive to use this informational advantage, complying with the government's requests at minimum but occasionally cutting corners to save money. It is worth noting that this principal-agent problem is not specific to prison privatization but is indeed a potential issue with each government service that is contracted out with incomplete monitoring.

It could also be the case that even the most robust, detailed contracts are controversial precisely because of the details found in them already. One study found that 65% of private prison contracts included occupancy guarantees—a requirement to keep the private prison or jail between 80 and 100% full at all times—or required payments for empty cells in these facilities (In the Public Interest, 2013). This ensures that the government pays for the private prison beds *regardless of whether or not they are being used*, which may provide an incentive for governments to incarcerate more people if they foot the bill for the contract anyway (Eisen, 2018, 186–187).

This discussion of continuing controversies, however, should not be taken as evidence that *public prisons* are particularly accessible to the public or scholars. Indeed, as I suggest in the conclusion of the book, private prisons tend to receive the most ire from the public, and we neglect to remember that governments are the ones that chose to contract with them to begin with. There is a transparency problem within *both* public and private prisons, though this problem is compounded in private prisons as these companies are largely not subject to Freedom of Information Act requests (see Chapter 2 for more details and see Eisen, 2018, 197). Moreover, our discussion of private prisons obscures the many profit motives in public prisons as well (see Chapters 2 and 6). Therefore, though nearly all correctional facilities are largely hidden from public view and scrutiny, private prisons in particular deepen this problem due to sometimes deliberate obfuscation and murky legal standards surrounding their use.

Not only are these concerns of accountability and transparency important to the government that contracts with these for-profit companies, but they are enduring problems that cannot easily be solved through methods like contract writing or appointment of contract monitors. In fact, I argue that these concerns of accountability and transparency are at the heart of the state's decision to privatize and that states are incentivized to privatize to shift accountability for poor prison conditions onto private companies.

The Modern Private Prison Landscape

In 1986, at least 1,600 inmates were held in privately operated state, local, or national prisons and jails. By 2016, that number had reached more than 160,000, a 100-fold increase in only 30 years (Gunderson, 2020c). In that year, nearly 18% of federal prisoners and approximately 9% of state prisoners were housed in private facilities (Carson, 2018). This growth represents a significant shift in the administration of punishment in the United States, even more significant considering that the first private prisons opened only in the 1980s.

This book analyzes state private prisons, *facilities that are managed by a publicly traded private prison company that houses at least some inmates under a state's jurisdiction.* Largely, these prisons operate after the government issues a request for proposal (RFP) and develops a contract for the management and/or operation of a facility with a third-party company. I describe this process in more detail in Chapter 2, and though privatization can (and frequently does) occur at the federal and local levels as well, this book considers state decision-making specifically to understand why a state would privatize its prisons.

A few states adopted private prisons and later eliminated them (like Wisconsin, Arkansas, and Nevada—see Chapter 2 for further details), but the majority of states privatized part of their corrections systems and did not later cease contracts with private prison companies entirely. Thirty-three states had a private prison facility, regardless of jurisdiction, operating within their borders at some point between 1986 and 2016, whereas 35 states contracted with a private facility to house a portion of their inmates (in- or out-of-state) in the same time period. Considerable diversity remains at the state level regarding the use of prison privatization, however. For example, Texas had the largest population of inmates in these private facilities between 1986 and 2016, at over 17,000 in any single year, while Hawaii had the highest proportion of inmates in private institutions relative to publicly run ones, at over 70% in any given year. The average state between 1986 and 2016 housed just over 4% of its inmates in private facilities. Though the share of inmates in these private facilities remains relatively low, the significant growth of this industry in only the last three decades warrants further study. This growth is even more stunning considering one of the preeminent private corrections companies, CoreCivic, was only founded in 1983 (Dolovich, 2005). Though modern privatization of corrections facilities at all levels, local, state, and national, began in the 1980s, carceral privatization has a long and torrid history in the United States.

Private companies had previously been involved with the operation of the corrections system beginning in the nineteenth century with the use of convict leasing (Dolovich, 2005). This system, in which state governments leased inmates to private companies to work on plantations, roads, or other projects, was the most common way private companies interacted with the corrections system prior to the 1980s (Dolovich, 2005). This was especially common in the South as Southern states effectively enslaved convicts to labor in coal mines, brickyards, and other projects to generate profit for the state (e.g., Gottschalk, 2006; Perkinson, 2010). This brutal tradition was eventually replaced first by chain gangs, which forced inmates to labor on road or infrastructural projects, then by more modern correctional facilities in which the state took the control of prisons back from private companies. Note, though, that public prisons still utilize prisoners for a variety of industries, so private prison companies are not alone in monetizing the labor of inmates (see Chapter 2 for more details on the long history of profit in American corrections).

The intense pressure of overcrowded prisons and jails encouraged the development of the modern private prison industry and the reemergence of profit in American corrections. In the words of one of the founders of CoreCivic, "we could sell [prison] privatization as a solution, you sell it just like you were selling cars, or real estate, or hamburgers" (quoted in Selman and Leighton, 2010, 48). The growth of the private prison industry since the 1980s has been exceptional. What is now a $5 billion industry dominated by two companies, CoreCivic and the GEO Group, began in the 1980s with dozens of companies vying for contracts with government partners. While there were once more than a dozen firms operating private correctional facilities in the United States (McDonald et al., 1998), that number has dropped dramatically. As of 2014, GEO and CoreCivic alone comprised approximately 85% of the market share (Mumford et al., 2016). The third largest competitor, the privately owned MTC, comes in a distant third, controlling approximately 11% of the market (Mumford, Schanzenbach, and Nunn, 2016). While 12 firms operated private prisons and jails in 1999, eight of those were eventually bought out by competing companies like GEO and CoreCivic, which have each acquired smaller for-profit prison companies steadily over the last few decades. The consolidation of the market has meant that the vast majority of government partners effectively have two, perhaps three, choices when privatizing a correctional facility: CoreCivic, the GEO Group, and, on occasion, MTC.

Regardless of the private company a government chooses to contract with, the process typically follows a common trajectory (see Chapter 2 for more details). Theoretically, a state's privatization process begins when politicians decide to privatize a particular government function. Then, the actual contracting process begins when firms submit bids for the maintenance or operation of prisons in response to a state's RFP[4] to shop around for the best proposal (Butler, 1991). In theory, contracting out encourages competition among firms, broadly theorized to result in more innovative and cheaper proposals (Butler, 1991). Gains in efficiency and quality are thus expected from services that are contracted out. More generally, contracts consist of a specification of the work to be done, a competitive climate resulting from a pool of potential producers, monitoring of the contractor's performance by the government, and enforcement of appropriate terms (Savas, 2000, chap. 7).

The Growth of the Carceral State and Carceral Governance

Private prisons are just one significant development in the criminal legal system[5] in the last few decades. As correctional privatization grew, so too did more general punitive policies aimed at incarcerating more individuals than ever before. The United States has experienced an unprecedented rise in the number of people directly affected by the criminal legal system: in 1968, there were approximately 780,000 Americans under correctional control, in prisons or jails or under community supervision; and in 2015 that figure was over 6.7 million (Kaeble and Glaze, 2016; Weaver and Lerman, 2010). The phenomenon of mass incarceration, as scholars call it, necessitated the construction of institutions to support surging populations in prisons and jails. These institutions make up the carceral state, the system of massive criminal legal institutions like prisons, jails, and surveillance systems like parole and probation, and individuals' contact with that system via actors like the police (Weaver and Lerman, 2010). As Figure 1.1 details, this growth has been expansive not only in prisons and jails but also among those under community supervision, on parole, or on probation. Less expansive but still a source of sudden growth over the last few decades are private prisons, the focus of this book. Carceral governance, in general, has been a growing topic of scholarly discussion as scholars seek to understand the causes and consequences of our massive criminal legal institutions.

The carceral state began to institutionalize as politicians used incendiary rhetoric regarding crime to justify more punitive policies, most notably the construction of prisons (Simon, 2007, chap. 3). This rhetoric was ubiquitous after the civil rights movement according to Vesla Weaver's concept of "frontlash," as the successes of that movement galvanized a powerful opposition to articulate a new problem of crime: the racial problem was redefined

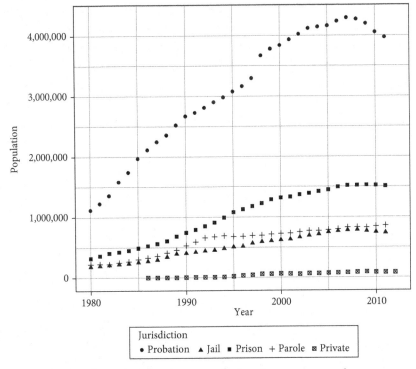

Figure 1.1 Population in jail, prison, or private prisons or on parole or probation. Data from the Bureau of Justice Statistics and the original data set detailed in Chapter 2.

as a crime problem (Weaver, 2007). Though this rhetoric was typically associated with members of the Republican Party (e.g., Beckett, 1999), recent studies of the development of crime policy, at least at the national level, suggest Democratic politicians were complicit in this rhetoric as well (e.g., Hinton, 2016; Murakawa, 2014). This support grew beyond rhetoric, however: stalwarts of the Democratic Party, including Bill Clinton, Joe Biden, and Ted Kennedy, were among the most strident supporters of national measures to impose mandatory minimum sentencing, increase the number of offenses to qualify for the death penalty, and lengthen prison stays (Murakawa, 2014, chap. 4). Democratic complicity in the growth of the carceral state extends even further back as former President Lyndon B. Johnson's Great Society initiative spurred the passing of the Safe Streets Act of 1968, an act that greatly increased the funding and resource capability of local police departments and thus the number of people arrested and convicted (Hinton, 2016, chap. 4).

This support also spreads beyond federal actors, to Democratic governors who are associated with increased corrections spending and incarceration rates in competitive gubernatorial races (Gunderson, 2021b). Therefore, the shift in rhetoric that occurred to "govern through crime" facilitated the construction of the institutions of the carceral state, rhetoric that was supported by both parties.

Democrats weren't the only strange bedfellows in the expansion of the carceral state. Feminist organizations played an integral role and formed an unlikely alliance with conservative politicians to promote mass incarceration and increased punishment for a variety of crimes, particularly for sexual violence (Gottschalk, 2006, chaps. 5 and 6). These organizations, in addition to those that represented battered women and victims of sexual assault, were broadly part of the victims' rights movement in the 1970s (Gottschalk, 2006, chaps. 4–6). These groups were loyal partners in the expansion of criminal sanctions for those convicted of rape or sexual or domestic violence. Correctional officers' unions also faced immense pressure to support punitive measures to ensure future employment (e.g., Page, 2011). And there is some evidence of Black elites pursuing punitive policies in their communities (e.g., Forman, 2017; Fortner, 2015), though I have found elsewhere that in the aggregate Black state legislators are associated with lower corrections spending in states (Gunderson, 2020b). The factors contributing to the growth in the government's ability to punish and incarcerate are not easily attributable to any single actor, political or otherwise.

Not only did the rhetoric surrounding the carceral state become more punitive beginning in the 1960s and 1970s but so too did the state's literal capacity to punish. States experienced a building frenzy of prisons in the 1980s and beyond, a necessary step to house the thousands entering prisons each year. This carceral capacity, as Schoenfeld (2018) calls it, then spurred the creation of new interest groups invested in the continuation of carceral expansion, as well as enhanced incentives for politicians to satisfy those interest groups with the growth of more punitive crime measures. This argument is similar in flavor to general theories of policy entrenchment or how reforms to existing policy survive even as others fail. The expansion of the carceral state was further entrenched as those involved made specific and extensive investments in those punitive reforms and thus developed consistent policy preferences in favor of higher incarceration rates and more punishment (Patashnik, 2014, 32).

Though the carceral state expansion encouraged the development of a myriad of interest groups, perhaps the one that has garnered the most public attention has been the private prison industry. The continued controversies about this policy, alongside the potential end of prison privatization at the federal level, mean that this book is extraordinarily relevant. In particular, by excavating the modern private prison industry, I aim to add essential context to conversations around profit, American corrections, and democratic accountability.

My emphasis on accountability in the decision to privatize has implications for several subfields. Most clearly, I speak to the growing literature on the political economy of the carceral state (e.g., Gilmore, 2007) in explicating the patterns in the adoption of punitive policy in the last few decades. Outside of that subfield, however, implications here are relevant for judicial politics, economics, state politics, policy, and law. My emphasis on inmate lawsuits and *all* lawsuits (not just those that are successful) provides essential insight into the role of the courts in altering the nature and character of other institutions, and correctional institutions in particular. Economics scholars studying privatization of any kind ought to situate politics squarely in the center of that decision, and the desire to evade accountability is a motivation that can be applied to other types of privatization like military contracting, education, or even benign government functions like garbage removal. Scholars in state politics or policy can readily use the data provided here to analyze prison privatization in the context of other policies and how the important incentive to limit democratic accountability may operate in other contexts. Finally, the important implications this project has for the legal rights of inmates, particularly of those incarcerated in private facilities, is a vital and understudied area in the law and legal politics literature. Though this book investigates one particular policy, I hope to provide essential context more broadly to those studying punitive institutions, litigation reform, policy creation and development, and inmates' power (or lack thereof) in our vast criminal legal system.

Looking Ahead

This book aims to shine a light on state adoption of private prisons. To fully explore this phenomenon, I develop an original data set of private prisons and describe interviews conducted with key government and industry partners in prison privatization (bureaucrats, legislators, governors, private prison companies, and advocacy groups; see the Appendix for more details) to demystify the process behind prison privatization. Next, I present the core theoretical argument of this book that emphasizes accountability as the crucial incentive in the decision to privatize prisons. I test and find evidence for my central argument, that more inmate lawsuits are associated with more prison privatization. Moreover, not only are successful lawsuits associated with less prison privatization, but private prison company investors punish those firms after a successful inmate lawsuit is announced in states where the company is operating. The unintended consequences of inmate litigation have contributed to a shift in the nature and character of state corrections systems and the administration of state punishment.

Chapter 2 describes the long history of profit in American corrections and introduces my data set, a longitudinally and geographically diverse source of information that contains information on the location of private prisons in the United States from 1986 to 2016, the most comprehensive data set of these institutions thus far developed (previously introduced in Gunderson, 2020c). I use this data set and excerpts from interviews with key government actors in the decision to privatize to describe the contracting process and how states privatize. I consider other commonly cited explanations for prison privatization (partisanship, economics, unionization, and campaign contributions) and highlight how those explanations alone are insufficient to explain prison privatization.

Chapter 3 introduces the central theoretical framework of this book and argues it is the advent of the prisoners' rights movement and inmates' use of litigation that prompted the rise of private carceral institutions. I review the historical development of prisoners' rights and the massive increase in inmate litigation before developing a set of hypotheses about how lawsuits influence the adoption of private prisons. I argue that more inmate lawsuits make a state more likely to privatize its carceral facilities to avoid legal and political accountability for poor prison conditions. Alternatively, the second hypothesis argues that an increase in the number of court orders against a state will make a state less likely to privatize. Because judicial decrees effectively force states to develop coherent rules and standards, the incentive to privatize to limit accountability is removed.

Chapter 4 then empirically tests these hypotheses using an instrumental variables design and the original data set of private prisons. I also develop a data set on both prisoner lawsuits filed in the federal district courts and successful jail and prison court orders from the Civil Rights Clearinghouse from the 1980s onward. I use these two novel data sets and the expectations laid out in Chapter 3 to test my hypotheses and find support for both empirically. States that experience a higher number of inmate lawsuits are more likely to privatize, whereas those states that face more court orders are less likely to privatize their correctional facilities. I ground these quantitative findings using historical examples of states' experiences with privatization.

Chapter 5 considers the activity of private prison firms from their perspective and analyzes how the stock performance of these companies varies as the settlements of successful lawsuits are announced. To what degree do stockholders pay attention to these lawsuits? I find no effect in the aggregate: lawsuits do not predict changes in stock prices. However, I do find a significant and negative effect of the announcement of a lawsuit in states that have increasing numbers of private prisons. This suggests that investors are savvy and particularly concerned about the legal climate in the states that privatize the most.

The final chapter concludes with some broad implications of this study, which extend far beyond private prisons specifically. If the rights revolution gave legal rights to inmates, and states privatized as a result, possibly leading to adverse consequences for inmates, how does that change our evaluation of this movement? Providing inmates with legal rights is normatively the appropriate choice, but this implication pushes us to think carefully about perverse incentives in our criminal legal system. Legal rights are fundamental for every American, rights that ought not to depend on criminal justice contact. While the rights revolution began the effort to enshrine incarcerated people with legal rights, the dueling interests of profit and accountability have made this a promise yet unfulfilled. Additionally, this book speaks to the literature on the utility of using courts for social change and suggests that the rights revolution has potentially adverse consequences for those who stand to benefit from it. That suggests not that the rights revolution was misguided but rather that it is an incomplete project that we must still fight to pursue on behalf of incarcerated people nationwide. This project points to the need to understand the dynamics at the heart of prison privatization, a policy that is only gaining in controversy and attention as states and the federal government continue to rely on it. Namely, there are four implications considered here: that the question of whether private or public prisons are worse is irrelevant; that the rights revolution for incarcerated people in public and private prisons is a promise yet unfulfilled; that profit is central to American corrections, and private firms will adapt to face the evolving needs of their government partners; and that, finally, privatization is merely a symptom and not a cause of the massive expansion of the carceral state in the latter half of the twentieth century, a "metastasis of the larger cancer of mass incarceration."

2

Profit in American Corrections

... these are amoral actors. It's not that they're evil people, but they will do what it takes to make a profit. And that's often not in the interest of incarcerated people.

—Advocacy director interview, 2020

... the expectations of this company [are] to provide a product.

—Private prison representative interview, 2020

The growth of the criminal legal system since the 1970s has been remarkable. This system, also referred to as the "carceral state," encompasses the police, courts, jails, prisons, as well as associated institutions and policies like legal financial obligations, probation and parole, and electronic monitoring (Schoenfeld, 2016). Though all of these facets have grown exponentially in the last few decades, perhaps the most peculiar development has been the introduction of private prisons. Companies, at the behest of government entities, run the day-to-day operations of prisons. This book aims to study this unique phenomenon since the 1980s as one of the most significant and controversial developments in modern American criminal justice.

I am certainly not the first, or the only, scholar to examine private prisons. Qualitative research has investigated the perils of private prisons (e.g., Selman and Leighton, 2010), whereas others have sought to understand questions like whether private prisons provide better care and experience judicial intervention at a lower rate than public prisons or whether private prison inmates recidivate at higher rates than their public prison counterparts (e.g., Bales et al., 2005; Blakely and Bumphus, 2005; Burkhardt, 2019; Burkhardt and Jones, 2016; Makarios and Maahs, 2012; Spivak and Sharp, 2008). Finally, others have theorized about the appropriate role of private goods provision in the criminal justice sector, the legal implications of that decision, and the historical development of this policy (e.g., Harding,

1997; Hart, Shleifer, and Vishny, 1997; Volokh, 2013). These are all important avenues to explore in the analysis of this complex phenomenon and help to contextualize our understanding of how private prisons work. However, studies thus far have suffered one significant obstacle to the study of private prisons: the lack of consistent, longitudinal data on the location, capacity, and customers of these facilities. This chapter describes a data set that helps scholars seeking to analyze this opaque policy choice by providing them with the information they need to do so.

This chapter introduces this source of data and shines a light on the lack of information on the involvement of profit in private prisons since the 1980s.This is not the first time private enterprise has been involved in the administration of American criminal justice, however. This chapter reviews the historical role that private interests have played in the administration of American carceral institutions before briefly discussing the limitations of existing theory and data in the study of private prisons. Finally, I introduce the data source and discuss the limitations of this data, particularly in regard to the semiprivatization of American criminal justice. What does an initial examination of this data tell us about broad patterns in the support and adoption of private prisons?

Private Interests and Carceral Institutions

Though the narrative of private prisons typically begins with President Ronald Reagan's push for privatization in all areas of government (e.g., Burkhardt, 2014; Henig, 1989; Sellers, 1993), profit has long been central to the management of American criminal justice. Though the *type* of privatization has evolved over time, governments have long partnered with private companies to facilitate the confinement and management of inmates (Feeley, 1991). As colonists arrived in America for the first time in the seventeenth century, convicted felons soon followed, with promise of a pardon if they agreed to be sold into servitude (Feeley, 1991; King, 2012). This pattern of servitude faded by the nineteenth century, though it was replaced with an brutal alternative, convict leasing and convict labor.

In 1825, Kentucky was the first state to lease the entire prison and its inmates to a businessman for a tidy sum (Feeley, 1991). This arrangement, reproduced in other states like Louisiana and Tennessee for individual facilities, had businesses assume the cost of running the facility in exchange for convict labor and the profits inmates produced (Dolovich, 2005). This system provided labor and bodies for often brutal projects like road and railway construction, coal mine operations, manufacturing operations, sawmills, brickyards, and even sugar and cotton plantations (e.g., Feeley, 1991; Mancini, 1996; Perkinson, 2010). This convict labor could take several forms—prisoners could work on projects within a prison's walls, inmates could be leased out to private businesses if they could not produce profitable items within the prison, or companies could pay the prison a fee or percentage of the profits for the right to employ convicts (Austin and Coventry, 2001)—though the operation of these enterprises often resulted in horrific conditions of abuse, corruption, neglect, violence, substandard living conditions, and death (Dolovich, 2005; King, 2012).

Perhaps most notable in the convict leasing system is the geographic concentration of this practice. Though areas across the country used this system throughout the nineteenth century, it was most widely used in the South, at least partially to rebuild the southern economy after the Civil War (Dolovich, 2005). This concentration was coupled with punitive laws aimed directly at newly freed slaves, resulting in the disproportionate incarceration of Black Americans, not unlike the current racial gap in sentencing and carceral confinement. Indeed, as one scholar suggests, convict leasing and the contemporary disparities in incarceration are similar in that "private entrepreneurs emerged to capitalize on strong public sentiment against a 'Black crime problem' " (Hallett, 2006, 9). And though important differences remain between convict leasing and slavery (Mancini, 1996, 20–28), the impact of both systems was felt most acutely and brutally by Black Americans.

The cruel system of convict leasing existed roughly from the end of the Civil War to the early twentieth century, though the dates and reasons for eliminating the system vary across states (Mancini, 1978). Largely, the racialized system of convict leasing was soon replaced with Jim Crow laws and other statutory forms of racial discrimination; profits from convict leasing diminished, thus reducing the incentive of private business to be involved with carceral management (Mancini, 1978). Following the elimination of the convict leasing system, private involvement in prisons lulled at least partially because of federal legislation that severely restricted the sale of prison-made goods, effectively crippling the production of products within prisons and, with it, the involvement of private enterprise in carceral institutions (Gill, 1931; Hawkins, 1983). This lull soon ended with World

War II when some prisons received wartime contracts to produce goods for the war effort (Conley, 1980; Hawkins, 1983).

Following the war, and with rising prison populations and growing unrest in the 1960s and 1970s, interest grew once again in the possibility of putting prisoners to work (Gallagher and Edwards, 1997). Prisoners across the country thus began working for private enterprises while incarcerated, producing goods for a variety of companies from the perspective that inmate idleness would deteriorate already unfortunate prison conditions (Gill, 1931; Hawkins, 1983). Companies like Texas Instruments, Boeing, Victoria's Secret, IBM, Microsoft, among many others, have used prison labor at some point (Davis, 2000). Federal legislation passed—notably, the Prison Industry Enhancement Act of 1979—that allowed states to sell prison-made products in the interstate market, pending safeguards to protect non-prison labor and industry (Gallagher and Edwards, 1997).

From the arrival of colonists to the United States to the development of prison industries and labor, American carceral history is characterized by the involvement of profit and private enterprise, even though that collaboration has taken on different forms. To be sure, the horrors of private involvement in practices like convict leasing do not exist in contemporary private *or* public prisons (Dolovich, 2005), a point that one state legislator made clearly: "we're not back in the twenties or teens where you had chain gangs, you had folks that were buying and selling pardons." Even though the conditions have undoubtedly improved, the effects of both systems are felt disproportionately by the Black community (e.g., Hallett, 2006). The legacy of that racial impact is felt by one advocacy director who mentioned, "the idea of profit on pain has deep roots . . . especially in the South, where we're literally talking about trafficking in Black and brown bodies." Another advocacy director echoed this sentiment, arguing that mass incarceration (and private prisons) is an evolution from Jim Crow laws and slavery, and that this legacy continues to shape carceral politics to this day. She laments that elected leaders say, " 'well, this is more of a business model. This doesn't have anything to do with mass incarceration, and it doesn't have anything to do with racism.' When, in fact, that's all it has to do with."

America's past experiences with profit and carceral institutions suggest that private enterprise has long been involved in the administration of American punishment and that this modern realization of profit in the carceral state should come as no surprise. Indeed, a former state bureaucrat references his state's legacy with convict leasing as a reason why he was skeptical of the policy to begin with: "there'll be trouble, we thought, if a private operator took over the prisons and the state walked away from it."

Modern Private Prisons

Though private enterprise was involved in prison labor projects in the midtwentieth century and even earlier (Gallagher and Edwards, 1997; Hawkins, 1983), it is in the 1970s and 1980s that a new form of carceral privatization emerged: the management and operation of prisons by a private company, contracted to do so by a government entity. This emergence began first with juvenile facilities in 1976 (the first was a treatment facility for male juvenile delinquents [Austin and Coventry, 2001]) and spread soon to the detainment of illegal immigrants in 1979 (McDonald, 1994). These developments received little attention, perhaps because these decisions were limited in size and scope (McDonald, 1994) and perhaps because they only affected disenfranchised and politically disempowered groups, immigrants, and children. Shortly after that, however, private industries began their involvement in adult correctional facilities, a development that received significant public scrutiny and controversy.

What Is a Private Prison?

Discussions around private prisons often conflate several different types of private prisons. Governments can have any number of arrangements with private vendors: the vendor can own the facility and manage it; the government can own the facility, and the vendor manages it; or some combination of both. An added complication occurs as to *how* the government is privatizing. Does the private vendor take over an existing facility or build an entirely new one (sometimes on spec, before the facility has a contract [McDonald and Patten, 2003])? Where does the government put these inmates—in private prisons within their own jurisdictions or in private prisons in other jurisdictions, via intergovernmental agreements?

Adding to this complexity is the expansive involvement of private companies in prison administration outside of prison management. A wide variety of services, from laundry service to healthcare to food, are often supplied by private companies in an otherwise publicly operated prison (Selman and Leighton, 2010, chap. 2). And prison labor is used by public and private prisons alike (Gallagher and Edwards, 1997). I return to this point in Chapter 6, when I discuss how the myopic focus on private prisons obscures the many other forms of privatization in American corrections.

The wide variety of institutional arrangements associated with so-called private prisons is a difficult theoretical and empirical task, and it becomes important to specify what kind of privatization is the focus. For the purposes of this book, a private prison refers to *a facility that is managed by a publicly traded private prison company that houses at least some inmates under a state's jurisdiction.* I am agnostic about whether the private company also owns the facility or whether it leases it from the state. I also exclude federal and local (city or county) private correctional facilities to understand the full scope of *state* decision-making on private prisons specifically (though the data set can be used to analyze federal and local decision-making as well and will be an important extension of this study).

Theory points to a compound process by which prison privatization occurs. First, the government must choose whether to contract out a service at all, before assessing proposals from private companies in a bidding process and choosing with whom to contract (Ferris and Graddy, 1986; Nicholson-Crotty, 2004). The second step in this process occurs when the state is determining the aggregate *level* of privatization. This second stage considers how state-level factors influence changing levels of prison privatization as it could be the case that once private prisons become institutionalized in a state, the factors that lead to the adoption of laws sympathetic to privatization may no longer be as relevant (Kim and Price, 2014). Theoretically, this perspective is consistent with the view that institutions are sticky in the long term, that once a framework is set up to facilitate privatization, few actors have an incentive to deviate from that process. Thus, this book considers the overall *level* of privatization as the important variable, not necessarily the initial decision to privatize, as it represents a continuing commitment to prison privatization.

Contracts

Key utilitarian questions at the heart of the decision to privatize have little public discussion: How do private prison contracts work? How does a private company sign, carry out, or even end a contract? How does the state government go about monitoring compliance with contracts? Briefly, it is useful to consider these questions using some insights from interviews conducted as part of this project (see Appendix for more details).

The typical contracting process begins with a request for proposal (RFP), whereby the state government releases a request for the kind of facility it is seeking bids for. The state then evaluates the bids before beginning the negotiating process. Subsequently, the state chooses its preferred bidder and moves forward with developing or specifying the monitoring structure of the contract.

Though this is typical of the privatization process of not only private prisons but other public–private partnerships as well, some firms bypass this process and instead build facilities "on spec." These facilities are built *prior to the establishment of a government contract* in "anticipation" of a successful contract bid (Harding, 2001). CoreCivic, for example, built the Northeast Ohio Correctional Center in Youngstown, Ohio, prior to a contract with the District of Columbia (McDonald et al., 1998). These risky initiatives are rare (especially in the contemporary era) as the massive cost of building or remodeling a facility bankrupted several firms that initially pursued this strategy (McDonald et al., 1998).

In most instances, private prison contracts begin only with an explicit request from the state in an RFP. RFPs, and subsequent negotiations with the state, specify contract requirements that can differ by state. One difference is contract length: successful contracts come up for re-bid at various time periods, though typically every two to four years. Another common contract component involves the financial requirements. Texas, for example, requires an individual private prison to be at least 10% cheaper than a similar state-operated facility (Ethridge and Marquart, 1993). One state legislator mentioned their state considered privatization, and the cheapest option was nearly $10 more per day than keeping the facility state-run: "why would you do that?" he asked. These cost-savings questions are at the heart of contract considerations, and some argue the savings come not from efficiency, as some private prison employees suggest, but from staffing issues or the "cherry-picking" of inmates.

Some argue that private companies save money by paying their staff less or offering fewer retirement or fringe benefits compared to the state. This can lead to problems for private companies in retaining employees and maintaining a quality workforce. One state bureaucrat noted that if private companies are "going to pay staff substantially lower wages than what they could make at or the same of what they could make working at Home Depot or Lowe's . . . you may not get the people you want to work there." Another interviewee argued the private prison company guards are "also in many ways exploited by that system [prisons] and were also victims of that system, not just enforcers of it." Not only may they pay their staff less, but they often do not staff sufficiently either. Shane Bauer, a *Mother Jones* journalist who went undercover as a prison guard at a CoreCivic facility in Louisiana, described in detail the chronic understaffing at his facility (Bauer, 2019). His experience at the facility was echoed by an advocacy director, who said it is an "open secret" that one of the ways private prison companies stay profitable is to never staff sufficiently. Some state bureaucrats disagree with this assessment, however. One acknowledges the pay gap but insists the quality of the prison is not affected: "and, well, yes, they may pay their staff a little bit less. The quality of what they do is exceptional." The private prison companies, for their part, argue they do not cut corners on staffing or training, suggest their facilities are newer and more modern than comparable public ones, and emphasize the job creation their facilities bring to communities across the country. One private prison company representative in particular emphasized the fact that their company's facilities in one (hot) state had air conditioning, whereas the state-run facilities did not.

Many also lament that private prison companies "cherry-pick" their inmates. Most private facilities are minimum- or medium-security, primarily because maximum-security facilities are more expensive to build and operate (Camp and Gaes, 2002; McDonald et al., 1998). This fact is a sticking point for those involved in the contracting and monitoring process. State legislators and bureaucrats mention that private facilities "cherry pick the best prisoners out there, the healthiest, the best behaviored, the ones that they're not going to have any problems with." Or, as another bureaucrat bluntly said, "Because they, like any private business, they want to make money, and *it's easier to make money housing well behaved people, relatively speaking, where it is housing people that are going to try to stab you in the eye*" (emphasis added). Another state legislator mentioned that private companies look to write the contracts in a way to only take relatively tame inmates and not high-risk ones. This division of inmates and the difference in inmate profiles is partially the reason why it is so difficult to compare the cost and performance of private prisons and public ones and why there is little scholarly consensus on whether private or public prisons perform better on a variety of metrics (Bauer and Johnston, 2019; Blumstein, Cohen, and Seth, 2008; Burkhardt and Jones, 2016). These evaluations, as one state bureaucrat suggested, need to make sure they are comparing apples to apples and oranges to oranges (i.e., comparing facilities with similarly housed inmates of similar security levels).

The final step in the contracting process is to develop or specify the monitoring and compliance structure of the facility. Most require the private facility to meet the laws and standards of the state they are operating in. However, one bureaucrat suggested that if the state is sending its inmates to private prisons *in other states*, it is much easier as there are fewer statutory requirements that govern the process of shipping inmates out of state. Some states require private facilities to receive accreditation from the American Correctional Association (ACA), or the companies voluntarily seek out accreditation (most, but not all, public facilities are accredited through ACA [Burkhardt and Jones, 2016]). Indeed, as one private prison representative argued, "we don't cut corners on care, staff or training, which meets, and in many cases exceeds, our government counterparts' standards."

Once the contract begins, there is variation in the degree of monitoring of the facility. Physical monitoring of the facility differs by contract regarding the frequency of check-ins and the precise institutional structure of those monitors (i.e., in which departmental agency they are housed). For example, one state bureaucrat mentioned that their state does monthly *and* daily reviews, both unannounced and announced. Other states that house some of their inmates in private facilities monitor their facilities relatively less, with an on-site monitor there constantly but state officials only inspecting the facility once every four months.

Occasionally, these monitors uncover problems with the contract if the private company is not providing services it promised. Though most of the state bureaucrats and legislators recalled that these instances were rare, monitoring of those contracts is essential for ensuring that facilities are operating to state and federal standards: one state bureaucrat mentioned, "we make sure that when they don't meet those standards, we have those discussions with them and then we hold them accountable through sanctions." Another private prison employee mentioned their company had only had this issue once in over 20 years and suggested a well-written and thorough contract is one way to prevent these disputes. This sentiment is echoed by various state partners with private companies: one state bureaucrat emphasized the importance of a "tightly written and tightly followed contract" and that they "rarely go outside [the] corners of the contract." Robust guarantees in this contract are desirable to both government and the private correctional partners, precisely because they govern the methods of solving any disputes that may arise.

Disputes are not always solvable, however, and can lead to the early or on-time termination of contracts with government clients. One state bureaucrat spoke of his experience with a private prison company, when the state released a budget that showed it would close a private facility over the next year. That private company then abruptly shuttered the facility prior to the contract's end, leaving the state in a lurch with 3,000 prisoners with nowhere to go and no staff to look over them. This sudden shift occurred because the contract specified that the contractor could give the state only 60 days' notice to close a facility. That bureaucrat was told privately by a company representative that the private prison firm had been hemorrhaging money and that they knew "this dog wasn't going to hunt." Firms can also simply choose not to renew their contracts, leaving states in a similar bind with potentially thousands of inmates with nowhere to go. At that point, the state needs to invest a significant amount to refit the facilities to state specifications, get employees on the payroll for public benefits, and the like. Either way, the choice to privatize can leave the state vulnerable to the whims of firms that may choose to leave contracts early or abandon the contract once it is completed. As one state bureaucrat said, "I'm not demonizing private prisons but the reality is what's in their interest may not be in the [state's] interest.... And of course it's not. And is that their fault or our fault? ... you can't buy a used car or something you're going to pay less for and expect it to operate like a new car."

Taken together, the qualitative evidence on the process and character of private prison contracting emphasizes the variety of state experiences with these firms. Some state bureaucrats and legislators mention their excellent experiences with their "privatized partners," whereas others mention specific, poor experiences with contract negotiations or terminations. A common thread, though, is the importance of a good contract that can govern a variety of desirable and undesirable situations and programmatically evaluate firm performance.

The details about these contracts, though, are few and far between in the public discourse on private prisons. Though some nonprofits and other advocacy groups have gained access to some contracts through sunshine laws (see MuckRock's Private Prison Project and In the Public Interest, 2013), the public does not have easy access to this information. This is part of a broader problem with examining private prisons: there is little systematic data, and the data that does exist is spotty at best. The next section considers the existing research on private prisons and the disappointing lack of information on the phenomenon, before I introduce a new source of data to help scholars seeking to study private prisons.

Existing Research and Limited Data

Some of the most common explanations of privatization put forth four main arguments to explain its rise and prominence: partisanship, economics, unionization, and campaign contributions (e.g., Kim and Price, 2014; Nicholson-Crotty, 2004; Page, 2011). Though I argue an important overlooked variable in the decision to privatize is the desire to limit legal and political accountability (see Chapter 3), these other explanations deserve brief mention here.

First, at its most extreme, privatization invokes an ideology that is anti-government and praises the benefits of market forces. These forces determine the allocation of governmental services and, according to this perspective, improve those services relative to those that are wholly government-run (Daley, 1996). Citizen support for privatization is driven by a general distrust of power, and government power in particular (Quinlan, Thomas, and Gautreaux, 2004). This political philosophy is heavily associated with conservative ideology, and the Republican Party specifically, as politicians under the conservative banner at the state, local, and national levels were the primary force behind the privatization of dozens of industries, including corrections, beginning in the 1980s (Daley, 1996; Schneider, 1999). Conservative groups and politicians led the campaign for more punitive criminal justice policies and the development of governmental capacity to punish and incarcerate criminal offenders (e.g., Gottschalk, 2006; Kim and Price, 2014). Following this logic, we may expect Republicans to be more supportive of policies that encourage both privatization and the further development of infrastructure to detain criminal offenders (Kim and Price, 2014).

Second, scholars and policymakers themselves often point to economic considerations to explain privatization. In the 1980s, governments were facing the dual pressures of the public's desire to incarcerate and its frugality in spending government money (e.g., Enns, 2016; Gilmore, 2007). States attempted to pass bonds to construct new prisons, but citizens repeatedly voted down these bonds or set controls on spending (Joyce and Mullins,

1991; McDonald et al., 1998). This theoretical intuition is bolstered by some scholarly evidence pointing to potentially millions in cost savings after contracting out to private companies (Savas, 1991; Stevens, 1984). Private prison companies take advantage of this belief by promoting themselves as frugal alternatives to the public sector. CoreCivic pledges to build a 1,000-bed prison for under $75 million compared to a public cost of more than $150 million (Corrections Corporation of America, 2013). This mechanism is also one identified by prison operators themselves: one 1998 report found that 57% of prison managers cited operational and construction cost savings as a reason why the facility or state privatized (McDonald et al., 1998).

Third, unions are associated with a decreased likelihood of privatization as unions often oppose privatization on the grounds that it increases both costs and the potential for corruption and decreases both accountability and job opportunities for union workers (Naff, 1991). Broadly, unions seek instead to raise wages and gain higher-quality insurance policies for their members, an effect that has been empirically confirmed at least for fire- and police-protection employees (Anzia and Moe, 2015). In particular, unionized corrections workers may be afraid that privatization will spur layoffs, along with lower wages and benefits (Brudney et al., 2005). In case studies, these dynamics appear to be at play: Page (2011) documents how the California Correctional Peace Officers Association (CCPOA) fought against private prison companies entering the state because private facilities do not use union labor, threaten the job security of its workers, and jeopardize the political legitimacy of the CCPOA as a union, one of the strongest in the country. Nationwide, bailiffs, correctional officers, and jailers have one of the highest rates of union membership, at 47.9% of those employed as of 2015 (Hirsch and Macpherson, 2003). In contrast, the rate of public sector union membership is about 12% lower, at 35.2% as of 2015; and corrections workers have a rate of union membership that ranks in the top 20 of nearly 500 occupations, after teachers, police officers, firefighters, and others (Hirsch and Macpherson, 2003).

Finally, the critiques of the private prison industry often cite their involvement in lobbying and campaign contributions to political candidates (Schneider, 1999). For their part, the private prison companies I interviewed for this book suggest that their lobbying activity is primarily informational, to provide details about privatization and not to lobby for increased sentencing or other punitive measures (information they say is "wrong" and "politically motivated"). This experience was echoed by at least one interviewee, who portrayed these lobbyists as "Johnny-on-the-spot, they're there to answer [our] questions." However, other government interviewees cited their experience with the lobbyists as more strategic with their behavior: these lobbyists "plant a seed as something in the legislator's hand and water it and make it grow" and are "very careful, they're very strategic, and they change legislators' minds." A state legislator recounted a time when they were drafting the budget and the lieutenant governor had called "begging" to add a budget item for privatization because the lieutenant governor was "buddies" with those companies and they had backed him in the election. Anecdotally, private prison companies engage in "lobbying blitzes" to defeat legislation antithetical to their business interests as these companies have much to lose from legislation that restricts the growth of incarceration (Schneider, 1999; White, 2001). CoreCivic's board is partially comprised of former government officials, which could reflect a strategy to make state governments more receptive to private prisons (Selman and Leighton, 2010, 95–97). Lobbying is a powerful tool of these companies, and the two largest private prison companies in the country, CoreCivic and GEO Group, both operate political action committees and regularly donate hundreds of thousands of dollars to candidates at the local, state, and national levels. The National Institute on Money in State Politics reports that for-profit correctional facilities construction and management contributed over $2,000,000 to candidates running for state office in 2014. According to Open Secrets, the CoreCivic Political Action Committee spent $264,697 on all candidates in the 2014 election cycle, while the GEO Group spent $518,390. It follows that we may expect those contributions to influence the policymaking decisions of those receiving the donations.

There are multiple reasons to think that these explanations alone do not predict prison privatization, however. First, though some argue that Republican states will be more likely to privatize, Republican *and* Democratic states currently have or had contracts with for-profit correctional companies and platforms, and all parties praised privatization at some point since the 1980s (Culp, 2005). This fits into the broader phenomenon of neoliberalism, a political shift in American politics that preferred the private operation of state responsibilities (Wacquant, 2009, 287–314). Republican and Democratic politicians alike championed neoliberal policies including prison privatization, and privatization of government services more generally (Gottschalk, 2016, 11). This is echoed by interviewees, who suggest that it does not matter if the government is Democratic or Republican, that privatization is dependent upon need. And general distrust of the public sector makes private enterprise appealing to a variety of Americans (Lerman, 2019, 12–13). Even public opinion points to a complex relationship between partisanship and support for private prisons: Republicans and Democrats are inconsistent in their approval of private prisons (Enns and Ramirez, 2018). Finally, the vast geographic scope of this policy makes it unlikely that this explanation alone prompts privatization. Liberal states like California and Hawaii use private prisons and at sometimes higher rates than more conservative states like Texas and Florida.

Second, the argument that privatization saves money is not borne out by empirical evidence (Selman and Leighton, 2010, chap. 5). There is also reason to believe that though governments experienced financial austerity in the 1980s, public desire and demand for increased incarceration helped politicians acquire the necessary capital to build and/or renovate prisons (e.g., Enns, 2016; Harding, 2001). States could also get creative with their financial solutions and circumvent voters altogether via lease revenue bonds for that construction, a method that does not require voter approval (Gilmore, 2007, 98–99). Therefore, it is not likely that economics is a primary driving force behind prison privatization, even though it is often cited as the exclusive or primary motivation by policymakers for this decision.

Third, though unions can be powerful actors in state policy, it is unlikely they alone are able to prevent states from turning to privatization. The prototypical example of the CCPOA perhaps the single most powerful corrections officers' union in the country, did not stop private prisons from opening in California (Page, 2011, chap. 6). Moreover, one interviewee mentioned that though their state had union opposition to privatization, they could simply house their inmates in a private prison *out of state* to bypass the complex union politics. It is thus not likely that unions are themselves preventing states from privatizing.

Finally, there is mixed evidence on the degree and nature of private prison lobbying. As with studies of campaign contributions more generally, there is inconsistent evidence on whether contributions actually translate into monetary gains for firms (Fowler, Garro, and Spenkuch, 2020). Also, it is unclear whether private prison firms are donating to create or maintain relationships with existing allies and how those relationships influence the awarding of contracts or other outcomes. One interviewee, a state legislator, remarked that he "didn't even know this myself until an article back during session," that he was not aware of the thousands that private prison companies had given to him throughout the course of his campaign. Though the largest private prison companies indeed contribute to politicians' campaigns at the state, local, and national levels, it is difficult to find direct, convincing evidence to suggest that private companies deliberately contributed to politicians to toughen criminal sanctions and grow their businesses (Dolovich, 2005). Rather, the growth of privatization was accompanied by other factors, like rising crime rates and public fears of criminals and violent crime, which most likely contributed to the expansion of incarceration. It is difficult to attribute the growth of incarceration to one variable, though private prison companies hire professional lobbyists and directly contribute funding to political candidates (Jones and Newburn, 2005). Empirical examinations of the relationship of those contributions to state private prison levels has not been undertaken, partially because of data limitations; but it is unlikely that campaign contributions and lobbying activity by these firms are alone significant drivers of the continued growth of privatization.

Taken together, the literature presents important theories about the growth of prison privatization, but they do not *alone* appear to explain the rise of prison privatization. That is, though they may be part of the prison privatization story, they themselves are not sufficient to explain growth in carceral privatization (and, indeed, empirical evidence suggests they are inconsistently related to privatization; see Chapter 4). Moreover, these studies suffer from a lack of systematic data on this phenomenon over time. Why is this data scarce, and what information is available for scholars to use?

A Source of New Data on Private Prisons

Data on private prisons is notoriously difficult to acquire and has been nearly impossible for scholars and the public alike to come by. Though private prisons have been of interest to scholars, policymakers, and the public alike for decades (e.g., Cody and Bennett, 1987; Selman and Leighton, 2010; Thompson and Elling, 2002), information on these facilities is relatively scarce. There are a few reasons for this opacity. For one, private prison companies were not subject to Freedom of Information Act (FOIA) or sunshine law requests at the state or national level for much of their history (Eisen, 2018,

197). It was only in 2013 or later that district court judges in states like Texas, Vermont, Tennessee, and Florida ruled that companies are subject to state public records laws about their facilities as these businesses effectively act as government bodies (Thompson, 2014). At the federal level though, the limited transparency forced upon these companies by the courts does not exist. Corrections companies are not subject to *any* federal FOIA requirements. Legislation to require FOIA compliance among nongovernmental entities that contract with the federal government to operate correctional facilities has been introduced in Congress every session since 2005, but that legislation, called the Private Prison Information Act, has always died in committee (Eisen, 2018, 128–130). Efforts by politicians to apply a universal FOIA requirement have so far been unsuccessful, but individual lawsuits against these companies at the federal level have gained more traction. Judges in the federal district and circuit courts ruled in 2016 and 2017 that private prison companies were mandated to share information about private facilities under FOIA (*Detention Watch Network v. United States Immigration and Customs Enforcement* 215 F.Supp.3d 256). Thus, at both the state and national levels, companies are only mandated to share pertinent facility information after the judiciary forces them to, which is by no means a universal application of FOIA law to private prison corporations. A researcher may be able to request contract information from these companies but only for certain states or locations and likely only for those contracts operating currently or relatively recently.

The opacity of the companies is a major roadblock to those seeking to study private correctional facilities. It is also not only official sources of data that are unavailable, though—even attorneys who represent clients in private facilities were barred from the facilities after the lawyers reported that officials forced detainees to sign documents without appropriate legal counsel (Eisen, 2017). One advocacy director mentioned that in her experience litigating against private companies they would often refuse to hand over documents like operations manuals or staff information (without a court order) because it was "proprietary information." This director described the litigation process as a "a war of attrition, and they fight it at every step of the way. Infuriating."

Therefore, those researchers who might rely on interviews, court records, or other qualitative research into these facilities are severely limited in the information available in public records.

What Information Currently Exists?

Faced with these challenges, researchers have used other sources to study private prisons, but none satisfactorily display over-time and across-state variation: how long a company has operated the facility for, whether the facility has undergone any capacity expansions, the customers of the facility, or the lengths of the contracts companies sign with government entities, among other information.

The most common source is the Bureau of Justice Statistics' (BJS) Prisoners series, which lists the number of private prison inmates a state has under its jurisdiction, housed both in- and out-of-state (e.g., Kim and Price, 2014). There are two significant flaws with this data, however. First, it does not provide any data on the *facilities* themselves, only on the prisoners housed in private institutions. Second, the BJS only began collecting this data in 1999, over a decade after the first private prison opened in the United States. A similar source also comes from the BJS, the Census of State and Federal Adult Correctional Facilities (e.g., Price and Riccucci, 2005), which identifies characteristics of individual private facilities like capacity, security level, and other information. There are two similar issues with this data, however. The series only began collecting facility-level data in 1990, so it also does not provide any information on private prisons in the 1980s. Additionally, this data is only recorded every five years, so an analysis of change in facilities and capacity over time would be difficult without some significant data interpolation, which would require additional assumptions about the growth of private prisons to be valid.

Another data source is information gathered from Professor Charles Thomas of the University of Florida (e.g., Nicholson-Crotty, 2004). Though this data is facility-level and longitudinal, problems remain. First, the information is not collected consistently, nor is it readily available for each year. Second, Thomas was a member of CoreCivic's real estate board and was partially funded to collect this information by the company (Nicholson-Crotty, 2004). While it is difficult to say whether and how much that fact could influence the collection or reporting of data, it does give me pause at using it as a source of unbiased data.

The existing data sources, therefore, are inadequate in a variety of ways. I develop an innovative data set on private prison facilities instead, using information found in the pages of shareholder reports of private prison companies from the 1980s to the present (introduced first in Gunderson, 2020c). This data set will allow scholars to examine the growth and character of private prisons since the 1980s for the first time.

An Original Data Set

I look to the Securities and Exchange Commission's (SEC's) 10-K reports, annual reports publicly traded companies are required to file with the SEC. These reports contain information on the location of companies' privately operated facilities and, for the most part, data on customers, design capacity, and contract length. My sample includes the facilities operated by the four publicly traded private prison companies that existed since the 1980s: CoreCivic, the GEO Group, Correctional Services Corporation (CSC), and Cornell Companies.[1] The entire sample encompasses private prisons from 1986 to the present, but the coverage differs across different firms. CoreCivic is included in the data from 1986 to the present, GEO Group from 1989 to the present, CSC from 1997 to 2004, and Cornell from 1996 to 2009. The GEO Group acquired both CSC and Cornell Companies in 2005 and 2010, respectively; and both CoreCivic and the GEO Group have acquired smaller, non-traded private prison companies since the 1980s. In fact, the industry has become smaller over time: in 1999, there were 12 private prison firms and by 2016, eight of the original 12 were absorbed by other companies, and only two new firms opened in that time period (Mumford, Schanzenbach, and Nunn, 2016).

Though the reports are fairly consistent over time, I filled in any missing data that occurred using past reports and other sources as a guide (more details in the Appendix). Additionally, this data encompasses only correctional facilities, like prisons and jails, and not community corrections facilities.[2] I chose to restrict the sample to only prison and jail facilities to measure the practice of *private corrections*, not private community corrections, which is a commonplace practice across all states (and evidence of the continued privatization of American corrections; see Chapter 6). The result is a data set of private jail or prison facilities, at the local, state, and federal levels, operated by publicly traded private prison companies in each state-year from 1986 to the present.

One important limitation with this data is that it only includes companies publicly traded on the stock market. This is likely not a significant concern, however. The businesses that are included represent the vast majority of the private prison market in the United States. In 1998, for example, these four companies together comprised more than 85% of the private prison market (Austin and Coventry, 2001). In 2014, after the GEO Group acquired the two smaller companies in my data set, GEO and CoreCivic comprised approximately 85% of the market share by themselves (Mumford, Schanzenbach, and Nunn, 2016). So, while this data set does not list every private prison since the 1980s, it provides the vast majority of them and the facilities that are operated by the largest, multibillion-dollar companies like CoreCivic and GEO Group.

This comprehensive data set improves on the existing data in several ways. First, it provides information on capacity, customer, and contract length for private prisons since the 1980s. No other data set contains consistent data on these facilities for that long of a time span. Second, not only does this data contain information on the location of these facilities, but it also lists contract data, information that was previously unavailable to researchers unless they chose to file FOIA requests with the state or federal government. Though this data source, like all others, is not perfect, it substantially improves the data currently available to researchers and helps us examine these facilities in more fine-grained detail than ever before.

What Does the Data Look Like?

What exactly do private prisons look like across the United States, and to what degree is there variation both over time and across states in the usage of this policy? Table 2.1 highlights the companies included in the data set, how many unique facilities they operated from 1986 to 2016, and the sum of the capacities of those facilities. CoreCivic has operated the most, with 158 unique facilities and over 1.5 million prisoners housed from 1986 to 2016, with GEO Group a distant second. Both Cornell and CSC operated fewer facilities for lower aggregate design capacities.

Table 2.1 Original Data Set of Private Prisons by Company, 1986 to 2016: CoreCivic Is Included from 1986 to 2016, GEO Group from 1989 to 2016, Cornell from 1996 to 2009, and CSC from 1997 to 2004.

Company	Number of Unique Facilities	Sum Capacity
CCA	158	1,586,256
Cornell	20	111,765
Correctional Services Corporation	20	38,470
GEO	137	949,555

Table 2.2 reflects the temporal variation in private prisons, listing the first year states placed any number of their inmates in private facilities. States could privatize a state prison and consequently house their inmates there, or states could house some of their inmates in an out-of-state private prison (recall how one

Table 2.2 Original Data Set of Private Prisons by State, 1986 to 2016.

State	First Private Inmates	First State Private Facility	First Local Private Facility	First Federal Private Facility
Alabama	2003			
Alaska	1994			
Arizona	1997	1994		1994
Arkansas	1996	1995		
California	1989	1989	1992	1997
Colorado	1996	1996	2016	1989
Connecticut				
Delaware				
Florida	1995	1995	1986	1996
Georgia	1997	1997	1998	1998
Hawaii	1998			
Idaho	1996	2000		
Illinois			2004	2004
Indiana	1997	2005	1997	
Iowa				
Kansas	1995	1995		1992
Kentucky	1998	1998	1998	
Louisiana	1990	1990	2007	2007
Maine				
Maryland				
Massachusetts				
Michigan	1997	1997		
Minnesota	1996	1996		1997
Mississippi	1995	1995	1997	2008
Missouri				
Montana	1997	1999		
Nebraska				
Nevada	1998	1998		2010
New Hampshire				
New Jersey				1996
New Mexico	1987	1987	1986	1990

(continued)

Table 2.2 *Continued*

State	First Private Inmates	First State Private Facility	First Local Private Facility	First Federal Private Facility
New York				1989
North Carolina	1994	1998		2000
North Dakota	1997			
Ohio	2011	1997	1998	2004
Oklahoma	1995	1995	2000	2014
Oregon	1989			
Pennsylvania			1995	1999
Rhode Island				1996
South Carolina	1996	1996		
South Dakota				
Tennessee	1991	1991	1986	1990
Texas	1987	1987	1994	1986
Utah	1999	1999		
Vermont	2004			
Virginia	1996	1996		
Washington	2005			1997
West Virginia				
Wisconsin	1997			
Wyoming	1996	2015		

"First Private Inmates" refers to the first year the state housed any inmates in private facilities, inside or outside their borders; "First State Private Facility" refers to the first private state facility in the state; "First Local Private Facility" refers to the first private local facility in that state; and "First Federal Private Facility" refers to the first private federal facility in that state.

interviewee suggested that housing inmates in an out-of-state private prison is much easier than doing it in their own state). There are some states like Alaska or Hawaii that utilize private prisons but do not physically have any within their borders, so those kinds of states will have an entry in the second column but not the third. Finally, the third and fourth columns list the first year a local or federal private facility opened within each state. From the table, the variation of prison privatization across states becomes obvious. Even if states do not explicitly allow state-run private prisons, they can still play host to either local or federal private facilities within their borders. At the very least, it is useful to see the vast geographic and longitudinal variation in this policy, particularly when it is broken down into the various kinds of prison privatization that can exist.

In addition to the temporal trends, the geographic distribution of the use of private prisons is fairly diverse. Figure 2.1 displays the logged number of

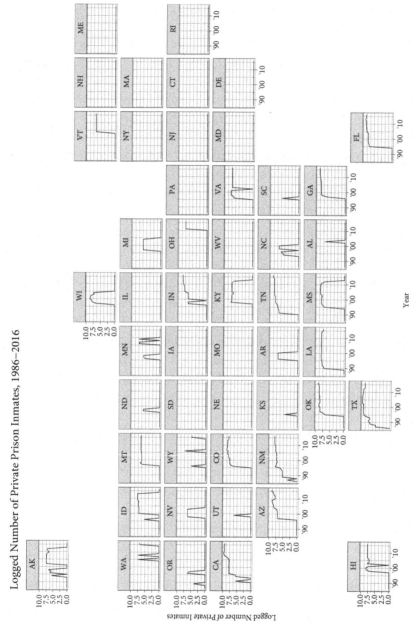

Logged Number of Private Prison Inmates, 1986–2016

Figure 2.1 Logged number of inmates held in private facilities, 1986 to 2016.

inmates housed in state-level private facilities since 1986. I chose to log the variable to highlight each state's relative usage of this policy over the last few decades since there are some states that vastly out-incarcerate others.

From the graph, there are a few evident patterns. First, for the most part, once a state decides to house inmates in private facilities, the government continues that policy. This is most obviously the case in states such as California, Arizona, Georgia, and Texas, all of which utilize private prison companies at least partially (and increasingly) throughout this time period. Though that is a general pattern, it is by no means universal. States like Wisconsin, Arkansas, and Nevada, among others, house some inmates in private facilities at some point throughout this time period but only do so temporarily, likely only to alleviate short-term overcrowding concerns in their corrections systems. Finally, there are some states that never utilize private prisons for their inmates, like most of the Northeast and states like Nebraska and Missouri.

A similar pattern emerges when evaluating the proportion of private inmates held in private facilities, as seen in Figure 2.2. This provides a more nuanced measure of each state's usage of this policy. For some states that are among those that house the most inmates in private facilities, like Texas and California, that choice is paired with an expansion of the incarceration rate overall. That is, the proportion of inmates held in private jails or prisons is fairly low even though the state relies on private prisons to incarcerate, as Figure 2.2 points out. Moreover, some states that have a lower overall number of private inmates still maintain higher proportions in these facilities, nearing 50% or more. These states, like New Mexico, Hawaii, and Alaska, among others, rely more heavily on private companies for incarceration than their capacity numbers would suggest.

One particular aspect of this map is worth considering. This graph represents only private inmates under state jurisdiction. Therefore, private facilities within the state that hold either inmates under jurisdiction of local authorities (like the city or county) or inmates under federal jurisdiction (of agencies like Immigration and Customs Enforcement [ICE] or the US Marshals Service [USMS]) are not included. In these circumstances, the state is not overtly involved in the administration of the private facilities because the inmates incarcerated are not under state jurisdiction. Local and federal jurisdictions can still operate private facilities within a state even if the state, like Illinois and New York,[3] statutorily prohibits state prison privatization (Quinlan, Thomas, and Gautreaux, 2004). So, to fully understand the scope

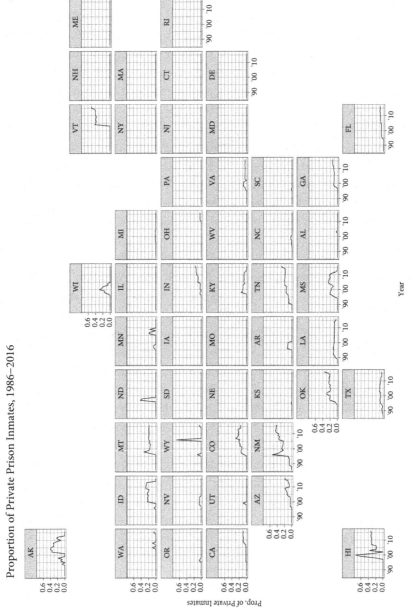

Figure 2.2 Proportion of inmates held in private facilities, 1986 to 2016.

of privatization at all levels of government, it is important to see the geographic pattern of not only private inmates but private facilities as well.

Figure 2.3 displays the logged number of private facilities in each state, from 1986 to 2016. This includes both local and federal facilities. For the most part, the pattern mirrors that in Figure 2.1: states like California, Arizona, Georgia, and Texas, which had some of the highest numbers of private prison inmates, also have some of the highest logged numbers of private institutions. Also, there are some states, like Alaska, Hawaii, and Minnesota, among others, that place some of their inmates in private facilities but not in their own states. Rather, states, particularly Alaska and Hawaii, house their prisoners as far as Arizona and Mississippi. Moreover, even the states that statutorily outlawed prison privatization, like New York and Illinois, contain private facilities within their borders. Though the customer base for those prisons is the federal government, even a prohibition against privatization cannot necessarily prevent other jurisdictions from placing private institutions in states that otherwise would not want them.

Similarly, Figures 2.4 and 2.5 represent the physical locations of these facilities in four different years across the data set—1986, 1996, 2006, and 2016. In the figures, larger circles indicate a higher density of private facilities at that location. Whereas the facilities were largely clustered in the South in 1986, for example, within 10 years more northern and western states had physical private prison facilities. By 2006 and 2016, locations such as Arizona, California, and Colorado had dense areas with at least five private facilities, though the geographic spread of private prisons remains extensive.

It is evident from the table and graphs that both the use of privatization and the placement of private facilities are geographically widespread and vary over time. These additional insights are only possible from the data collection effort described here and help to address a few myths about privatization: that it is exclusive to the South and that states that adopt privatization do not later change their mind and move away from prison privatization.

In addition to the number of facilities by state, another useful piece of information found in my data set considers the mix of intergovernmental agreements to share correctional facilities. In the data, less than 10% of the prisons or jails have more than one customer (see Figure 2.6). When the facilities have more than one customer, though, the customer type is nearly always different. These prisons or jails often house federal prisoners alongside state or local ones or can house customers from multiple of the same type of

Logged Number of Private Prison Facilities, 1986–2016

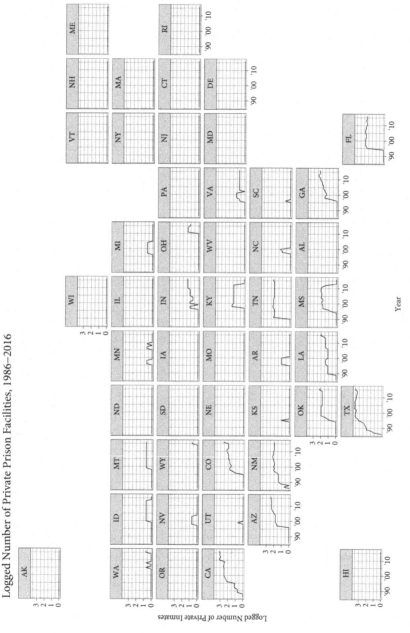

Figure 2.3 Logged number of private facilities in each state (including federal and local facilities), 1986 to 2016.

(a)

(b)

Figure 2.4 Location of private facilities in 1986 (a) and 1996 (b). Larger circles represent more private facilities at that location. This map includes all private facilities that held local, state, or federal inmates.

(a)

(b)

Figure 2.5 Location of private facilities in 2006 (a) and 2016 (b). Larger circles represent more private facilities at that location. This map includes all private facilities that held local, state, or federal inmates.

Distribution of Number of Customers by Year

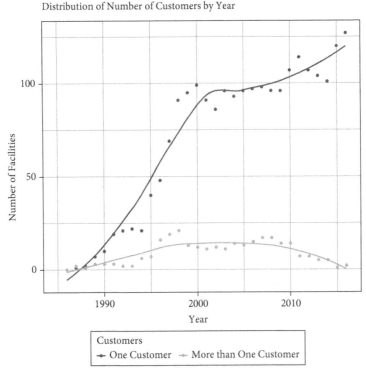

Figure 2.6 Sum of all facilities that have either one or more than one customer, 1986 to 2016.

customer: federal inmates from both the USMS and ICE, for example. Either way, it seems that these companies use these facilities as much as they can to ensure that capacity is reached and the company makes the most money as possible.

Finally, it is worth considering how the data set developed here corresponds to existing measures. By far the most comprehensive, and the one that provides the highest amount of longitudinal and spatial detail, is the annual BJS data on the number of private prisoners per state. That data is only available consistently after 1999, so this section will only consider the correspondence between the BJS data and the original data set from 1999 to 2015. Figure 2.7 offers visual evidence of the high correlation between these measures.

The two lines of the figure are nearly identical, and the correlation between them is extremely high at 0.844. Moreover, the divergence in the lines could be attributed to the variation in coding schemes that the BJS uses versus what

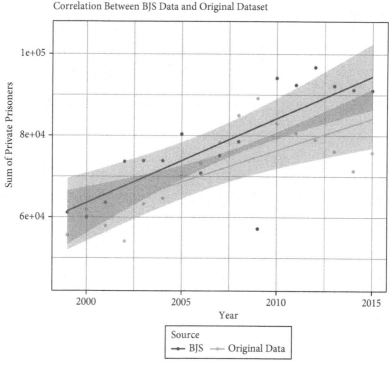

Figure 2.7 Comparison of Bureau of Justice Statistics (BJS) and the original data set data on prisoners in private facilities, 1999 to 2015. This represents the sum of all state prisoners in each year who are housed privately.

I used. While my original data set only considers those privately incarcerated in prisons or jails, the BJS data also includes those in privately operated halfway houses, treatment centers, and hospitals. It is likely, then, that some (or most) of the divergence found in this graph is because of that slight difference in coding. As states experiment more with privately operated halfway houses in lieu of incarceration, the gap between the BJS data and mine should get larger (and it does, in the 2010s) since I do not include those kinds of facilities in my counts. Additionally, my data set only considers the four companies that were traded publicly on the stock market. The BJS data makes no such distinction, so part of the divergence is additionally explained by the inclusion of smaller companies that are not in my data set. Finally, though the lines themselves diverge somewhat over the time period, the confidence intervals are nearly identical, which helps assure that the small discrepancies between the two data sets are not massively significant. Overall, though, the extremely high correlation is encouraging evidence that my data collection is mostly accurate in its representation of private prisons in the United States.

This novel data set highlights the temporal variation in the use of this policy overall. Though some interviewees spoke of their states' retrenchment in private prisons once they opened a facility, the data shows that states did and continue to either ramp up their use of privatization or eliminate it altogether in the last few decades. Private prisons burst onto the carceral scene nearly four decades ago, and states have certainly made wide and varied use of their presence. These patterns, though illustrative, do not provide a sense of explanation for this variation in patterns. Moreover, the cursory common explanations do not seem to map neatly onto the patterns of adoption we see from the data. What explains why states choose to privatize their prisons? The next chapter introduces a novel theoretical explanation for why this choice occurs, emphasizing the key role of accountability in the choice to privatize.

3

The Rights Revolution and
Prison Privatization

... what you see when they're private is they try to throw the buck back and forth to each other, right? And you will have them literally saying to you, "Well, I don't control that, they control that." In the same room as people like, "No, we don't control that." And then you're like okay, who controls that? Like somebody's in charge of transport, right? ... But the buck passing is like, honestly, it just ends up being terrifying, because you realize like, oh my God, who is in control? ... Like how is this not utter chaos? And the truth is, we're all lucky that more bad things don't happen more often.

—*Advocacy director interview, 2020*

In 1986, the first annual report from CoreCivic (formerly the Corrections Corporation of America [CCA]) after the company went public on the stock market made the case for stockholders that their company would succeed by providing solutions to the corrections industry. The report mentions overcrowding, greater financial flexibility, and more administrative efficiency as some of the benefits of privatizing. It also, however, explicitly mentions legal liability: "the company assumes the primary exposure of legal liabilities, leaving the contracting agency in a secondary position. CCA reduces potential liability" (Corrections Corporation of America, 1986). A year later, the annual report re-emphasized this important role of limiting accountability for the company's government partners: "the market segment with the most potential for the private sector is that portion which has the greatest need to relieve overcrowding, comply with court orders, and operate with greater efficiency" (Corrections Corporation of America, 1987).

I argue that the desire to limit both legal and political accountability is an important overlooked factor in the decision to privatize prisons at the state level. I put forward two hypotheses: first, I argue that more prisoner lawsuits, regardless of outcome, make it *more* likely a state will privatize its prisons. Privatization helps states evade legal and political accountability for prisoner lawsuits. The legal environment around privatization is murky, with inmates seeking to sue a variety of actors: private corrections officers, private companies, government monitors, or governments themselves (or all four) (Tartaglia, 2014). States thus benefit from an added layer of bureaucracy that limits their legal accountability for lawsuits. Second, the opaque chain of responsibility for private prisons encourages states to privatize and shift political blame for poor prison conditions away from themselves, to private companies.

My second hypothesis considers the rare instance of successful prisoner lawsuits. I hypothesize that more successful lawsuits make states *less* likely to privatize. Under the watchful eye of lawyers and attorneys, the state bureaucracy professionalizes and builds or expands existing facilities to adhere to judicial decrees. The state no longer has a need for new, updated facilities as the bureaucracy reforms to accommodate the growing problem of overcrowding. Additionally, judicial decrees often mandate that the state decrease prison populations, which has a direct and negative effect on private prison business. This fact is recognized by companies themselves as they write of the negative effect of successful lawsuits on their business in annual shareholder reports (Corrections Corporation of America, 2012).

This chapter expands on this argument by, first, reviewing the historical background of the prisoners' rights movement in the judiciary and other institutions, before discussing the rise of mass incarceration and the shifting nature of the criminal legal system since the 1970s and 1980s. I then describe how these changing dynamics affected prisoner lawsuits, and states' decision-making around prisons. Finally, I discuss the incentives to privatize when states are facing more lawsuits or a rare successful one. How did state governments, in concert with actions undertaken by prisoners, lawyers, and judges, decide to privatize their correctional institutions? How did the actions of these four actors change as the legal environment for prisoner petitions shifted, ultimately resulting in the unintended consequence of the adoption of prison privatization?

The Judiciary's "Hands-Off" Attitude
and Slaves of the State

A convicted felon [is one] whom the law in its humanity punishes
by confinement in the penitentiary instead of with death. For the
time being, during his term of service in the penitentiary, he is in a
state of penal servitude to the State. He has, as a consequence of his
crime, not only forfeited his liberty, but all his personal rights except
those which the law in its humanity accords to him. He is for the
time being the slave of the State.

—*Ruffin v. Commonwealth (1871)*

American jurisprudence ignored prisoners for much of the country's history.
The judiciary was not alone, however: for centuries, prisoners were relegated
to dark cells, in a mass of violence and darkness. It is not until the development of the penitentiary, aiming to rehabilitate offenders jointly through
solitude and labor, that governments gave much thought to the fate of the
incarcerated (de Tocqueville and de Beaumont, 2014, chaps. 1 and 2). Given
the scarcity of attention to the plight of prisoners, it is no surprise that courts
followed the lead of both the federal and state governments in their neglect of
inmates. When the courts did consider prisoners, that consideration largely
occurred to cement the incarcerated's place at the bottom of the social and
political hierarchy. *Ruffin v. Commonwealth* (1871), a Virginia court case that
occurred shortly after millions of Black Americans were legally freed from
slavery, retained the slave concept to apply it to those confined in prisons
and jails. Slavery was legally outlawed in the United States in 1865, but for
prisoners, state-sponsored confinement continued long after.

After the Civil War, states subjected prisoners to horrific conditions not
much distinct from the conditions of slavery. Particularly in the South, the
development of the convict-leasing system allowed private companies to effectively enslave convicts to labor in coal mines and brickyards and on other
projects (see Chapter 2 for more details; Gottschalk, 2006; Perkinson, 2010).
This brutal tradition was outlawed by most southern states by the mid-1920s
and replaced by chain gangs that developed the South's infrastructure by
forcing convicts to work mainly on road projects (Gottschalk, 2006, 51–52).
The most brutal conditions, like those in chain gangs, slowly disappeared
from states' criminal legal systems; and in their place, states developed a

variety of prison management styles. Some states, like California, embraced the rehabilitative aspect of incarceration and provided more educational and re-entry services, while others, like Texas, instead preferred inmates to learn discipline, primarily via labor in the fields (e.g., Perkinson, 2010). Though the administration of corrections varied across states, many state corrections bureaucracies took a laissez-faire, hands-off attitude to their prisons, allowing prisoners themselves to run vital operations within facilities rather than trained corrections officials (e.g., DiIulio, 1987; Feeley and Rubin, 2000). This practice, called the "trustee" or "building-tender system," was at the heart of many prisoners' rights cases as inmates argued that this hierarchical system, in which chosen prisoners administered punishment at the behest of corrections officers, resulted in incredibly violent prison conditions (DiIulio, 1987, chap. 5). It is in this environment, in which states variously sought to control and rehabilitate offenders often through punishment administered by prisoners themselves, that the prisoners' rights movement and the increase in prison litigation began.

For the first half of the twentieth century, the courts largely deferred to state governments in the administration of correctional facilities in an approach termed the "hands-off" doctrine.[1] Officially, this doctrine stemmed from the court's perceived lack of jurisdiction in supervising prisons or interfering with the daily activities within correctional institutions ("Beyond the Ken of the Courts," 1963). The judiciary largely followed this doctrine for some or all of the following five rationales: first, a concern about separation of powers; second, the lack of expertise in penology; third, fear that judicial action would be counterproductive in maintaining prison discipline; fourth, the view that federalism prohibited federal courts from intervening in state prisons; and fifth, a concern that allowing these petitions would subsequently trigger a domino effect, overwhelming the federal judiciary in prisoner petitions (Goldfarb and Singer, 1970; Haas, 1977). Though the courts considered prisons virtually outside their jurisdictional purview for the first half of the twentieth century, sympathetic language crept into court opinions beginning in the 1940s and 1950s that indicated a changing attitude toward prisoners and their right to litigate (Feeley and Rubin, 2000, 35). This hands-off approach eroded piecemeal in the evolution of law surrounding prisoners as the federal judiciary took particular interest in promoting the rights of the incarcerated.

Though the hands-off doctrine constrained judges in their ability to grant prisoners relief for constitutional violations occurring within prisons, inmates did not stop filing lawsuits altogether. Hundreds of cases were filed in the first half of the twentieth century as prisoners sued for perceived grievances against the state (Feeley and Rubin, 2000, chap. 1). The early lawsuits were by and large unsuccessful and very uncommon, but they paved the way for the watershed prisoners' rights cases, beginning with *Cooper v. Pate* in 1964. This Supreme Court decision gave state prisoners protections guaranteed in the Civil Rights Act of 1871[2] (Goldfarb and Singer, 1970). This case, brought by a Black Muslim prisoner housed in Illinois, centered around the plaintiff's claim of discrimination as prison officials would not provide him with a Qur'an (Losier, 2013). The Supreme Court decision permitted Muslim prisoners to sue prison officials for religious discrimination under Section 1983 of Title 42 of the US Code (Chase, 2015). Thomas X. Cooper, the plaintiff in this case, filed the lawsuit pro se, without the aid of an attorney, after consulting with the leader of the Nation of Islam (NOI), Elijah Muhammad, and other inmates (Losier, 2013). Though Cooper filed this lawsuit by himself, he connected his experience while incarcerated to the plight of other Muslim inmates, and his case illustrated a typical strategy of the NOI to utilize networks both within and across prisons nationwide to expose inhumanities within correctional facilities to the broader public. Thus, while this particular case is often heralded as the first modern prisoners' rights case, it is emblematic of the beginning of a larger mobilization effort on behalf of prisoners nationwide and, in particular, mobilization efforts begun by minority advocates to highlight racial discrimination running rampant in prisons and jails.

Racial disparities in incarceration and punishment that exist in contemporary America[3] did not always exist as starkly. In the late 1930s, Black Americans comprised approximately a quarter of the prison population; and in contemporary America, they comprise about *half* of all people in prison (Gottschalk, 2006, 2). The timing of this shift, shortly after the civil rights movement, is no coincidence. Some scholars argue that the losers of the Civil Rights Movement? segregationists and other actors who wanted to maintain White supremacy in social and political life, turned to criminal justice policy in the aftermath of the successful movement to champion tough-on-crime policies that effectively controlled the minority population by sending more of them to prison (Weaver, 2007). This discrimination also did not stop at the prison walls. Prisons all across the country continued to be heavily segregated, both informally in terms of which groups inmates aligned with but also formally as prison officials gave the higher-paying, more prestigious prison jobs to White inmates and, in the South, enlisted the majority-Black prison population to pick cotton and other crops at the behest of White overseers. It is likely no surprise, then, that the increasing number of minority inmates flooding into prisons who encountered additional discrimination at the hands of prison officials felt that this discrimination stemmed directly from their race. Many Black and Latinx inmates merged their individual experiences within prisons to the struggle of minorities more broadly.

Black inmates who organized both inside and outside of prisons to protest the conditions within these facilities largely organized under the umbrella of two groups: the NOI and the Black Panthers. Incarcerated members of the NOI were at the forefront of the prisoners' rights movement, as *Cooper v. Pate* illustrates, largely to win religious accommodations denied to them (Berger, 2014, 58). This litigation effort was coordinated and intentional, a strategy pursued by the NOI which served as a catalyst for non-Muslim prisoners to file cases (see Felber, 2019, chap. 2). The movement begun by the NOI, followed by the efforts of the Black Panthers, sought to illuminate the growing racial disparities in prison and the idea that Black Americans were incarcerated to maintain the system of White supremacy, which was in decline after the civil rights movement (e.g., Berger, 2014). Both movements attracted media attention to the plight of incarcerated minorities, through media movements and publicity of high-profile lawsuits against the criminal legal system.

It wasn't solely litigation prisoners turned to in their efforts to reform the system, however. Some prisoners turned to bloody and brutal riots in an effort to attract media attention to the horrors within correctional facilities and, in particular, to racism within prisons (e.g., Thompson, 2016). Though these events are much different than prisoners filing lawsuits in federal court, the aim was the same: to attract public attention to substandard conditions within prisons. These riots generally began in an effort to secure better living and working conditions within prisons, an outcome similar to the one sought by prisoners filing lawsuits (e.g., Thompson, 2016). Moreover, the number of riots was burgeoned by the writings of convict revolutionaries like Eldridge Cleaver, Angela Davis, and George Jackson (e.g., Berger, 2014). Jackson's death while he was incarcerated in disputed circumstances in August 1971 was a major contributing factor to the notorious September 1971 riot at Attica prison in New York, a four-day standoff that left over 40 people dead, prisoners and prison workers alike (see Thompson, 2016). This riot was certainly exemplary in its massive media coverage and high death toll, but it was a part of a larger movement among prisoners to riot to attract public attention to horrific prison conditions: in 1967, there were only five prison riots; in 1971, the year the Attica riot occurred, there were 37. By 1972, that number had risen to 48, the highest number of prison riots in American history at that time (Gottschalk, 2006, 178–179). Prisoners rioted to achieve changes within the criminal legal system but also to garner political and social support for their cause through the media reports of horrific conditions at their facilities (Rosenberg, 2008, 308–309). In this way, lawsuits and riots were inextricably linked, as both strategies sought to attract attention to the brutalities within prisons and gain sympathy for the prisoners' cause.

The external mobilization of these advocacy groups to attract attention to the inequalities within correctional institutions was matched by internal mobilization of the prisoners themselves. Prisoners who wanted to file lawsuits but were inexperienced with the criminal legal system often sought help from jailhouse lawyers, inmates who took a special interest in litigation and aided other inmates in the filing of lawsuits and other legal actions (Berger, 2014; Jacobs, 1980; Thomas, 1988). Though prisons were initially hostile to jailhouse lawyers, often painting them as agitators and punishing them for aiding fellow inmates in filing petitions, *Johnson v. Avery*, a 1969 Supreme Court case, held that state correctional officials could not punish jailhouse lawyers for providing legal assistance when the facility itself did not provide those services (Jacobs, 1980). As a result, jailhouse lawyers proliferated, helping prisoners file lawsuits when they would otherwise not.

Jailhouse lawyers were only so effective at aiding inmates' legal claims, however. Greater attention to the plight of the incarcerated was also particularly useful at attracting legal advocates to prisoners' causes. Many of the first prisoners' rights cases were filed pro se, without the aid of an attorney, and often as part of a greater litigation campaign by organizations like the NOI. However, as the federal courts stepped away from the hands-off doctrine and began issuing decisions maligning state corrections systems, the fate of prisoners was linked to a broader struggle for rights in the United States. This larger mobilization effort occurred as other disadvantaged groups were similarly utilizing the judiciary to acquire rights previously denied to them. This movement is known as the "rights revolution," which expanded civil rights and liberties in the judicial context (Epp, 1998, 7). Though this term is often used in reference to previously underrepresented groups gaining additional liberties, as in the case of prisoners or women, at its simplest, it refers to the increased judicial attention to the protection and establishment of individual rights. For prisoners, activists were crucial to the success of this litigation campaign as they linked the prisoners' cause to that of other powerless groups, ensuring that inmates were part of a larger rights movement (Rosenberg, 2008, 308). The most involved activists nationally worked with the New York City Legal Aid Society, the National Association for the Advancement of Colored People (NAACP) Legal Defense Fund, and the American Civil Liberties Union's (ACLU's) National Prison Project, though there were smaller regional and local organizations that aided prisoners in filing lawsuits as well (Jacobs, 1980; Schlanger, 2006). These organizations, and the lawyers within these groups, were previously part of the struggle for civil rights, highlighting how they viewed prison conditions as a question of fundamental rights (Jacobs, 1980). This framing reached far outside these activists and caught the attention of law schools and the law profession itself. The University of Tennessee was the first law school to open a prison legal services program in 1947, but those programs soon proliferated across the country in the 1960s and 1970s (Cardarelli and Finkelstein, 1974). Further, the American Bar Association created the Commission on Correctional Facilities and Services in the 1970s to pursue correctional reform (Jacobs, 1980). Thus, legal advocacy on behalf of prisoners was in full swing, with multiple national organizations using the courts to push for the protection of prisoners' civil liberties while incarcerated.

The involvement of a network of national advocacy organizations altered the makeup of prisoner litigation claims more broadly. Lawyers were able to collate individual claims into large lawsuits, pushed for class action status on behalf of prisoners, and largely sought to generate outcomes that placed entire prison systems under court order (Justice, 1990; Schlanger, 2006; Schoenfeld, 2010). In some cases, judges themselves indicated to lawyers that they were open to charges against state prisons and even contacted sympathetic attorneys to represent prisoners in their cases against the state (e.g., Feeley and Rubin, 2000; Justice, 1990; Schoenfeld, 2010). As a result, lawyers were intimately involved in the strategy of the prisoners' rights movement and could serve as a signal to judges of the quality and legitimacy of prisoners' complaints. Because there were far more prisoner complaints than advocacy organizations designed to help them, involvement of any group of this type signals the merit of those prisoners' lawsuits.

The 1960s and 1970s are considered the heyday of the prisoners' rights movement as both public and legal attention was devoted to the inhumane conditions within correctional facilities. Even after public attention to the cause waned, however, the impacts of the movement were largely positive. Generally, prisoners had greater access to educational programs, medical treatment, and accommodations for religious practices (Jacobs, 1980). Additionally, the most obvious physical brutality and torture faded. What soon replaced the draconian, chaotic prison system was a comprehensive bureaucracy that governed prison life. These highly detailed standards covered the management of residence facilities, sanitation, food, clothing, medical care, discipline, staff hiring, libraries, work, and education, among other facets of prison life (Feeley and Rubin, 2000, chap. 6). More recent research on the longitudinal effects of federal court intervention suggests that this intervention improved prison conditions, increased operating and capital expenditures within prisons, and decreased the number of inmate deaths (Boylan and Mocan, 2014). Thus, it seems the aggregate effect of the rise in prisoners' legal claims is positive as state bureaucracies devoted more resources to ensure prisoners' constitutional rights while incarcerated.

The involvement of prisoners, lawyers, judges, and the state government prior to the 1970s soon changed, however. Prisoners had the same incentive to file lawsuits to protest inequities within prisons and were even more interested in doing so after both the likelihood of success increased and their access to the federal judiciary, via jailhouse lawyers and other legal groups, expanded. Lawyers from the civil rights movement became involved in prison litigation and advocacy, helping collate individual claims and pursuing wide-ranging decisions against entire prison or jail systems. Judges shifted from virtually no acknowledgment of prisoner complaints against the state to more wide-ranging jurisdiction on these issues. Finally, state governments that once operated their correctional institutions often with little oversight and control that led to widespread physical abuse were now forced to professionalize and develop bureaucratic standards for prison governance. It is in this evolving interaction between these four actors that an additional challenge came to bear on all of them: mass incarceration.

The Rise of Mass Incarceration

For state prisoners, eating, sleeping, dressing, washing, working, and playing are all done under the watchful eye of the State, and so the possibilities for litigation under the Fourteenth Amendment are boundless. What for a private citizen would be a dispute with his landlord, with his employer, with his tailor, with his neighbor, or with his banker becomes, for the prisoner, a dispute with the State. (*Preiser v. Rodriguez* 1973)

The 1980s heralded a monumental shift in criminal justice policymaking in America. Prior to the 1970s, states largely relied on the rehabilitative approach to corrections. Governments used indeterminate sentencing, which allowed administrative authorities like parole boards to personalize offenders' sentences based on capacity for and evidence of rehabilitation, to reduce recidivism and ease the formerly incarcerated person's transition back into the community (Gottschalk, 2006, 37–39). Simultaneously, states employed education and vocational programs, substance abuse treatment and other counseling, therapeutic communities, and other residential programs to prepare an inmate for release (Seiter and Kadela, 2003). Sociologist Robert Martinson's infamous declaration that "nothing works" in the field of criminal rehabilitation in 1974 galvanized the critics of indeterminate sentencing and rehabilitative re-entry policies into action. In the next 10 years, indeterminate sentencing was abolished at the federal level[4] and replaced by determinate sentencing, mandatory minimum drug laws passed with sweeping congressional majorities, and truth-in-sentencing laws mandated that offenders serve at least 85% of their sentence (Gottschalk, 2006, 14). These radical changes in the criminal legal system pushed hundreds of thousands of people into prison and community supervision programs like probation and parole each year who would previously be diverted or released early.

Incarceration rates were largely stable in the first half of the twentieth century, increased slightly in the 1960s and 1970s, before exploding in the 1980s (see Figure 3.1). The incarceration rate rose precipitously as punitive laws passed legislatures at the state, national, and local levels to criminalize drug possession and dealing and to increase mandatory minimum sentencing for a variety of crimes (Murakawa, 2014, chap. 1). This shift vastly expanded the reach and scope of the criminal legal system as thousands of people, the majority of whom were Black or Latinx, were swept into prisons and jails (Alexander, 2010, chap. 1). This nationwide change is partially attributable to the wide support for the expansion of the criminal legal system across political and social lines: Republicans, Democrats, White Americans, Black Americans, and others all supported the expansion of the carceral state, at least at the beginning of the 1980s (e.g., Beckett, 1999; Enns, 2016; Forman, 2017; Fortner, 2015; Greenberg and West, 2001; Gunderson, 2021b; Murakawa, 2014; Smith, 2004). Thus, while variation existed in states' criminal justice

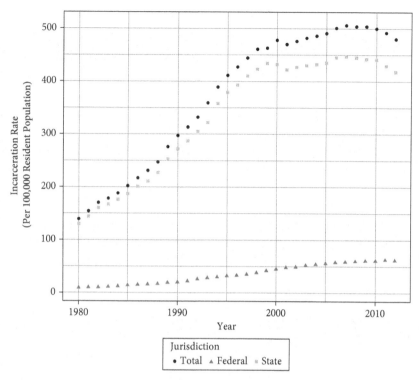

Figure 3.1 Incarceration rate of prisoners under jurisdiction of state and federal correctional authorities, 1980 to 2016. Data from the Bureau of Justice Statistics.

policy, swelling prison populations and no place to put incoming inmates meant that all states were facing similar difficulties as the 1980s began.

Prisoners, Lawyers, and Judges in an Era of Mass Incarceration

The difficulties introduced by mass incarceration led to a commensurate increase in the number of prisoner lawsuits filed in federal courts. Lawsuits about continuing fights for liberties such as healthcare and food grew even higher in number as prisons exceeded their capacities. In 1960, prisoners filed only 872 claims in federal court, just 2 percent of the total docket (Feeley and Rubin (2000, 45). That number soon exploded: by 1965, prisoners filed 12% of all filings in federal courts; and by 1971, they filed 18% of all filings, more than 12,000 individual complaints (Feeley and Rubin, 2000, 45). Though the majority of these claims were filed pro se and often dismissed quickly, the federal judiciary still faced a mountain of litigation that they previously did not.

Prisoners did not substantively change their strategy as mass incarceration grew. Still armed with an abundance of time, low or nonexistent filing fees, and the aid of either jailhouse lawyers or lawyers representing advocacy groups, inmates took advantage of their ability to sue and did so in greater and greater numbers. Though the quality and nature of these suits differed slightly from the lawsuits filed by the pioneers of the movement, more access to the courts resulted in more petitions filed overall.

Lawyers involved in prisoners' cases also changed somewhat. Whereas the beginning of this movement attracted attorneys from the ACLU and NAACP who had come directly from the civil rights movement—sometimes "follow[ing] their clients into jail" (Schlanger, 1999, page 2017)—these national organizations soon took a step back from this approach. The NAACP ended its involvement in these cases in the late 1970s, federal funding for prison legal aid groups decreased in the 1980s, and decreasing foundation support for groups like the ACLU's National Prison Project soon followed (Schlanger, 2006). Though these nationally minded lawyers gradually limited their involvement in prisoners' cases, reform-minded attorneys began to form regionally focused organizations like the Southern Center for Human Rights in Georgia and the Southern Poverty Law Center in Alabama to continue fighting for prisoners' legal rights (Schlanger, 2006). The commitment to prison reform did not change as the literal composition of the lawyers representing prisoners shifted, but it placed increasing importance on case selection: attorneys from these groups increasingly chose cases that had broad implications for the law more generally, rather than taking on individual complaints of inmates (Sturm, 1994).

The legal strategy also shifted. Because the most horrific conditions were the first to be litigated, the questions of conditions that remained after the initial blockbuster cases were qualitatively different from before or, as one lawyer from the ACLU National Prison Project said, "cheap victories are now nonexistent" (Schlanger, 2006). Cases left to be litigated after the larger cases were more difficult and represented individual complaints rather than cases with wide-ranging policy implications. Prisoners' rights cases have also become more rigorous over time as standards for evidence of deliberate neglect within these facilities have increased (Schlanger, 2006). As a result, lawyers shifted their strategy from challenging entire court systems like in the large cases in the 1960s and 1970s to more specific claims about particular correctional institutions and discrete actions taken by officials within those facilities (Schlanger, 2006). Despite this change in lawyers' litigation strategy, their motivations remained the same: litigate the most egregious of offenses to provide the most relief for the highest number of inmates as possible (Sturm, 1994).

Not all lawsuits were legitimate, however. Prisoners alleged cruel and unusual punishment because they received melted ice cream, believed the facility planted mind control devices in them, or gave them the incorrect ratio of chunky to smooth peanut butter jars from the canteen (Schlanger, 2003). These kinds of lawsuits are often cited by proponents of limiting inmate access to the courts, but these kinds of lawsuits are often dramatized by the media to make it seem like the only lawsuits inmates file are frivolous, which is not the case (e.g., Calavita and Jenness, 2015; Hanson and Daley, 1995). Also, frivolous lawsuits are not the only kind of prisoner petitions that do not get much traction in the legal system. Prisoners representing themselves or those who are assigned attorneys with little experience and incentive to fight for their rights within prisons and jails are likely falling through the cracks of the judicial system if they have a simple, individual complaint against a facility (Gunderson, 2021a; Sturm, 1994). Often, the frivolous and potentially legitimate individual claims alike are dismissed quickly as judges face a mounting number of cases they must process quickly.

Prisoners, a group previously largely absent from the judiciary, now filed tens of thousands of lawsuits each year. While some judges still felt it necessary to correct abuses occurring within prisons, others felt fatigue at the growing number of petitions. Some judges believed that the blockbuster prisoners' rights cases betrayed the hands-off doctrine and that legal rights levied to prisoners to sue states while incarcerated went too far[5] (Feeley and Rubin, 2000, 46–50). There are some judges who never saw a problem with the hands-off doctrine, instead preferring to defer to the authority of corrections officials. Others saw the benefit of correcting the most egregious of issues, but as the 1980s continued and the worst practices faded away, judges questioned the utility of further litigation as prisoners had won such significant victories already (Feeley and Rubin, 2000, 46–50). Judges' reticence to prisoner claims was further supported by the increasing number of frivolous lawsuits filed by inmates that some judges viewed as a waste of time and judicial resources. Finally, judges' natural skepticism toward prisoner petitions has always been the most pronounced among conservative justices. Critics of providing further rights to prisoners grew as President Ronald Reagan's judicial appointees joined the bench in the early 1980s, at the same time as the number of prisoner petitions swelled (Schlanger, 2006). Through the increased skepticism of all judges to prisoners' claims of abuses and the influence of conservative judges, courts began scaling back prisoner victories in free speech, due process, legal access, and free exercise of religion in the 1980s and 1990s (Feeley and Rubin, 2000, 46–50).

States' first, initial responses to the growing number of prisoner lawsuits involved simply making do with their outdated and small facilities. Once inmates began filing more petitions protesting this and other practices within prisons, however, governments were forced to proactively address these concerns before being sued by prisoners. Officials possessed one clear option to ameliorate their overcrowding concerns without expanding or constructing new prison facilities—the release of existing prisoners onto parole or probation to make room for new entrants. In fact, some court cases mandated precisely this action, requiring states to provide early release mechanisms and inmate population limits to prevent dangerous overcrowding (Taggart, 1989). Though this was an occasional tactic utilized by judges in their orders against states, it became less common as the decade wore on and as the opinion of both the general public, media, and politicians at that time heavily favored keeping inmates *inside* prisons, rather than letting them out to potentially endanger citizens (Enns, 2016, chap. 2).

Corrections departments could not ignore overcrowding because of the intense pressure the judiciary placed on the bureaucracy. In some states, entire corrections systems were placed under court order to reform their prisons. A federal judge placed the entire Arkansas prison system under a court order for violating the Eighth Amendment rights of prisoners in 1970, the first comprehensive court order of its kind (Feeley and Rubin, 2000, 39). Following the landmark Arkansas decision, entire prison systems across the country were declared unconstitutional,[6] reaching 9 states in 1983, 13 in 1990, and 15 by 1995 (Schlanger, 2006). The effect of the court orders was not always so dramatic, though. In other states, individual facilities were the only ones judicially mandated to mitigate overcrowding and other inhumane conditions. Forty-four states had a court order against at least one of their state prisons in 1984, and the same number faced at least one court order against a local jail within the state in 1983. Eventually, 48 out of the 53 jurisdictions in the United States had at least one facility declared unconstitutional, highlighting the broad scope of this litigation and its wide-spread geographic impacts (Feeley and Rubin, 2000, 40).

Thus, states released prisoners less frequently for two main reasons: it was politically unpopular to do so and was unlikely to solve the significant overcrowding problem within state prison systems. The most logical re-sponse after releasing prisoners is to instead construct new facilities to ac-commodate the thousands of new prisoners entering the system each year, a strategy undertaken by most state corrections' bureaucracies (Vaughn, 1993). However, the option to build a new, publicly run facility is not nec-essarily desirable because of the immense cost of doing so. Often, states funded the construction of new prisons through the issuance of bonds and ballot initiatives sent to the voters requiring them to approve the likely multimillion-dollar cost of building a new facility.[7] Citizen opinion shifted to prefer government austerity, and bond initiatives aimed at funding prisons specifically were repeatedly voted down even as citizen concern about crime grew (Selman and Leighton, 2010, 43). Indeed, retributive measures like the three strikes laws were passed via initiative in states like California, even as the state government was suffering economically (Barker, 2009, chap. 3).[8] Thus, politicians were running out of options to fund needed expansions to the prison system. These restrictions were only magnified by the signif-icant decrease in federal block grants to the states beginning in the 1980s. The amount of federal grants to state and local governments in fiscal year 1987, for example, was 14% lower than the comparable number in 1981 (Haughwout and Richardson, 1987). Additionally, state revenue from federal block grants decreased by 5% in only 10 years, from 1980 to the early 1990s (Poterba, 1994). This effect was magnified even further by the dismantling of the Law Enforcement Assistance Administration (LEAA), an agency within the Justice Department, in 1982. The LEAA was created in 1968 and resulted in massive transfers of federal monies to state and local law enforcement agencies with little regulation on what the governments could do with the funds (Gottschalk, 2006, 80). Thus, state governments faced massive strains on their criminal legal systems without the federal assistance they had previ-ously had.

These changes made it difficult for states to manage growing prison populations and limits on the construction of new correctional facilities. Beginning in the 1980s, however, there were two main avenues to new con-struction: either the state built or renovated new facilities themselves or the state could instead rely on an alluring new prospect to take on the physical and financial burden of construction: private prison companies. I argue that states responded to these difficulties in two distinct ways, either pursuing or avoiding privatization, depending on the outcome of prisoner litigation.

Inmate Lawsuit Growth and Private Prisons

Though successful prisoners' rights lawsuits changed the composition of states' correctional systems in many cases, states faced a larger issue than just the implementation of court orders. The number of lawsuits prisoners filed reached the tens of thousands in the 1980s as inmates took advantage of the more favorable legal climate to litigate their grievances. Briefly, I argue that the pressure of mounting lawsuits, regardless of the outcome of these cases, made it more likely for states to turn to private companies to alleviate the temporary stress on the criminal legal system. I suggest that this dynamic is driven by a desire to limit political and legal accountability for prisoner lawsuits.

It is useful to begin by revisiting the characteristics of lawsuits. While some are successful, most are not. A higher number of lawsuits in a given state-year is some mix of failures and successes, but the percent of victorious cases is much lower than the percent of failures—88% by one estimate (Schlanger, 2015) and even higher failure rates like 98.4% in others (Ostrom, Hanson, and Cheesman, 2003). The rate fluctuates slightly over the years but is always biased against prisoners: inmates are vastly more likely to fail in their litigation attempts than to succeed. There are a few reasons for this. First, "cheap victories are now nonexistent" (Schlanger, 2006), suggesting that the most egregious of violations were addressed in large lawsuits and only individual complaints remain. One advocacy director echoed this sentiment in her interview, saying that while they get "many, many" individual complaints, her organization would not take the case unless they see a pattern and practice they could litigate to impact many prisoners. Second, though the federal courts supported the expansion of prisoners' rights, retrenchment of those liberties soon followed. The Supreme Court raised evidentiary standards for prison cases, making them increasingly complex and expensive for attorneys to litigate (Schlanger, 2006; Sturm, 1994). Finally, the passage of the federal Prison Litigation Reform Act (PLRA) in 1996 (and similar measures at the state level [Brill, 2008]) added further legal obstacles for prisoners. This act sought to stem the mounting pressure placed on the corrections system by decreasing the number and severity of lawsuits prisoners filed against the state. The PLRA had numerous provisions: it required prisoners to exhaust any administrative remedies within prisons prior to filing an outside lawsuit in the federal system, limited both the damages inmates could receive and prisoners' attorneys' fees, and finally, imposed filing fees even on indigent inmates (Schlanger, 2006). These restrictions immediately decreased the number of lawsuits prisoners filed—by 40%, even as the incarceration rate continued to climb—as most of the requirements were so high as to effectively ensure that thousands of filings wouldn't be processed or even filed each year (Schlanger, 2006).

It is thus not a surprise that inmates have a relatively low likelihood of success. These lawsuits have some effect on states' responses to overcrowding, however. Even if the state is not under some sort of court order, how does the presence of these petitions alter states' behavior? States unburdened by judicial and legal surveillance of their activities chose privatization as the most logical response to their overcrowding problems. This dynamic is driven by all lawsuits, not just lawsuits filed to protest overcrowding, because any lawsuit filed has the potential of revealing the poor state of the prison system. Whether it be overcrowding concerns or inadequacies in medical care or other complaints, these lawsuits highlight the inadequacy of the existing prison system to accommodate the current prison population. This argument is similar in flavor to those of others who argued that successful court orders promoted prison expansion and increases in spending on prison capacity (Boylan and Mocan, 2014; Guetzkow and Schoon, 2015; Schoenfeld, 2010), but this study emphasizes the role of *all* lawsuits in this process, not just successful ones. Without the bargaining chip of a successful lawsuit to prompt public prison expansion, states needed an alternative source of revenue for this expansion: partnerships with private prison companies.

From a theoretical perspective, prison privatization allows the state to shift accountability away from the government to the private sector (Kay, 1987; White, 2001). States can shift the blame for poor conditions onto private prison companies. This mechanism is similar to the debate at the core of the use of private military contractors abroad (Leander, 2010). And similar to the legal murkiness described in more detail below in regard to private prisons, the legal uncertainty around the use of private military firms has also been a source of much controversy (Minow, 2004).

Within the broad concept of accountability, there are several ways in which privatizing helps state government. First, there is the question of political accountability. In this vein, a growing number of inmate lawsuits brings public scorn and attention to poor conditions within prisons (Jacobs, 1980). Privatizing prisons, then, allows states to shift political accountability to these private companies and the negative media attention that comes with horrific prison conditions. Similarly, privatization is often accompanied with the appointment of a contract monitor or other government official, whose responsibility it is to oversee the private operation of the prison. The appointment of this person, who in theory is supposed to ensure that the government keeps a close eye on any problems happening within the facilities (Selman and Leighton, 2010, 118–119), in fact helps lessen governmental accountability (Raher, 2010). Adding a layer of bureaucracy diffuses the blame for poor conditions within prisons—with the addition of the monitor, who is to blame for problems within prisons? It is thus more difficult, if not impossible, for voters to hold governmental representatives politically accountable for poor conditions in prisons as there are multiple layers of bureaucracy to contend with and no clear attribution of responsibility for institutional failures. Not to mention, governmental officials may be reticent to question the contractor's operations if the state is heavily reliant on them to manage their prisons (Raher, 2010). Thus, privatizing prisons allows state governments to shift accountability away from themselves and add a complex layer of bureaucracy to make it even more difficult to hold the state responsible for poor conditions in these facilities.

Do citizens actually care about the problem of prison overcrowding enough to prompt state action? That is, public officials should only care that privatization diffuses blame if voters know about deficiencies in prison operations and are willing to hold politicians responsible for those deficiencies. Though public opinion polls on this issue are few and far between, one poll conducted by the National Center for State Courts Inter-Branch Relations Survey in 2009 is suggestive: 39% of respondents thought state legislators should respond to the problem of prison overcrowding, with 27% thinking the governor should respond and 22% placing responsibility for prison overcrowding problems on judges. About 84% of respondents also had "personally seen, heard or read about the problem of prison overcrowding in [the] state," suggesting the wide scope of public knowledge about the issue (National Center for State Courts, 2009).[9] Though comprehensive data does not exist on public opinion on prison overcrowding, this poll implies, first, that citizens demand accountability from *multiple institutions and political actors* for prison conditions and overcrowding and, second, that they are knowledgeable about this issue.

Not only do people care about the issue of prison overcrowding, but in practice policymakers firmly attach blame for poor prison conditions within private facilities to the private companies. In the late 1990s, both CoreCivic and GEO Group experienced violent events at their facilities in Ohio and New Mexico, respectively. After these events, politicians went public with their concerns about private facilities, conducted investigations into their activity, and made it clear the private companies (and those companies alone) were the ones responsible for those violent altercations (McDonald and Patten, 2003). In New Mexico, after GEO Group–operated facilities there experienced riots and murders of guards and inmates, the New Mexico Department of Corrections Commissioner was "reported in the press as saying that hardcore inmates take 'special management,' something that private prisons 'are not really designed to do' " (McDonald and Patten, 2003, xxiii), placing the blame squarely on GEO Group. Moreover, the New Mexico governor publicly warned GEO Group that if any more inmates were killed, he would order all private inmates transferred to public facilities, a warning repeated in the press under the headline "Private Prisons Warned" (Useem and Goldstone, 2002). Using the media to publicly name and shame these private companies all but guarantees that the public attributes blame for these incidents to private companies. Moreover, privatizing allows policymakers to gain political capital from appearing as the "heroes" in that they are taking action on the failed criminal legal system and the evils of private prison companies (Schneider, 1999). Some experimental evidence suggests that this strategy is successful, with respondents assigning more blame to private military companies in the face of civilian casualties when compared to a similar situation with the US government (Ramirez, 2021). Indeed, the more modern movement demanding divestiture from private prison companies is evidence of the continued demonization of these firms and an absence of state responsibility for continuing contracts with them (Eisen, 2018, chap. 6).

Also, there is a question of legal accountability, a complex question in the context of private prisons. In public prisons, inmates can bring claims against corrections officers, wardens, or the state itself for unconstitutional conditions of confinement. When a state holds some of its inmates in private facilities, the question of who the inmate can sue is a difficult one—a private corrections officer,[10] the private company, a government monitor, or the government itself (Tartaglia, 2014). However, court decisions since the advent of private prisons have declared that private prisoners cannot sue the private guards or the private companies when there are sufficient state tort remedies, if the prisoner were to sue under Section 1983 of Title 42 of the US Code, the most common legal avenue for inmates (Tartaglia, 2014). Similarly, inmates can only hold government monitors legally accountable if that monitor is actively and personally involved in depriving a prisoner of some right, an extremely high burden to prove. All that said, the law surrounding who is exactly responsible for events within private prisons (and in other realms of government privatization more generally) is far from settled, making an already opaque litigation system even more inaccessible to inmates seeking to sue (Gilmour and Jensen, 1998; Raher, 2010). By privatizing, states receive two potential significant benefits: it is perhaps even more difficult to hold them responsible legally for actions that happen within private prisons, and it makes the litigation process even more difficult for inmates to access, thus stemming the flow of litigation overall.

Limiting state liability for privatization is evident in the construction of private prison contracts that require private companies to indemnify states of problems that occur within private prisons. As one example, a 2009 contract, collected by In the Public Interest, between CoreCivic and Nashville-Davidson County reads, "The Contractor shall *protect, defend, indemnify, save and hold harmless Metro, all Metro Departments, agencies, boards and commissions, its officers, agents, servants and employees, including volunteers, from and against any and all claims, demands, expenses and liability* arising out of acts or omissions of the Contractor, its agents, servants, subcontractors and employees and any and all costs, expenses and attorney's fees incurred as a result of any such claim, demand or cause of action" (In the Public Interest, 2013, emphasis added). These clauses are commonplace in both the contracts and any enabling legislation of privatization, specifically codifying that states are indemnified from legal action and only the private companies are responsible instead.

The limited liability also has financial benefits: states are incentivized to avoid further prisoner litigation to save money[11] and personnel time (Burkhardt and Jones, 2016). Though there is no concrete source on the precise costs of inmate litigation, the estimates reported in journalistic accounts are significant: California, for example, spent over $200 million over 15 years on legal fees and costs of providing inmates with attorneys to sue the government (Associated Press, 2013). Florida spent about $2 million on these lawsuits annually in the 1990s ("Law Aims to Reduce Prisoner Lawsuits; Top 10 Frivolous Lawsuits," 1996). One inmate in Wisconsin alone filed 117 lawsuits in the 1990s, costing the state $1.7 million ("Stopping Inmates' Silly Lawsuits," 1998). And, of course, while this is not a significant proportion of state budgets, it nevertheless represents an unecessary cost for the states to absorb.

Private companies entered the market expressly promising to alleviate the financial and legal stress on state governments. This was a conscious marketing decision by these companies: a 1988 annual report from CoreCivic (formerly CCA), one of the largest private prison companies in the United States, confirms the intuition that these companies provide flexible financing for states that need it. As the report reads, "CCA's combined design-build-finance capabilities permit government to build, renovate, or add beds quickly without upfront capital outlays" (Corrections Corporation of America, 1988). Similarly, the other largest private prison operator in the country, GEO Group, offers a similar promise in its annual report from 1990: they are "particularly adept and experienced in assisting and advising government agencies and community representatives on methods of financing new facility construction, such as tax exempt municipal bonds or certificates of participation, and has developed relationships with major public finance underwriters" (Wackenhut Corporation, 1990). Private prison companies marketed themselves as helpful in finding financial solutions for states' prison funding problems, but also highlighted existing issues within public correctional systems.

CoreCivic argues in its 1986 annual report in response to concerns of overcrowding that "government response to this growth has been hampered by the administrative and budgetary problems traditionally plaguing public sector facilities" (Corrections Corporation of America, 1986). Similarly, "many jurisdictions have placed a low priority on corrections funding. The outcome has been a proliferation of outdated facilities with a lack of sufficient capacity to meet constitutional standards" (Corrections Corporation of America, 1986). CoreCivic's and GEO Group's promises of fast-track construction techniques and flexible financing are incredibly alluring to state officials struggling with how to find the funds to build new prisons. Their lobbying efforts, described by CoreCivic, specifically state the company was targeting politicians in states that have considered legislation to allow privatization or in those states that are sympathetic to privatization for some reason (Corrections Corporation of America, 1986).

Private companies concentrated their lobbying and marketing efforts in states most conducive to privatization, and these companies highlighted the cost savings and efficiency they would bring to prisons. This was a conscious marketing decision by these companies: a 1988 annual report from CoreCivic confirms that these companies provide flexible financing for states that need it. This intuition is nicely captured from CoreCivic's annual report in 1988: "in short, the additional contracts that have been awarded to CCA in the past year represent, in part, a lack of viable alternatives for government in a 'must do' environment" (Corrections Corporation of America, 1988).

Interviewees echoed this sentiment as well, suggesting that privatization was a way to "wash their hands of it" (the prison overcrowding problem); and for one state bureaucrat, that was especially important as privatization helped the state stay out of federal oversight due to prison overcrowding. Another state legislator mentioned this incentive but argued that this appeal was made behind the scenes to legislators rather than in public: "the arguments then that saw the light of day the most were those that suggested financial benefit for the taxpayer as opposed to what I would suspect would be a more private argument to policymakers about the benefit of shifting responsibility. But I'm certain that those arguments were made at one time or another." Private prison companies themselves also emphasized this point in explaining the benefits of privatization: the "contract process shifts public functions, responsibilities, and possibly capital assets, in whole or in part, from the public sector to the private sector" and "[our company] takes the burden off the government or municipalities. Instead of all the business that goes along with running a detention facility, the government simply must supply the population and oversee the contract requirements." Therefore, these dynamics are explicitly cited by those involved in the privatization process as prompting state action on these issues.

Taken together, these dynamics suggest that prison privatization is beneficial for states facing more litigation as it helps limit their legal and political accountability in doing so. The opaque legal rules surrounding prison privatization and the complex chain of blame attribution that occurs when a state privatizes contribute to this incentive and form the basis for my primary hypothesis.

Hypothesis 1: *States in which prisoners filed more lawsuits, regardless of outcome, are more likely to privatize their corrections systems.*

What About Successful Lawsuits?

The widespread geographic impact of successful prisoners' rights cases prompted state action in response (Feeley and Rubin, 2000, chap. 3). Briefly, I argue that successful lawsuits make it *less* likely for a state to privatize its prison system. The state is held accountable for poor prison conditions within the corrections system, and thus no longer has the incentive to privatize to avoid legal and political accountability concerns of these lawsuits. To illustrate the common dynamics at play in these successful lawsuits it is useful to revisit three blockbuster lawsuits that were typical cases in the beginning of the prisoners' rights movement: *Holt v. Sarver I* and *II* in Arkansas in 1969 and 1970, *Pugh v. Locke* in Alabama in 1976, and *Ruiz v. Estelle* in Texas in 1980.

The first comprehensive prisoner rights case occurred in Arkansas, *Holt v. Sarver* in 1969. Judge J. Smith Henley appointed local attorneys to represent the group of inmates suing the state government and consequently relied heavily on the expert testimony presented in the case to issue the resulting court order, which acknowledged the horrific conditions within state prisons and provided a general set of recommendations to improve existing problems (e.g., Feeley and Rubin, 2000; Feeley and Swearingen, 2004). The recommendations from the judge not only covered overcrowding within the state's prisons but also ordered the elimination of the trustee guard system and the establishment of higher standards for inmate safety, health, and sanitation (Harriman and Straussman, 1983). Henley handed down his order in 1969, but his involvement did not stop there. He ordered the state to report back on its progress toward sufficient health and safety standards for inmates, but lack of action by state officials prompted Henley to declare the entire system unconstitutional in *Holt v. Sarver II* in 1970. For nearly a decade afterward, the judge heard a barrage of additional cases after appointing two new lawyers to the case including Philip Kaplan, an attorney experienced with the civil rights movement (e.g., Feeley and Rubin, 2000; Feeley and Swearingen, 2004). These additional lawsuits accused the state corrections system of violating prisoners' constitutional rights even after the disposition of the original case, which culminated in Henley then ordering reports and updates[12] on the state's progress in meeting the judge's recommendations. In the years following this blockbuster decision, Henley issued several supplemental decrees, kept close tabs on corrections officials, and even toured the prisons himself (Feeley and Rubin, 2000, chap. 3). The close surveillance of the corrections bureaucracy continued for over a decade as the judge and lawyers alike continued to ensure compliance with the court's order.

Another early successful prisoners' rights case is *Pugh v. Locke*, an Alabama decision handed down in 1976. Frank Johnson, a district judge in the state, received several complaints from inmates in state prison systems and responded by bringing in private counsel, the ACLU National Prison Project, the US Attorney's Office, and the Department of Justice's Civil Rights Division to investigate these claims (Schlanger, 2006). The subsequent trial was short as the state essentially admitted it had not provided adequate conditions for its prisoners (Robbins and Buser, 1977; Yackle, 1989). Johnson issued a highly detailed order, demanding the establishment of a classification system and even a minimum size of state prison cells (Yackle, 1989, 130–131). Johnson's extensive involvement was instrumental in ensuring the wide scope of the order, and his willingness to include experienced counsel for the plaintiffs signaled his commitment to improving prison conditions. *Pugh* lasted for years, as the state negotiated[13] with prisoners' lawyers and Judge Johnson. After Johnson was replaced by Robert Varner when Johnson moved to the US Circuit Court of Appeals, the case culminated in judicial mandates to release prisoners and improve conditions within the existing facilities (Yackle, 1989). These actors entered a protracted battle to ensure state compliance with the court order, but the sweeping order against the prison system came to an end in 1984 as the state had made enough progress to limit judicial supervision of the carceral system (Yackle, 1989, 251).

Finally, the paradigmatic prisoners' rights case is arguably *Ruiz v. Estelle*, a Texas case decided in 1980. Judge William Wayne Justice sought out complaints from prisoners in state facilities and asked his law clerks to find representative plaintiffs to sue the state government for deficiencies in safety and health within prisons (Justice, 1990). Then, Justice asked William Bennett Turner,[14] a seasoned civil rights lawyer from the NAACP Legal Fund, to represent the plaintiffs, who were now organized into a large class action suit against the state of Texas (Justice, 1990). This lawsuit detailed the horrific and violent conditions within Texas prisons, most notably the building-tender system that imbued some prisoners with power over others, resulting in mass physical and sexual abuse of those inmates not in a position of power (DiIulio, 1987, chap. 5). Justice's order against the state furiously detailed the abuses prisoners underwent while incarcerated and ordered the state to fix these problems (Feeley and Rubin, 2000, 84–85). Afterward, the judge also appointed a special monitor to ensure compliance with his court order shortly after his decision. Over the next decade, the Texas Department of Corrections experienced a period of instability as multiple directors of the department resigned under pressure to conform to the court order, an order which the department resisted at every turn (Ekland-Olson and Martin, 1988). Eventually the state adapted to the new requirements, but it took more than a decade: Justice didn't relinquish his court order until 1992 (Feeley and Rubin, 2000, 94–95).

These three cases—*Holt v. Sarver I* and *II*, *Pugh v. Locke*, and *Ruiz v. Estelle*—are paradigmatic of the earliest successful lawsuits against state prison systems. The similarities among the lawsuits, as well as states' responses to these victories, are essential for understanding why a state with more successful lawsuits will be *less* likely to privatize its corrections systems. Most notably, lawyers, judges, prisoners, and the state bureaucracy are in constant communication to ensure state compliance with any and all judicial requests regarding the prison system. There are three commonalities between these cases that ensure the state is held accountable for poor prison conditions: the judge is intimately involved in prison reform, continued monitoring of state actions within prisons, and the establishment of bureaucratic standards in response to the court order. Taken together, these commonalities ensure that the incentive to privatize to limit accountability is moot as the state is already being held accountable for poor conditions within prisons.

First, judges were instrumental in bringing in successful lawyers, experienced with litigating cases regarding civil rights, signaling both their willingness and commitment to ensuring that prisoners are substantively represented. Moreover, once the judge handed down the court order, he worked with the attorneys to ensure state compliance with judicial recommendations. Judges heard appeals from prisoners in the system, even touring the facilities themselves and keeping abreast of the contemporary challenges inmates faced (e.g., Feeley and Rubin, 2000; Justice, 1990; Yackle, 1989). The continued involvement of the judge meant the state could not shirk from its responsibilities to improve the corrections system, and the judge's continued involvement held the state truly accountable for actions that occurred in these prison systems, at least while the court order was in place.

Second, judicial involvement ensured continued monitoring of state action in the corrections system, but others more broadly were involved in confirming compliance with court orders. In a variety of cases, most notably *Ruiz v. Estelle*, the court appointed a special master to report to the judge on the Department of Corrections' progress in adhering to the court order (Justice, 1990). These monitors provide an additional layer of accountability in which judges are able to check compliance without monitoring the bureaucracy themselves. Not only were monitors instrumental in ensuring compliance, but the lawyers in the cases also had a keen interest in the court order's implementation. Whereas the prison litigation in Arkansas was piecemeal prior to *Holt v. Sarver II*, for example, it became more holistic and effective once more experienced lawyers stepped in to represent prisoners (Schlanger, 1999). Lawyers were in touch with their clients and able to alert the judge quickly if the state did not follow through on its promises. Continued attention to public prisons shone a spotlight on an otherwise opaque system and provided an opportunity for judges and lawyers alike to keep tabs on the bureaucracy.

Finally, these court orders ensured that the state was accountable for these poor prison conditions via the actual translation of the court order to policy. Prolonged attention paid to the corrections systems makes compliance with court orders, whether they mandate new construction of prisons[15] or more vague requirements to alleviate overcrowding and horrific conditions, all the more likely. Because state bureaucracies are forced to heed the requests of both the judge and the attorneys involved in the process, they are more likely to professionalize their prison systems and incorporate the requests of judges into the design of corrections systems (Feeley and Rubin, 2000, chap. 6). To respond to the orders placed on the corrections systems, bureaucrats must fundamentally alter their operations in response. This environment provided a venue for national correctional leaders to institute more professional and expansive standards across the country and attracted a new kind of correctional administrator, reform-minded and skilled bureaucrats who possessed more expertise than their previous counterparts (Feeley and Swearingen, 2004). Additionally, the court orders were not only tolerated and adapted by prison officials but welcomed by these administrators. The orders effectively gave bureaucrats within corrections departments leverage in the budget process, to procure additional resources for the facilities (Rosenberg, 2008, 312). They additionally insulated these officials from negative public opinion on prison conditions: by allowing corrections bureaucrats to blame new unpopular rules on judicial mandates rather than decisions made by the department, it shifted the blame for horrific conditions away from bureaucrats to other actors (Rosenberg, 2008, 312–313). Finally, the bureaucratization of prison guidelines, ensuring written, uniform, and reasonable rules within these facilities, helped protect against future charges of unfairness (Jacobs, 1980). Court orders additionally motivated the department to innovate in its activities and provide adequate resources to prisoners (Feeley and Rubin, 2000, chap. 6). Judicial action now, though occasionally undesirable in its scope and magnitude, can help prevent even bigger problems from occurring later and prevent the additional involvement of the judiciary in the prison system.

These three factors—judicial involvement, continued monitoring of court order compliance by other actors like special masters and lawyers, and the development of clear bureaucratic standards—ensure that the state is held accountable for poor prison conditions. Whereas privatization is attractive to limit political and legal accountability, *if the state is already held accountable for improving prison conditions, it no longer has the incentive to privatize to avoid this responsibility.* States are forced to accommodate reforms via the expansion of existing prisons or construction of new facilities, a process conducted under close attention of the judge and attorneys. It is thus unnecessary to export the operations of prisons to private companies: the state implements court orders and builds or renovates public facilities itself. The promises of private companies, to save money, build new facilities easily and cheaply, and limit states' legal accountability, thus fall on deaf ears in states with successful litigation. Additionally, because the bureaucracy professionalizes, recruiting reform-minded corrections officials who initiate the adoption of national standards, the department has no need for outside managers of these facilities. The antiquated workforce is replaced by professional workers who are reluctant to hand over operations of correctional institutions to private companies.

This dynamic is also one recognized by private companies themselves. In response to a 2011 court case about prison overcrowding in California, *Brown v. Plata*, reports to shareholders from private prison companies indicate their unease about this successful lawsuit (see Chapter 5 for more details). In each of the company's annual shareholder reports, it cites the strict 137.5% capacity limit promulgated in *Brown* and specifically mentions the negative effect this successful lawsuit will have on business. CoreCivic's report for fiscal year 2011 reads, "In an effort to meet the Federal court ruling, the fiscal year 2012 budget of the state of California calls for a significant reallocation of responsibilities from state government to local jurisdictions. . . . The return of the California inmates to the state of California would have a *significant adverse impact on our financial position*, results of operations, and cash flows" (Corrections Corporation of America, 2012. emphasis added). The

GEO Group's annual report for shareholders in fiscal year 2012 is similarly negative: California "discontinued contracts with Community Correctional Facilities which housed low level state offenders across the state . . . a material decrease in occupancy levels at one or more of our facilities could have a *material adverse effect on our revenues and profitability*, and consequently, on our financial condition and results of operations" (GEO Group, 2012, emphasis added).

States' responses to successful lawsuits and companies' negative responses to these lawsuits lead me to my second hypothesis.

Hypothesis 2: *States with any federal court orders about prison or jail conditions are less likely to privatize their corrections systems.*

Accountability and Privatization

A state is not at liberty to afford its citizens only those constitutional rights which fit comfortably within its budget.
—Pugh v. Locke (1976)

I propose that prisoner lawsuits, and the concepts of legal and political accountability, are important overlooked factors in the decision to privatize. My primary hypothesis argues that states will be more likely to privatize their prisons in the face of mounting lawsuits to limit their legal and political accountability. The legal murkiness around lawsuits in private prisons and the opaque nature of these contracts mean it is difficult, if not impossible, to know who to hold responsible for problems that occur within private prisons. These for-profit companies then present themselves as panaceas to the problems of publicly run prisons and concentrate their marketing efforts to those states. The second hypothesis considers what happens when states are held accountable for poor prison conditions when a court order about prison or jail conditions is handed down. I hypothesize that any successful prisoners' rights lawsuits are associated with less prison privatization. Successful lawsuits involve the judge, outside monitors, and attorneys in the monitoring of state corrections systems to ensure compliance with the terms of the court orders. States respond by professionalizing their corrections bureaucracy and complying with the court order via new construction or expansion of facilities in line with judicial recommendations. Because the state is held accountable for poor prison conditions, it no longer has the incentive to privatize.

This chapter suggests that prison privatization is an active strategy pursued by state governments to evade democratic accountability and the burden of providing legal rights to prisoners. These legal rights are the bedrock of American democracy, and incarcerated people deserve those rights. These unintended consequences hold significant implications for the people who are incarcerated within private and public prisons. Do these patterns show up empirically, however? The next chapter takes up this question and finds support for an association between inmate litigation and privatization, suggesting, as one interviewee argued, "the litigation is necessary to light a fire and make us do more."

4

Inmate Lawsuits and Private Prisons

... So you really see them trying to pass the buck ... delay, delay, delay, obfuscate, obfuscate, obfuscate, obfuscate. So the buck passing is something that you get when you have a private involved, whether they're a defendant or not.

—Advocacy director interview, 2020

The last chapter laid the theoretical groundwork for this book, to suggest that the prisoners' rights movement and the litigation it spurred influenced a state's decision to privatize its prisons, a story largely about accountability. I proposed two hypotheses: primarily, a state that faces more prisoner lawsuits, regardless of outcome, will be more likely to privatize its prisons. Privatizing helps states avoid legal and political accountability for the claims raised in these lawsuits. Conversely, the second hypothesis argues that a state with successful lawsuits will be *less* likely to privatize. Judges, outside monitors, and the establishment of clear rules and procedures for prison life ensure that the state is already held accountable for poor prison conditions. States experiencing successful lawsuits therefore have no incentive to privatize to avoid accountability as they are already held accountable for deficiencies in conditions of confinement. Taken together, the main theoretical argument presented here posits that prisoner lawsuits are instrumental in the choice to privatize.

This chapter evaluates these hypotheses empirically. First, I present some descriptive data on inmate lawsuits and private prisons, using the data introduced in Chapter 2. Next, I consider my explanations along with other common explanations of privatization (partisanship, economics, unionization, and campaign contributions). I then consider an instrumental variables (IV) analysis to combat the likely endogenous relationship between inmate lawsuits and private prisons (i.e., more lawsuits could spur privatization, as I argue, but privatization may result in changes in lawsuits as well). I find broad support for both hypotheses from the previous chapter, that more litigation increases the likelihood a state will privatize and any successful court orders decrease the likelihood a state will privatize. I present some additional tests of the theory and robustness checks, along with some contextual examples of my hypotheses to further emphasize these dynamics. Finally, I evaluate my theoretical claims in the face of the quantitative evidence I marshal and offer implications for the results presented here. If efforts to enshrine populations with rights previously denied to them contributes to unintended and perhaps unwanted consequences, what effect, if any, does that have on our evaluation of the rights revolution writ large? How does our evaluation of the success of the prisoners' rights movement change if that revolution shifted penal policy in an unexpected, and perhaps negative, way? This suggests not that the rights revolution was misguided but rather that it is an unfulfilled promise of legal rights for every American, even those who are incarcerated. States have perverse incentives to privatize in order to evade accountability for inmate litigation.

Data: Private Prisons and Inmate Litigation

This chapter uses the original data introduced in Chapter 2 to evaluate the effect of either successful lawsuits or more lawsuits overall on prison privatization. I read dozens of Securities and Exchange Commission (SEC) reports to develop a comprehensive data set on private prison adoption since 1986. These data comprise only those for-profit correctional institutions operated by publicly traded companies, representing the vast majority of the private prison market, approximately 85% of all private prisons in the country (Mumford, Schanzenbach, and Nunn, 2016). In my analyses, I use three separate dependent variables to reflect variation in private prison adoption: the sum of all inmates under a state's jurisdiction held in private facilities, the proportion of all prisoners under a state's jurisdiction in these private facilities, and the number of private prisons in the state that hold a state's inmates from 1986 to 2016 for all states (see Chapter 2 for maps of these variables). Since 1986, all three variables are increasing. There are quite a few states that consistently have zero values for all three of these variables, but there is great variation in how much the states use private prisons in the aggregate and as a proportion of their total prison system. While California and Texas, for example, hold the highest number of inmates in private facilities, it is smaller states like New Mexico and Hawaii that use private prisons at the highest percentage of their total prison system.

The second step in estimating this relationship is the collection of data on inmate litigation. To test both hypotheses from Chapter 3, we need two separate sources of information on inmate litigation: the sum of all lawsuits filed by prisoners and the number of successful lawsuits.

First, to test the effect of a higher amount of inmate litigation on private prison adoption, I constructed a large data set of all the "Prisoner Petition" cases[1] filed in the federal district courts from 1986 (the first year of available SEC data for private prisons) to 2016. I utilized two separate sources, the Federal Judicial Center's Integrated Database (FJC) and Bloomberg Law, to create a comprehensive data set of each court case filed and terminated in each state-year. I merged these two sources together to create a data set of 866,755 court cases filed by prisoners in all states[2] from 1986 through 2016. Each court case contains information about a battery of case outcomes: who won the case (plaintiff, prisoner, or defendant; the state or local correctional institution) and the damages awarded to the plaintiff (if applicable), among other characteristics. The outcome is a state-year data set with information on the sum of the number of inmate lawsuits terminated in each year from 1986 to 2016.

Figure 4.1 represents the number of prisoners' lawsuits terminated in the district courts each year, from 1986 to 2016. In any given year, inmates nationwide file tens of thousands of lawsuits to protest conditions of their incarceration. There is a large uptick in the beginning of the time period, the 1980s to the mid–1990s, until the Prison Litigation Reform Act (PLRA) was passed in 1996. Recall from the last chapter that the PLRA severely curtailed inmates' ability to file lawsuits in federal courts, which gives substantial leverage to state governments in these litigation proceedings,[3] all the while limiting power inmates have in the system (Schlanger, 2015). That sharp break is followed by a fairly consistent amount of inmate litigation through the first decade of the 2000s, with another sharp dip beginning in 2015. It is unclear why this sharp decrease occurred, but overall district court filings decreased by over 2% in 2016, so perhaps the decline reflects a general downturn in the district court filings. Moreover, the FJC's data on district court filings by inmates also shows a sharp decrease for that year, so for some reason prisoners were less litigious in 2016 than in previous years. Either way, there is variation over the time period of this study as prisoners used litigation more heavily in the earlier period, the PLRA limited their

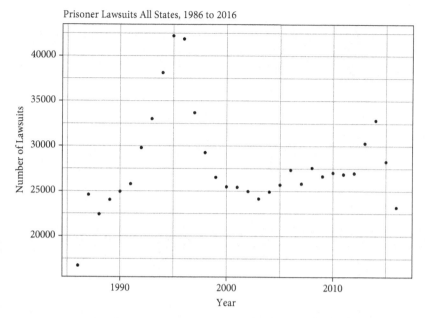

Figure 4.1 Prisoners' lawsuits terminated in each year 1986 to 2016. Data from the Federal Judicial Center.

legal options, then the level of inmate lawsuits reached a lower, rough equilibrium afterward.

These kinds of demands appear fairly static across states: Figure 4.2 shows a distribution of the number of lawsuits filed per prisoner across the states, 1986 to 2016. Inmates' litigiousness appears fairly even across states, with lawsuits peaking in the 1990s and dropping off more recently. This helps to assuage concerns that some states' inmates are suing more than others: rather, prisoner litigiousness appears fairly consistent across states.

For the secondary hypothesis, which analyzes the effect of successful lawsuits on prison privatization, I need data on the court orders issued against the state for poor prison conditions in the last few decades. Scholars seeking to understand the comprehensive effect of successful court cases on state corrections administration typically take a qualitative approach through the use of case studies (e.g., Schoenfeld, 2010, 2018; Yackle, 1989). This method is particularly useful for tracing the complicated and multipronged effect one court case could exert on a variety of institutions as court orders are often complex in their scope

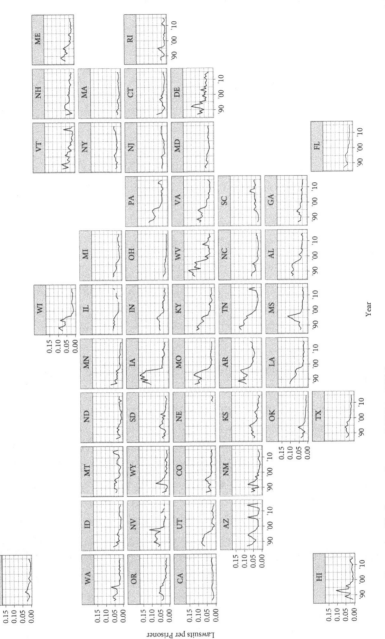

Figure 4.2 Lawsuits filed per prisoner, 1986 to 2016.

and implementation. The drawback of this approach lies in its limited external validity as it is unclear to what extent the lessons gleaned from court cases in Alabama or Florida, for example, travel to other states. Other large-N examinations of the effects of successful court cases identify a small number of individual court cases that were significant in their scope and analyze how outcomes shift when a state is under a comprehensive court order versus when it is not (e.g., Boylan and Mocan, 2014; Fliter, 1996; Levitt, 1996). Often, these analyses only cite those cases in which entire states' corrections systems were placed under court order, which does not allow scholars to identify the effects of not only the most comprehensive court orders but also the smaller cases that still mandate some improvement in conditions or treatment within corrections facilities.

These two approaches are useful, but they are less amenable to large-N studies of a host of court cases, prisoner litigation that includes not only blockbuster cases but also those that achieve smaller goals for inmates. For information on successful lawsuits, I rely on the Civil Rights Clearinghouse (CRC) database[4] housed at the University of Michigan Law School and founded by Margo Schlanger. The CRC is an online database of important court case outcomes filed in a variety of case categories, such as elections and voting rights, presidential authority, and public housing, among about a dozen other law areas. Scholars at the CRC scour legal filings in these categories and find the most important cases, injunctive litigation that seeks real policy or operational change, rather than those that simply seek damages. The CRC data contains a battery of information on these cases, on case characteristics of the attorneys representing the plaintiffs, whether the lawsuit was certified as a class action lawsuit, among other information. Therefore, the cases included in this data set are the most consequential cases filed in each of these different case types, as determined by a number of law experts. This fits nicely with the expectations laid out in Hypothesis 2 as these experts selected only those cases that yielded policy change, and thus were the most likely to alter the behavior of corrections departments.

For the purposes of this analysis, I focus on the CRC's coding of important cases in either the "Jail Conditions"[5] or "Prison Conditions" category. These particular categories mostly include those cases prisoners or jail inmates won or settled for a decree of some kind to improve prison or jail conditions.[6] This encompasses more than 1,300 cases filed in district courts in all 50 states from the 1950s to the present. Because the private prison data begins in 1986, I truncate this data set to fit that time frame and only consider those cases that were resolved from 1986 to the present, resulting in a final collection of more than 400 of those cases.

The main independent variable of analysis is a binary variable, *Court Order Began*, which takes on the value of 1 if one (or more) court orders began in that state-year over the period 1986 to 2016. See Figure 4.3 for a map of the sum of these court orders since 1986. These 442 total cases cover 46 states (with the exception of Alaska, Minnesota, North Dakota, and West Virginia) and range in number in each state-year from 1 to 10 (hence why I dichotomize this variable). More than half of the states only experience one injunctive court order in each year, so this data set is likely only capturing the most significant prisoners' case annually in each state. Finally, though the CRC includes important inmates' rights cases from all jurisdictions, this analysis only considers those filed in the *federal district courts*, to facilitate the empirical analysis and ensure appropriate comparison between the cases across states. Moreover, most prisoners file their cases in federal court because of the allegations that prison officials are violating their federal, constitutional rights (Piehl and Schlanger, 2004). Because approximately two-thirds of all inmate litigation is filed in federal courts, I look at this venue[7] as a prisoner's primary legal pathway to relief.

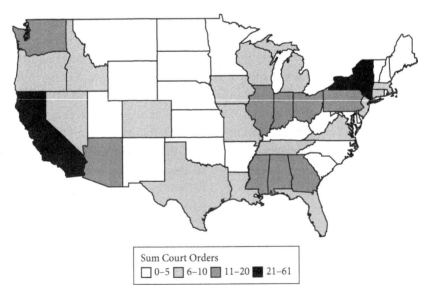

Figure 4.3 Sum of court orders issued, 1986 to 2016. Data from the Civil Rights Clearinghouse.

For the most part, these successful lawsuits are filed under Section 1983 of Title 42 of the US Code, which gives prisoners the right to sue the government for constitutional violations while incarcerated. The topics of these lawsuits are diverse and range from religious accommodations to deprivation of healthcare to segregation, among other concerns. There is diversity in the content of the orders depending on whether the inmates were suing state prisons or local jails, however. Most decrees handed down to state prisons alleged unconstitutional confinement but were geared more toward the long-term health and comfort of the inmates. These decrees mandated actions such as more diversity in the religious services offered to inmates, more recreation time for inmates in solitary confinement, and availability and quality of health and dental care.[8] These kinds of cases in state prisons prompted corrections departments to professionalize and develop guidelines with respect to the rights of the confined. Jail court orders, on the other hand, were more specific as to the remedies the government needed to undertake. Some of these decrees required the closure of the jail facility until it met minimum legal standards, placed population caps on the facility, gave the sheriff legal ability to release prisoners if and when the facility reached a certain population, or mandated the construction of a new jail.[9] Therefore, while the content differs slightly across the facility type, the decrees mandate some action from the government, whether it be through the development of new guidelines or the construction of a new facility. All the cases included in my sample resulted in some kind of court order, imposed on the state either by a judge or via a consent decree, which is negotiated and agreed upon by both the government and the inmates' lawyers. Moreover, the scope of these orders differs. Some place strict caps on the prison population, others mandate the construction of new facilities, whereas others task the corrections departments with developing a comprehensive set of guidelines to accommodate inmates' grievances. Though these successful lawsuits differ with the precise details of the complaint, they all result in some kind of court order on the system, and the government is prompted to develop professional, clear guidelines on different facets of prison life.

Lawsuits and Other Explanations for Privatization

As an initial examination, I evaluate my two hypotheses alongside other common explanations for privatization, namely partisanship, economics, and unionization.[10]

Hypothesis 1

I estimate an ordinary least squares model (OLS) using the following equation:

$$y_{i,t} = \alpha_i + \delta_t + \beta_1 SumLawsuits_{i_{t-1},t_{t-1}} + \beta_z OtherTheories_{i_{t-1},t_{t-1}}$$
$$+ X_{i_{t-1},t_{t-1}} + \epsilon_{i,t} \tag{4.1}$$

In this equation, $y_{i,t}$ is a set of dependent variables concerning private prisons: *Private Design Capacity, Proportion Inmates in Private Facilities,* and *Number of Private Facilities—State Only,* all of which are calculated using the original data set collected as part of this project. *Private Design Capacity* reflects the sum of inmates under a state's jurisdiction who are confined in a private prison operated by a publicly traded company. For those facilities with multiple customers, I averaged the total bed capacity across the jurisdictions. For example, North Lake Correctional Facility (operated by the GEO Group) lists both Vermont and Washington as its primary customers in 2016, but it is unclear how many of the prison's inmates are under either state's jurisdiction. This variable averages the total capacity, 1,748, across the two jurisdictions. Thus, both Vermont and Washington are assigned 874 inmates (though I re-visit this calculation in the Appendix). Second, I also calculate *Proportion Inmates in Private Facilities,* the percentage of the total prison population that has been privatized. Third, I use *Number of Private Facilities—State Only,* a sum of state private facilities[11] in each state-year, regardless of which company operates them. This dependent variable only considers those private facilities in a state that house that state's inmates, though the results are similar if the variable is instead just the sum of all private facilities in a state, regardless of whether they house state inmates or not.

The main explanatory variable of interest is *Sum Lawsuits Terminated,* the sum of all prisoner lawsuits terminated[12] in each year, from the FJC data set. This represents all lawsuits filed in the district courts in each state-year, though this effect seems primarily driven by small, quickly adjudicated lawsuits (see the Appendix for more information). The results are also robust when using a proxy for the number of lawsuits filed by state inmates only.

I also evaluate other explanations for privatization, in *Other Theories.* I include a dummy variable for Republican governor, a dummy variable for the presence of a Republican-controlled legislature (i.e., both chambers); a dummy variable for the interaction of these two, unified Republican government; budget gap per capita; and the number of unionized corrections officers. The partisanship variables come from the National Conference on State Legislatures and the *Book of the States*, and budget gap per capita is the per capita difference between revenue and expenditures in any given state-year from the Census Bureau. The number of unionized corrections officers is a proxy I calculate. First, I use Page (2011)'s classification of which states had a corrections officers' union as of 2011. Second, I use Hirsch and Macpherson (2003)'s data on the nationwide percentage of unionized corrections officers measured annually from 1986 through 2016. I then multiply the national percentage of corrections officers who are unionized by the total number of full- and part-time corrections employees in each state-year from the Bureau of Justice Statistics (BJS), before finally multiplying that number by the dummy variable of whether the state had a union in 2011 or not. I divide the final measure by 1,000. Though this is a proxy, it provides a rough estimate of the number of unionized corrections officers, data that is not readily collected by the states. I consider campaign contributions and lobbying activity in the Appendix as data availability severely curtails the sample size. The variable is positive and significant in some specifications, but its magnitude is extremely small, indicating that campaign contributions are not a primary driver of prison privatization.

All explanatory variables are lagged by one year. So, *Sum Lawsuits* in one state-year is matched with the set of dependent variables—either *Private Design Capacity, Proportion Inmates in Private Facilities*, or *Number of Private Facilities—State Only*—in the following year, reflecting the time lag of the effect of court decisions.

Finally, I also include state and year fixed effects, α_i and δ_t, and cluster the standard errors by state. The model also contains two control variables in $X_{it-1,tt-1}$, violent crime rate, the number of violent crimes per 100,000 population from the Federal Bureau of Investigation, and incarceration rate, the number of prisoners in each state per 100,000 state population from the BJS. These control variables help to mitigate concerns about additional omitted variable bias (see the Appendix for additional variables like economic policy liberalism, prison overcrowding, deaths in custody, and campaign contributions).

Table 4.1 estimates Equation 4.1. The common explanations of privatization—partisanship, economics, or unionization—do not appear to significantly drive state prison privatization, whether it be the number of inmates

Table 4.1 Hypothesis 1: Prisoner Lawsuits and Private Prisons

	Private Design Capacity		Proportion in Private Facilities		Sum State Private Facilities	
	(1)	(2)	(3)	(4)	(5)	(6)
Sum lawsuits		1.503***		0.00003***		0.001***
		(0.406)		(0.00001)		(0.0004)
Republican legislature	−29.151	162.236	−0.006	−0.002	−0.417**	−0.235
	(281.499)	(272.620)	(0.013)	(0.013)	(0.198)	(0.169)
Republican governor	118.295	139.480	0.018*	0.018*	−0.052	−0.032
	(143.788)	(136.696)	(0.010)	(0.010)	(0.117)	(0.103)
Unified Republican gov't	238.898	149.217	−0.005	−0.007	0.218	0.133
	(330.027)	(342.027)	(0.016)	(0.015)	(0.211)	(0.193)
Budget gap per capita	13.003	3.779	−0.015**	−0.015**	0.038	0.029
	(89.918)	(82.612)	(0.007)	(0.007)	(0.057)	(0.050)
No. unionized corrections officers (1000s)	298.209*	182.470	−0.003	−0.005**	0.346*	0.236*
	(173.056)	(139.107)	(0.002)	(0.002)	(0.180)	(0.137)
Incarceration rate	7.566***	7.756***	0.0001	0.0001	0.008***	0.008***
	(2.786)	(2.309)	(0.0001)	(0.0001)	(0.003)	(0.002)
Violent crime rate	−3.887**	−3.385**	0.0001	0.0001	−0.002*	−0.002*
	(1.852)	(1.594)	(0.0001)	(0.0001)	(0.001)	(0.001)
N	1,417	1,417	1,417	1,417	1,417	1,417
R^2	0.734	0.756	0.565	0.570	0.841	0.857
Adjusted R^2	0.718	0.741	0.538	0.543	0.831	0.848
Residual SE	1,245.408 (df = 1,333)	1,193.720 (df = 1,332)	0.064 (df = 1,333)	0.064 (df = 1,332)	1.061 (df = 1,333)	1.006 (df = 1,332)

$*p < .1; **p < .05; ***p < .01.$

Standard errors (SEs) clustered by state.

df, degrees of freedom.

in private facilities, the proportion of a state's inmates in private facilities, or the sum of state private facilities. The unionized corrections officers variable is significant in column 1 but becomes insignificant with the addition of the lawsuits variable in column 2. The Republican governor dummy variable is significant and positive in columns 3 and 4, indicating a positive relationship between Republican governors and the proportion of a state's inmates in private facilities. Some of these results are contra to the expectations of the literature. The Republican legislature variable, for example, is *negatively* related to the number of state private facilities in column 5. Perhaps this is due to the bipartisan nature of prison privatization and criminal justice policy in particular (Gunderson, 2021b). The budget gap per capita variable is *negatively* associated with the proportion of inmates in private facilities. This could be due to overall reticence to privatize from a moral perspective: as one state legislator suggested, "If you're going to make it about making money or losing money, you're losing track of what the scales of justice are asking us to do." Though economics may be a driver for this decision for some, it is unclear whether other considerations matter above and beyond the budget. Similarly, though the literature would predict a negative association between unionization and prison privatization, some of these variables are significant and *positive*. Though it is difficult to say why this is so, perhaps the reason is the potential weakness of these unions. Comprehensive studies of corrections officers' unions have not been undertaken to my knowledge, and while the prototypical example is the California Correctional Peace Officers Association, the strength of that union may be an outlier in the context of the other state-level organizations. This suggests that if these common explanations are associated with prison privatization, they may not be associated in the ways that we have theorized thus far.

The prisoner lawsuits variable, on the other hand, is significant and positive in each specification. This table indicates that with each additional prisoner lawsuit filed, there is an associated rise of more than one inmate in private prisons, an increase of 0.003% of inmates in private prisons as a percentage of a state's inmates, and 0.001 more state private facilities. Though some of these coefficients are small in magnitude, they present a strong correlation between these variables that suggests that inmate lawsuits is an important, and overlooked, variable in the decision to privatize prisons. And, importantly, this variable is significant at predicting privatization even after accounting for the other common explanations.

Hypothesis 2

Next, I test Hypothesis 2 using Equation 4.2.

$$y_{i,t} = \alpha_i + \delta_t + \beta_1 CourtOrderBegan_{i_{t-1},t_{t-1}} + \beta_z OtherTheories_{i_{t-1},t_{t-1}}$$
$$+ X_{i_{t-1},t_{t-1}} + \epsilon_{i,t} \tag{4.2}$$

Equation 4.2 is identical to Equation 4.1, save for the inclusion of a different independent variable, *Court Order Began*. This variable is from the CRC and is a dummy variable for whether any court order was initially issued in that state-year. Because I do not expect a state to respond differently to one court order than it may respond to more than one court order, I dichotomize this choice here, though the number of court orders in any given year ranges from 0 to 10. This variable represents any new court orders issued in each state-year, to reflect the new judicial pressures states face. Otherwise, the estimation is identical. In the Appendix materials, I also add control variables and a lagged dependent variable model.

Table 4.2 highlights, once again, the primary insignificance of the other explanations of privatization—partisanship, economics, or unionization. Unlike Table 4.1, none of these explanations reach traditional levels of statistical significance.

Budget gap per capita, as in Table 4.1, is *negatively* associated with private design capacity, the opposite expectation from the literature, which emphasizes that financial stress will make a state more likely to privatize (though this variable does not reach statistical significance). The beginning of at least one court order is significantly associated with fewer private facilities in-state, though the coefficient does not reach statistical significance for the other two dependent variables (though they are negatively signed following Hypothesis 2).

The OLS specifications provide support for Hypothesis 1, but the results are more tentative when considering Hypothesis 2. There is one issue with the analysis thus far, however: endogeneity.

Table 4.2 Hypothesis 2: Successful Prison Lawsuits and Private Prisons

	Private Design Capacity		Proportion in Private Facilities		Sum State Private Facilities	
	(1)	(2)	(3)	(4)	(5)	(6)
Court order began		−1,035.954		−0.021		−2.449***
		(669.192)		(0.017)		(0.810)
Republican legislature	208.172	204.152	0.014	0.014	0.065	0.055
	(336.314)	(338.265)	(0.016)	(0.016)	(0.325)	(0.328)
Republican governor	−234.179	−262.919	0.005	0.004	−0.317	−0.383
	(332.608)	(347.962)	(0.010)	(0.010)	(0.412)	(0.432)
Unified Republican gov't	−25.464	1.653	−0.015	−0.014	−0.073	−0.011
	(445.423)	(452.598)	(0.017)	(0.017)	(0.473)	(0.487)
Budget Gap Per Capita	−389.936	−382.230	0.003	0.003	0.058	0.076
	(246.560)	(251.677)	(0.005)	(0.005)	(0.056)	(0.060)
No. unionized corrections officers (1000s)	−12.812	−13.174	−0.002	−0.002	−0.025	−0.026
	(48.601)	(48.508)	(0.003)	(0.003)	(0.045)	(0.045)
Incarceration rate	0.166	0.246	0.0002	0.0002	0.002	0.002
	(3.121)	(3.154)	(0.0001)	(0.0001)	(0.002)	(0.002)
Violent crime rate	0.409	0.319	−0.00001	−0.00001	−0.001	−0.001
	(1.536)	(1.584)	(0.0001)	(0.0001)	(0.002)	(0.002)
N	1,376	1,376	1,375	1,375	1,417	1,417
R^2	0.349	0.350	0.239	0.240	0.388	0.393
Adjusted R^2	0.307	0.308	0.190	0.190	0.350	0.355
Residual SE	1,963.434 (df = 1,292)	1,962.759 (df = 1,291)	0.084 (df = 1,291)	0.084 (df = 1,290)	2.062 (df = 1,333)	2.055 (df = 1,332)

***$p < .01$.

Standard errors (SEs) clustered by state.

df, degrees of freedom.

Instrumental Variables Estimation

Hypothesis 1

Evaluating whether prisoners' rights lawsuits caused a state to privatize part of its corrections systems is a difficult methodological task. Endogeneity likely exists as prisoners' lawsuits could lead to a higher degree of privatization within the state or higher prison privatization could alter the pattern of prisoner-driven litigation. Though I expect the causal direction of the first possibility, the theorized relationship, to show up empirically, the argument presented in Chapter 3 suggests that the opposite relationship is likely true, that privatization stems the flow of prisoner lawsuits. Indeed, at least part of the attraction of privatization for state governments is transfer of liability, so governments are relieved of the responsibility of defending themselves against costly and extended periods of litigation involving prisoners (Kay, 1987). Despite that belief, there is mixed evidence as to whether private facilities have a lower likelihood of being subjected to a court order (e.g., Burkhardt and Jones, 2016; Makarios and Maahs, 2012), but nevertheless the possibility remains that prisoners are litigating complaints in a different way when incarcerated in private facilities. Legally this is correct as inmates in private facilities have the power to sue individual officers for civil rights violations[13] and the companies that operate those facilities, but those same inmates are unable to sue the federal government directly for negligence and are only permitted to sue the company itself (Volokh, 2013). Therefore, it is likely that the relationship between prisoners' lawsuits and prison privatization is an endogenous one, complicating any methodological strategy for estimating this relationship. In particular, this issue can result in the independent variable, the sum of inmate lawsuits, being correlated with the error term in any estimation, resulting in biased estimates. To overcome this problem, I utilize an IV approach.

The key advantage this approach provides is that it uses an IV in place of the independent variable, successful lawsuits, that only influences the dependent variable, prison privatization, via the independent variable (Sovey and Green, 2011). A valid instrument additionally is independent of other preexisting determinants of the dependent variable, prison privatization. A valid instrument in this case must fit several characteristics, the most important of which is that the instrument must serve as a source of exogenous variation that is currently missing from the analysis. In essence, an IV model finds a variable that is a plausible source of exogeneity to use in place of the independent variable. To fit this characteristic, I look to the exogenous imposition of caseloads across the district courts.

Scholars often assume that district court judges are randomly given cases ("from the wheel").[14] Though this practice is often taken as a given by scholars studying the effects of district judges' characteristics on outcomes like sentencing disparities (e.g., Payne, 1997; Schanzenbach, 2005), it may be of practical importance that cases are not truly assigned randomly. Some studies have found non-random practices in assignment procedures in individual district courts (Ashenfelter, Eisenberg, and Schwab, 1995; Macfarlane, 2014), so the assumption of random assignment is not always supported by the evidence. Indeed, scholars studying a similar phenomenon at the Court of Appeals have cautioned against using random assignment as a cure-all for causal inference identification problems in analyzing the effect of judges' characteristics on various outcomes (Boyd, Epstein, and Martin, 2010; Hall, 2010). Despite these legitimate concerns of non-random assignment, there are a few reasons to believe this is not a significant problem for the analysis presented here.

First, the analyses that cast doubt on the true random assignment of judges to cases often cite the Court of Appeals as the venue (Chilton and Levy, 2015; Hall, 2010). There hasn't been a conclusive declaration about non-random problems in the district courts. Second, though the concerns of non-random assignment are important because of causal inference issues, it seems that the assignment is random in the aggregate, at least in most districts (Ashenfelter, Eisenberg, and Schwab, 1995; Hall, 2010). Each judge in the district likely hears at least one prisoner case per year, so the composition of the pool of judges likely reflects the true distribution of judges in the circuit. Thus, it is likely the case that judges are not selecting into any cases writ large and specifically prisoners' rights cases, allaying any concerns about non-random assignment.

The assignment of judges being random allows me to use that exogeneity to find an instrument for my independent variable, *Sum Lawsuits*. To do this, I consider the caseload facing district court judges. Because judges are assigned randomly to these cases, it is unlikely that they are actively manipulating their caseload. I therefore use *Weighted Cases per Judge Serving* as my IV, which represents the weighted number of cases both active and senior judges hear in each state-year (Habel and Scott, 2014).[15] This is a plausible instrument because one may expect judges who hear more cases each year to terminate more cases and vice versa as an overburdened judge has an incentive to terminate cases quickly to clear the docket. Finally, it is important that the exclusion restriction is satisfied, which means the IV must not have any independent effect on prison privatization other than through the independent variable, the sum of all prisoners' lawsuits (Sovey and Green, 2011). This exclusion restriction is likely satisfied as *Weighted Cases per Judges Serving* only influences prison privatization through *Sum Lawsuits*. It is unlikely that the varying number of cases heard prompts judges to alter a state's corrections policy as judges do not possess this policymaking power and cannot easily modify the number of cases they hear. Additionally, it is highly unlikely that states will modify the character of their prison systems due to the number of cases judges terminate in each year.

The following IV analysis uses two-stage least squares (TSLS) equations on the data. Equation 4.3 refers to the first stage, and Equation 4.4 refers to the second stage, in which I use the fitted values from the first equation in place of *Sum Lawsuits*.

$$\text{Sum Lawsuits}_{i_{t-1}} = \alpha_i + \delta_t + \text{Weighted Cases Per Judges Serving}_{i_{t-1}, t_{t-1}} + \epsilon_{c_1, t_1} \tag{4.3}$$

$$\gamma_{i,t} = \alpha_i + \delta_t + \widehat{\text{SumLawsuits}}_{i_{t-1}, t_{t-1}} + \epsilon_{c_2, t_2} \tag{4.4}$$

In Equation 4.4, $\gamma_{i,t}$ is a set of dependent variables concerning private prisons: *Private Design Capacity, Proportion Inmates in Private Facilities,* and *Number of Private Facilities—State Only*, as described in the previous section. The main explanatory variable of interest is *Sum Lawsuits*, the sum of all prisoner lawsuits terminated in each year. The IV is *Weighted Cases per Judge Serving*, the weighted number of cases district court judges hear in each year. α_c refers to a vector of circuit intercepts, δ_t is a vector of year intercepts, and ϵ_{c_2, t_2} is a matrix of error terms. Finally, I cluster by circuit to reflect the systematic differences between various circuits. I use circuit fixed effects and clustered standard errors[16] rather than state, as in the earlier analysis, as nearly one-third of the states have *no* variation in the dependent variable. No control variables are exogenous[17] and can be included in the TSLS estimation. A smaller number of circuits do not vary over time, and while that is not ideal, it at least allows me to control for some geographic heterogeneity. Finally, all explanatory variables, including the IV and the endogenous variable, are lagged by one year. So, *Sum Lawsuits*, and thus *Weighted Cases per Judge Serving*, in one state-year are matched with the set of dependent variables in the following year, reflecting the time lag of the effect of court decisions and matching the previous analysis.

The results from both the IV and OLS designs for the first dependent variable, the lagged number of inmates in private facilities, are in Table 4.3.

The results corroborate the intuition behind Hypothesis 1—as the sum of all prisoners' lawsuits increases, so too does the lagged number of inmates in private facilities. Encouragingly, the results from the OLS and IV estimations are fundamentally identical, highlighting that whether or not the estimation accounts for endogeneity does not substantively alter the findings presented here. Of note also is the F statistic presented in the first-stage IV results: *Weight per Judge Serving* is a significant predictor of *Sum Lawsuits*, with an F statistic of 19.32, suggesting that it is a strong instrument for the key independent variable of interest (the rule of thumb is to aim for an F

Table 4.3 The Effect of Terminated Prisoner Lawsuits on Lagged Private Design Capacity

	Lagged Private DC	Sum Lawsuits	Lagged Private DC
	OLS	First Stage IV	IV
	(1)	(2)	(3)
Sum lawsuits	1.761***		2.093***
	(0.494)		(0.747)
Weight per judge serving		1.075**	
		(0.441)	
Constant	−693.351***	−511.281***	−605.951***
	(194.637)	(180.162)	(152.185)
N	1,501	1,400	1,400
R^2	0.498	0.362	0.497
Adjusted R^2	0.484	0.345	0.483
Residual SE	1,644.950 (df = 1,459)	519.587 (df = 1,361)	1,608.332 (df = 1,361)

**p < .05; ***p < .01.

Standard errors (SEs) clustered by circuit. F statistic is 19.32.

DC, design capacity; df, degrees of freedom.

statistic over 10 [Sovey and Green, 2011]). These results suggest that states are utilizing privatization more in the aggregate as the stress on the criminal legal system more broadly increases.

An identical analysis using the lagged proportion of inmates in private facilities is in Table 4.4. These results are not robust but are suggestive of an opposite relationship to the results presented in Table 4.3: as prisoners' lawsuits increase, the proportion held in private facilities decreases. Table 4.4 suggests that states that use private prisons to alleviate overcrowding also expand their public capacity at an even higher rate. However, because the OLS results are barely significant and the IV results do not rise to traditional significance levels, it is difficult to make a definitive conclusion about the effect of more prisoner litigation on the proportion of a state's inmates held in private facilities.

Finally, the third dependent variable I examine is the sum of state private facilities. These results are in Table 4.5. Similar to Table 4.3, there is a significant and positive relationship between the number of state private prisons

Table 4.4 The Effect of Terminated Prisoner Lawsuits on Lagged Proportion of Inmates in Private Facilities

	Lagged Proportion in Private	Sum Lawsuits	Lagged Proportion in Private
	OLS	First Stage IV	IV
	(1)	(2)	(3)
Sum lawsuits	−0.00002*		−0.00002
	(0.00001)		(0.0001)
Weight per judge serving		1.075**	
		(0.441)	
Constant	−0.046***	−511.281***	−0.045***
	(0.013)	(180.162)	(0.015)
N	1,500	1,400	1,400
R^2	0.231	0.362	0.239
Adjusted R^2	0.210	0.345	0.218
Residual SE	0.082	519.587	0.080
	(df = 1,459)	(df = 1,361)	(df = 1,361)

*$p < .1$; **$p < .05$; ***$p < .01$.

Standard errors (SEs) clustered by circuit. F statistic is 19.32.

IV, instrumental variable; df, degrees of freedom.

Table 4.5 The Effect of Terminated Prisoner Lawsuits on Lagged Number of State Facilities

	Lagged Sum State Facilities	Sum Lawsuits	Lagged Sum State Facilities
	OLS	First Stage IV	IV
	(1)	(2)	(3)
Sum lawsuits	0.002**		0.003**
	(0.001)		(0.001)
Weight per judge serving		1.075**	
		(0.441)	
Constant	−0.560***	−511.281***	−0.385***
	(0.173)	(180.162)	(0.137)
N	1,550	1,400	1,400
R^2	0.542	0.362	0.496
Adjusted R^2	0.530	0.345	0.482
Residual SE	1.701 (df = 1,508)	519.587 (df = 1,361)	1.820 (df = 1,361)

$**p < .05; ***p < .01$.
Standard errors (SEs) clustered by circuit. F statistic is 19.32.
IV, instrumental variable; df, degrees of freedom.

and inmate litigation. States house more private facilities within their boundaries when the sum of lawsuits filed by prisoners increases. This suggests another aggregate shift in the priorities of prison systems, to construct private facilities overall to mitigate the pressures of overcrowding.

I find support for Hypothesis 1 in the analyses presented in Tables 4.3, 4.4, and 4.5. The results from the OLS and IV estimations are substantively identical, providing encouraging evidence that the relationship posited in Hypothesis 1 persists even after accounting for endogeneity. However, the contradictory results in Tables 4.3 and 4.4 again suggest that states are utilizing both private and public facilities to mitigate concerns of overcrowding in correctional institutions. While states are building more private facilities and housing more of their inmates in those kinds of institutions in the aggregate, the population in publicly run facilities is still increasing at a higher rate than the private rate. This is in line with states' priorities as the incarceration rate rose precipitously—to house more inmates, public or not. Even states with the highest aggregate levels of privatization over this time period, like Texas and New Mexico, also vastly expanded their public system. The effect of more lawsuits on prison privatization is at least partially dependent on whether we are examining aggregate or proportional levels of privatization.

To ground these empirical results in context, we can consider a few states' experiences with privatization. New Mexico is one typical example of a state with few successful lawsuits as only five suits prisoners brought in this state were successful from 1986 to 2016 according to the CRC. Despite this, New Mexico has one of the highest proportions of inmates in private facilities. How do we explain this divergence? I argue, via Hypothesis 1, that states facing more litigation overall will turn to the private sector in an effort to deal with overcrowding crises brought to public attention through lawsuits. Privatization helps the state avoid the costly expense of opening new prisons and helps it pass the buck of poorly operated prisons. As one editorial in the *Santa Fe New Mexican* put it in 1987, "the real force behind the attempt to push corrections operations into private industry might be to save politicians from the embarrassment and blame when incidents occur . . . with a private prison, it would be convenient to blame all the problems on the contractor" ("Private Industry Won't Solve Woes," 1987). This particular example concerns the operation of private prisons within a state's jurisdiction, but concerns about sending inmates to out-of-state facilities also follow a similar logic. Alaska, which has housed anywhere between 20 and 40% of its inmates in private prisons in other states, contemplated opening a facility of its own in the late 1990s to accommodate concerns of overcrowding ("Some Towns Looking," 1997). However, that expansion never occurred as costs of opening a public prison were just too high (in both start-up and maintenance), and the state continued to use private prisons out of state to provide an interim solution to the overcrowding problem. Both of these states illustrate the potential motivations behind privatizing: to shift blame away from the state for problems occurring within prisons and to provide an interim solution that does not require professionalization or the development of new prisons or guidelines.

Another state's experience with privatization (and subsequent elimination of privatization) is also illustrative. Idaho began contracting with CoreCivic to operate the Idaho Correctional Center in 2000. For the next decade, the state knew the facility was violating the contract and misrepresenting staff hours, but it was not until extensive litigation occurred that the state acted and took back ownership of the facility (Tartaglia, 2014). This is an example of the political accountability mechanism working in reverse: the state privatized initially to avoid the problems associated with prisoner litigation, but soon that litigation got so severe that the state was facing media and public scorn about it. The state then took control of the facility back as privatization no longer helped the state avoid accountability for these lawsuits. This example helps to provide context for the results in the tables, but it cannot tease out which mechanism is at play, whether states are avoiding legal or political accountability. Future studies of these mechanisms, and case study analyses in particular, may help to illuminate these considerations.

Hypothesis 2

Similar to the approach in the previous section, I use an IV regression to limit the effect of endogeneity on my estimations. Because judges are in theory assigned randomly to cases, the background characteristics of judges can be considered similarly randomly assigned. The IV is *Proportion Prior Prosecutor*, the proportion of prisoners' rights cases heard in each state-year that were heard by judges who were formerly prosecutors or district attorneys. I expect the relationship between *Court Order Began* and *Proportion Prior Prosecutor* to be positive for a few reasons. First, while it is often taken as a given that prosecutors will be less amenable to the requests of prisoners, it is likely that this assumption is false. For one, as Myers (1988) points out, prosecutors are more likely to apply the law uniformly than other judges. Their prior legal experience lends them a healthy respect for the law and its application. Because so many of the prisoners' rights cases, particularly at the beginning, had egregious violations of inmates' rights at the core of the cases, it is likely that prior prosecutors would take these violations of the law more seriously than judges without that experience. Additionally, some empirical work follows this intuition: prior prosecutors are more likely to decide a case in the plaintiffs' favor in civil rights cases, including those involving prisoners (Ashenfelter, Eisenberg, and Schwab, 1995).

An IV analysis requires the exclusion restriction to be satisfied, which mandates that the IV, *Proportion Prior Prosecutor*, has no independent effect on prison privatization other than through the independent variable, successful lawsuits (Sovey and Green, 2011). From a narrative perspective, this is likely. For one, the judiciary is not a policymaking institution, so judges cannot directly aid in the adoption of private prisons. The only mechanism of control judges have over state corrections is via their judicial decisions and court orders, which is precisely why this variable is an appropriate instrument for successful lawsuits.

To assess the causal effect of successful lawsuits on prison privatization, I use an IV approach, instrumenting for successful lawsuits via the proportion of judges who were prior prosecutors in each state-year. I estimate using the following TSLS equations on the data. Equation 4.5 refers to the first stage, and Equation 4.6 refers to the second stage, in which I use the fitted values from Equation 4.5 in place of *Court Order Began*.

$$\text{CourtOrderBegan}_{i,t-1} = \alpha_c + \delta_t + \beta_1 \left(\text{PropPriorProsecutor}_{i_{t-1},t_{t-1}} \right) + \epsilon_{c_1,t_1} \quad (4.5)$$

$$\gamma_{i,t} = \alpha_c + \delta_t + \beta_2 \left(\widehat{\text{CourtOrderBegan}}_{i_{t-1},t_{t-1}} \right) + \epsilon_{c_2,t_2} \quad (4.6)$$

As in the previous section, $\gamma_{i,t}$ is a set of dependent variables concerning private prisons: *Private Design Capacity, Proportion Inmates in Private Facilities,* and *Number of Private Facilities—State Only.* The variables are similarly lagged, as well as the inclusion of common fixed effects: α_t, circuit intercepts; δ_t, year intercepts (i.e., two-way fixed effects); and ϵ_{c_2,t_2}, a vector of error terms.

The IV is *Proportion Prior Prosecutor,* the proportion of all prisoners' cases in each state-year heard by judges who were previously prosecutors. I relied on the Bonica and Sen (2017) data set of federal judges, matched those judges with the data set on prisoners' rights cases, and examined the composition of the judges' prior experiences. I then searched the prior employment field of the Bonica and Sen (2017) data set to find those who were previously prosecutors and calculated the proportion of these cases heard by those who had been employed as prosecutors. I was unable to match approximately 44% of the original prisoner petitions data set, but there is at least one matched judge per state-year and thus a value for the *Proportion Prior Prosecutor* variable. The bulk of the missing data, however, is still in the first few years of the data set. [18] *Court Order Began* is from the CRC and is a binary variable for whether that state had at least one court order begun in that year.

This hypothesis considers the effect of successful lawsuits on *Private Design Capacity.* I display the results using regular OLS, along with the first and second stages of the TSLS estimation in Table 4.6.

Table 4.6 The Effect of Court Orders Begun on Lagged Private Design Capacity

	Lagged Private DC	Court Order Began	Lagged Private DC
	OLS	First Stage IV	IV
	(1)	(2)	(3)
Court order began	320.788		−1,522.019
	(303.487)		(3,978.326)
Proportion prior prosecutor		0.506**	
		(0.210)	
Constant	−1,000.730***	0.181***	−702.315
	(311.008)	(0.052)	(695.591)
N	1,550	1,550	1,550
R^2	0.324	0.084	0.221
Adjusted R^2	0.305	0.060	0.200
Residual SE (df = 1,508)	1,883.735	0.396	2,021.762

$**p < .05; ***p < .01.$

Standard errors (SEs) clustered by circuit. F statistic is 19.61.

DC, design capacity; df, degrees of freedom.

Of note is the first stage of the IV regression in column 2. The F statistic for this instrument, which helps to differentiate between weak and strong instruments, is more than 10, indicating that the instrument here is fairly strong (Sovey and Green, 2011). The first-stage IV is significant and positive, though, suggesting that a higher proportion of judges who were prior prosecutors are associated with the imposition of one or more court orders in each state-year. Though the OLS and IV specifications are not significant, the direction of the results support the intuition of Hypothesis 2, that court orders issued in a state-year make it less likely for states to privatize. Moreover, the results from a Wu-Hausman test, which tests whether the IV regression is as consistent as OLS and whether the variable I am instrumenting for is endogenous and would bias OLS results, were highly significant, indicating that IV is consistent and OLS is not. This may explain why the OLS results in column 1 are not significant: since OLS is not consistent, the results reported there may be biased. Overall, it seems there is some support for the hypothesis that court orders issued in each state-year in prison and jail conditions cases make it less likely for individual cases in the 1980s.

The identical analysis run using the dependent variable of *Lagged Proportion in Private Facilities* is in Table 4.7. Encouragingly, Table 4.7 highlights a similarity among the OLS and IV results in their magnitude—a higher number of court orders issued in the district courts results in a lower percentage of a state's prisoners in private facilities. I take this as tentative evidence of Hypothesis 2, though the variable does not reach traditional levels of statistical significance. The results indicate that the announcement of *any* court order is associated with a lower proportion of a state's inmates in private facilities. There is evidence for Hypothesis 2—states seem to be decreasing not only the number of inmates in private facilities (as in Table 4.6) but also possibly the overall percentage of their inmates in private facilities.

Finally, the analysis run using the third dependent variable, *Lagged Number of Private Facilities—State Only*, is reported in Table 4.8. Similar to Table 4.6, a higher number of court orders in a given state-year is associated with a lower number of private facilities in the IV analysis. The Wu-Hausman

Table 4.7 The Effect of Court Orders Begun on Lagged Proportion of Inmates in Private Facilities

	Lagged Proportion in Private	Court Order Began	Lagged Proportion in Private
	OLS	First Stage IV	IV
	(1)	(2)	(3)
Court order began	−0.015		−0.181
	(0.011)		(0.194)
Proportion prior prosecutor		0.511**	
		(0.211)	
Constant	−0.040***	0.181***	−0.013
	(0.012)	(0.052)	(0.036)
N	1,548	1,548	1,548
R^2	0.228	0.085	−0.279
Adjusted R^2	0.207	0.060	−0.314
Residual SE (df = 1,506)	0.081	0.395	0.105

**$p < .05$; ***$p < .01$.

Standard errors (SEs) clustered by circuit. F statistic is 19.98.

df, degrees of freedom.

test is significant, suggesting that the IV estimation is more consistent than OLS because of the endogeneity of the court orders variable. This is more encouraging evidence of Hypothesis 2 that states utilize private facilities less often as the court gets more active in the administration of prisons.

Collectively, the results from Tables 4.6, 4.7, and 4.8 provide some, but not total, support of Hypothesis 2, that states with successful prisoners' rights litigation privatize at a lower rate. The narrative laid out in the previous chapter therefore finds some support in these analyses, though some of the specifications do not reach statistical significance. Nevertheless, I take this as initial, tentative evidence for my claims. Most importantly, it identifies the effect of the most important prisoners' rights cases, as determined by subject matter legal experts, and shows that states are indeed responsive to the orders of the judicial system. This not only provides encouraging evidence for the existence of checks and balances and cross-institutional enforcement of orders but also suggests that problems identified within the system are recognized by the state and institutionalized as reforms. The state is being held

Table 4.8 The Effect of Court Orders Begun on Lagged Number of State Facilities

	Lagged Sum State Facilities	Court Order Began	Lagged Sum State Facilities
	OLS	First Stage IV	IV
	(1)	(2)	(3)
Court order began	0.355		−0.880
	(0.286)		(3.629)
Proportion prior prosecutor		0.506**	
		(0.210)	
Constant	−0.945***	0.181***	−0.745
	(0.345)	(0.052)	(0.621)
N	1,550	1,550	1,550
R^2	0.347	0.084	0.309
Adjusted R^2	0.330	0.060	0.290
Residual SE (df = 1,508)	2.031	0.396	2.089

$^*p < .1; ^{**}p < .05; ^{***}p < .01.$
Standard errors (SEs) clustered by circuit. F statistic is 19.61.
df, degrees of freedom.

accountable for poor prison conditions and thus has no incentive to privatize its prisons.

It is useful to ground these empirical results with substantive examples. Much like the Arkansas case described in the previous chapter, *Holt v. Sarver I* and *II* , states professionalize after a court order is handed down. The continued attention of the judge and attorneys involved in the litigation ensures compliance with the court order, that the state is truly reforming its prison facilities. It is likely because of this extended third-party enforcement of the court order that states, rather than waste their time and resources outsourcing carceral activities to the private sector, choose instead to reform inhouse and not privatize.

If a state is actively turning away from privatization in the face of successful lawsuits, what does this look like in practice? One colorful example is *Tillery v. Owens*, a case filed by inmates in the US District Court for the Western District of Pennsylvania in 1987 alleging unconstitutional conditions of confinement at the maximum-security State Correctional Institution in Pittsburgh (SCIP). This case is prototypical and follows the reasoning laid out in the previous chapter, for a few reasons. First, attorneys within larger community organizations represented these prisoners as lawyers from the National Prison Project at the American Civil Liberties Union (ACLU) along with lawyers from the Neighborhood Legal Services Association represented the inmates. This bolsters the narrative that the most successful lawsuits are successful because of the involvement of larger organizations that help collate prisoners' claims. Second, Maurice B. Cohill, Jr., the judge on the case, became personally involved when he toured SCIP unannounced before the bench trial. Finally, when Cohill sided with the plaintiffs, he appointed a special monitor to submit reports regarding the compliance of the prison officials, ensuring that the court kept a watchful eye on the prison to determine whether it made the appropriate administrative changes. Judge Cohill lambasted the prison officials for unconstitutional conditions, writing, "we might very well order that SCIP be closed immediately; it is an overcrowded, unsanitary, and understaffed fire trap." Altogether, this prototypical case helps to bolster the empirical claims here: the involvement of judges, attorneys, and sometimes special monitors prompted (or forced) the state to professionalize at least some part of its operation to stay in compliance with the court order. Indeed, Pennsylvania never adopted private prisons at the state level, even though one federal private facility, the Moshannon Valley Correctional Center that holds Federal Bureau of Prisons prisoners, opened in 2006 after years of local opposition to the project. It seems that the state is following the narrative sketched out in the previous chapter by professionalizing only in response to a successful lawsuit and not privatizing as a result.

Accountability and Privatization in Context

Both dynamics of Hypotheses 1 and 2 are illustrated fairly well by Hawaii's experience with both privatization and inmate lawsuits. In 1984, inmates at two prisons in the state sued, alleging that correctional officials were in violation of prisoners' constitutional rights regarding overcrowding, healthcare, and sanitation, among other concerns. The case, *Spear v. Waihee*, began with the help of the ACLU and resulted in a broad court order that lasted from 1985 to 1999 (State of Hawaii Auditor, 2010). In the meantime, the state accommodated the broad requests of the judge, but 10 years after the imposition of the court order, Hawaii began its first private contract. The court order was soon lifted after the state sufficiently complied and Hawaii continued to sign private prison contracts. This example nicely illustrates the dynamics of Hypotheses 1 and 2. Whereas the state's initial response to the court order is to professionalize and adapt correctional standards to the lawsuit, the effect of more lawsuits over time forced the state's hand in privatizing part of its corrections systems. Or, as noted by the state auditor in a report on the status of Hawaii's contracts with private prison companies, "what started as a temporary solution to relieve prison overcrowding is today a matter of state policy" (State of Hawaii Auditor, 2010).

Empirical testing resulted in strong support of Hypothesis 1 and tentative evidence of Hypothesis 2: privatization is more likely in states facing a higher number of lawsuits and less likely in states facing any successful court orders. In the aggregate, a higher number of prisoner lawsuits results in higher numbers of private inmates and facilities. When examining the overall level of prison privatization, however, the relationship was negative. This indicates that states are increasing their use of correctional privatization, but the expansion of publicly run prisons was growing at a faster rate. Collectively, these results suggest a two-pronged approach to prison overcrowding, that states rely partially on privatization but more so on publicly run facilities. They do this to limit accountability as more lawsuits overall make a state more likely to seek out methods to reduce its legal and political accountability. On the other hand, successful lawsuits are holding states accountable for these conditions already, thus removing the state's incentive to do so.

These results are in line with other theoretical and quantitative work on the effects of prisoner litigation on various outcomes. States are responsive to litigation and change their corrections policy as a result (e.g., Levitt, 1996; Schoenfeld, 2018). This theoretical intuition is bolstered even further by the nature of the successful lawsuits in this study. These orders specifically mandate the construction of new guidelines over inmate grievances, place specific population caps on prisons, or even mandate the construction of new facilities. Successful lawsuits prompt institutional change within the states that experience them, as evidenced by the development of new rules and procedures, massive changes to a state's corrections bureaucracy, in the face of court orders (e.g., Justice, 1990; Schoenfeld, 2018; Yackle, 1989).

States face perverse incentives to privatize their prisons in order to avoid protecting and providing incarcerated people with legal rights. This suggests that the rights revolution, at least for those who are incarcerated, is incomplete. Public and private prisons alike ought to consider and protect these essential rights for incarcerated people as they are at the core of American democracy.

Though this evidence suggests that states are indeed responding to lawsuits filed by prisoners, is there any reaction from private prison companies? Even if litigation is promoting favorable (or unfavorable) outcomes for private prison companies, that outcome is unimportant if these businesses do not consider political or institutional factors throughout their decision-making process. In particular, how do the fortunes of private prison companies change as the political environment shifts under them?

5

Do Private Prison Firms Respond
to Successful Prison Litigation?

... in an effort to meet the Federal court ruling, the fiscal year 2012
budget of the state of California calls for a significant reallocation of
responsibilities from state government to local jurisdictions. ... The
return of the California inmates to the state of California would have
a significant adverse impact on our financial position, results of operations, and cash flows.
—*Corrections Corporation of America Annual Report, 2012*

The previous chapter analyzed the effect of inmate litigation on prison privatization and found support for the two central hypotheses: primarily, that
a higher number of lawsuits in the aggregate makes it more likely for states
to privatize their prisons. Moreover, I found support (though more tentative) for my second hypothesis, that states with a higher number of federal
court orders about prison or jail conditions are less likely to privatize their
corrections systems. Those analyses considered the prison privatization process from the perspective of state actors, how institutional constraints from
the judiciary prompted state representatives and bureaucrats to act in particular ways. This chapter instead focuses on how prison litigation informs the
behavior of the other actors in this relationship, private prison companies.

To what degree do these companies react to political events like the announcement of prison consent decrees? It is of vital importance to ask this question to
further illuminate the arguments presented in previous chapters. Even if state
governments react in certain ways to particular events like prison overcrowding
and inmate litigation, that behavior means next to nothing unless private prison
firms, and their investors, *acknowledge the importance of these events*. Specifically,
the theory in Chapter 3 suggests a mutual relationship between politicians and
firms, that governments are sometimes forced to privatize in response to carceral

pressures but also that these companies actively seek out expansion opportunities, especially with sympathetic political representatives. This chapter considers the performance of private prison firms and seeks to discover the degree to which their finances are dependent on particular political events.

Unlike Chapters 3 and 4, the focus of this chapter is exclusively on the announcement of *successful lawsuits* as those events are newsworthy and likely to catch the attention of investors. More lawsuits is likely not interesting to these investors because they cannot readily observe it happening—they would need to be watching district court dockets to see if any prisoner litigation was filed each day, which is unlikely given the high frequency of this litigation and the difficulty of doing so. Therefore, I focus on the implications of Hypothesis 2 from Chapter 3, that successful court orders make a state *less* likely to privatize its prisons. I consider the behavior and character of investors of private prison companies and develop some hypotheses about how those investors will respond to the announcement of successful lawsuits. I argue that there will be no unconditional effect of successful lawsuits on stock performance in the aggregate, but there will be a significant and negative effect of the lawsuits on companies' stock behavior in states with private facilities. These results are confirmed empirically, suggesting that investors are the most savvy at responding to threats to business in states that have the most private prisons.

The Obama Department of Justice and Private Prisons

On August 11, 2016, the Office of the Inspector General (OIG) in the US Department of Justice (DOJ) released a blockbuster report that maligned the private operation of several federal correctional facilities, revealing that these prisons had comparatively more safety and security incidents than similar publicly operated facilities. The OIG noted the privately operated prisons—run by the three largest private prison operators in the country, CoreCivic, the GEO Group, and Management and Training Corporation (MTC)—had more assaults, uses of force, lockdowns, and contraband finds, among other safety and security incidents (US Department of Justice, 2016). The damning report generated a wave of controversy about the role of private prisons in the federal prison system and reached an inflection point seven days later, on August 18, 2016, when Deputy Attorney General Sally Yates released a memorandum in response to the report's findings, recommending that the federal government either decline contract extensions or dramatically reduce their scope (Yates, 2016).

There were quite a few reasons the report was not as dire for private prison business as the news implicated. For one, Yates' directive was only directed toward the Federal Bureau of Prisons (BOP), which accounted for only 9% of CoreCivic's revenue and 14% of GEO Group's revenue in 2016.[1] Far more of the revenue from the federal government for each of these companies is concentrated in other branches not covered by this report, including the US Marshals Service (USMS) and Immigration and Customs Enforcement (ICE), which together account for 43% of CoreCivic's revenue in 2016, 33.2% of GEO Group's revenue in the same year, and three of MTC's 57 facilities in 2016 (information from MTC's website [Management and Training Corporation, 2016]).

Even though BOP's business is not the majority of the business these companies are engaged in with either the rest of the federal government or state governments, these companies immediately suffered at the hands of their shareholders at the otential loss of these contracts. Figure 5.1 highlights how

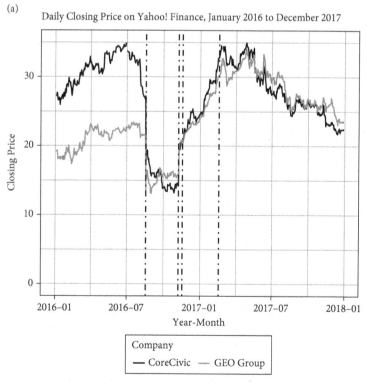

(a)

Daily Closing Price on Yahoo! Finance, January 2016 to December 2017

Figure 5.1 Closing prices of CoreCivic's and GEO Group's stock. In (a) across two years and in (b) across eight months. The four dotted lines are Yates' announcement, Trump's election, Trump's nomination of Jeff Sessions as attorney general, Sessions' confirmation as attorney general.

(b)

Daily Closing Price on Yahoo! Finance, July 2016 to March 2017

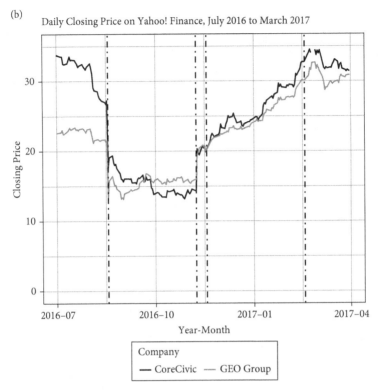

Figure 5.1 Continued

the returns of the two publicly traded companies[2] that had contracts with the federal government at the time of the 2016 announcement—CoreCivic and the GEO Group—dropped precipitously with the DOJ report release and the Yates announcement a week later.

Figure 5.1(a) shows the two-year period that covers the DOJ announcement, whereas Figure 5.1(b) is the approximate six-month period around that announcement. The first dotted line in Figure 5.1 represents the Yates announcement of the rollback of the use of private prisons on August 18, 2016. The closing price of both companies' stocks dropped precipitously after the announcement, even though these companies still retained their most valuable federal customers, USMS and ICE. CoreCivic and GEO Group did not rebound quickly from this announcement until the second dotted line three months later, on November 8, 2016, when Donald Trump was elected president. Shortly thereafter, Trump nominated Alabama senator Jeff Sessions to be his attorney general, on November 18, 2016 (the third dotted line), an announcement that continues the upward trajectories of the companies' closing stock prices. The rising closing stock prices of these companies are indicative of private prison firms' expectations that both Sessions and Trump would be supportive of federal carceral privatization. The final dotted line in Figure 5.1 is February 8, 2017, when Sessions was confirmed as the attorney general. Sessions soon rescinded the Yates memo and reasserted the federal government's support of private prisons, thus providing these companies and their shareholders reason to celebrate the election. The end of 2017 brings the closing prices of these firms to pre-Yates memo levels, indicating that shareholders are at least as confident in the future of their business as they were prior to that announcement.[3]

Examining the stock performance of private prison firms is particularly illustrative of shareholder expectations about the companies' futures: are investors confident in the future of the business and in the viability of the government as a customer, at least for the foreseeable future? This short anecdote, though only one of many political events that can affect the financial performance of private prison firms, indicates a close relationship between politics and business in the realm of carceral privatization (Collingwood, Morin, and El-Khatib, 2018). And though this one example is particularly stark, it is only one event of many that provides prima facie evidence not only that private prison firms and their investors pay attention to politics but that their business depends on it.

Investors and Company Stock Performance

Companies that are publicly traded on the stock market—in this case, private prison firms—often go public initially to get an infusion of capital from selling shares. This capital can then be used to build the business, via the purchase of property, resources, or the like. After the initial public offering (IPO), however, stocks become less directly important to the fiscal health of the firm and instead act as important signals to investors of the company's health and well-being, particularly as compared to the competitors.

Stock prices are therefore a useful barometer for investors to assess a company's health and how confident investors appear to be in the future of the company. Though stock prices by themselves do not make firms money after the IPO phase (unless they release new shares for investors to purchase), there are a few reasons why these prices are so integral to the future of the business. First, investors who are unhappy with stock market performance can take drastic measures to alleviate that concern, through actions like a takeover of the board or forcing through changes to improve company performance. And because companies are required to file public documents with the Securities and Exchange Commission once they go public, shareholders have access to a multitude of financial data they can use to force changes within the company if necessary. The second reason why stock prices are so important to company health is that so many board members also hold massive amounts of stock in their own company. Whether they are incentivized to do so via stock incentive programs or choose to invest in their own company by themselves, company employees who own stock are financially invested in ensuring that those stock prices remain high. Finally, lower stock prices could result in unintended financial consequences elsewhere: banks that are considering lending to a company will often take the firm's share price into account when making that decision. Therefore, the new acquisition of loans or capital to build the business is at least partially dependent on stock prices.

Because the performance of stock prices is an overall indicator of economic health, with investors and company employees alike relying at least partially on rising stock prices to make money and build the business, fluctuations in these prices on the stock market are of particular import to study. The key question underlying analyses of stock prices then has to grapple with a tough puzzle: what explains changes in firm's stock prices over time? The explanations for stock price fluctuations are many and diverse, from general macroeconomic changes in economic activity like inflation or interest rates to unobserved, private decisions made by shareholders.[4]

This chapter considers how changes in stock prices are altered by political events. Specifically, I engage with the argument presented in Chapter 3 to hypothesize that private prison firms' stocks suffer in response to the announcement of successful prisoners' rights lawsuits. In particular, I argue that shareholders will respond negatively to announcements of successful prisoners' rights lawsuits *but only in those states that have at least one private facility*. I expect a negative reaction to the issuance of a court order because of the reasoning behind Hypothesis 2. Successful prisoners' rights lawsuits prompt the state to professionalize and bureaucratize in response to the often very specific requests of the judiciary. The governments therefore have little incentive to outsource their carceral operations to the private sector as corrections departments adapt their behavior to the court orders and no longer need to look to the private sector for quick and easy solutions to prison overcrowding. I argue that the key motivation behind privatization is the limitation of accountability, and successful court orders already ensure that the state is held responsible for prison conditions. That argument, detailed in Chapter 3, found tentative empirical substantiation in Chapter 4. I found that states with a higher number of successful court orders were less likely to privatize prisons. Because of these theoretical and empirical expectations, therefore, I hypothesize that shareholders will respond negatively to the announcement of these court orders.

There is an important caveat to this argument, however. I do not expect that all lawsuits, in the aggregate, will shift stock prices because not all these judicial orders will have a bearing on the business of the private firms. If a private company has no business in Washington State, for example, it likely matters little what the court rulings are in that state. I develop two separate expectations about the stock market behavior of these companies in response to the announcement of a judicial court order:

Hypothesis 1: *The stock market prices of private prison firms will not be affected, on average, when a federal court order about prison or jail conditions is announced.*

On the other hand, companies rely heavily on signals from state governments in which they operate to determine the future of their business. If a court ruling is handed down in California, for example, it bears on both CoreCivic's and GEO Group's business as both companies have multiple facilities located there. Therefore, the second hypothesis argues that the influence of the announcement of court orders on stock prices is conditional on whether that company has business there to begin with.

Hypothesis 2: *The stock market prices of private prison firms will be negatively affected when the federal court order about prison or jail conditions occurs in a state with at least one existing private facility.*

These two hypotheses reflect the savviness of private prison investors, that only those legal orders that are the most important for the continuation of business will affect the stock price. The mechanism of investors responding quickly to the announcement of a court order is a general hypothesis put forth by the finance literature, but the specific aspects of the private prison industry illustrate how this intuition operates in practice.

Private Prison Firm Stocks and Politics

The private prison industry is a massively profitable one but is dominated by two firms, CoreCivic and the GEO Group. In 2016, these companies listed over $1.8 billion and $2.1 billion in revenues, respectively, from the operation and maintenance of dozens of private prisons and community corrections centers in the United States and abroad. These businesses are traded publicly and therefore are fixtures on the stock market, with CoreCivic and the GEO Group having over 118 million and 123 million shares outstanding as of 2018, respectively (figures from the NASDAQ profiles of these companies).[5] Though this chapter is primarily tasked with analyzing the effects of Hypotheses 1 and 2, its goal is also to illuminate the stock performance and characteristics of these firms. With that in mind, what characterizes the stock performance of these companies?

As with other companies, private prison firms like CoreCivic and the GEO Group issue stock that is held by both individuals and institutions, such as investment companies and large banks. Though individuals can and do hold stock in both firms, the vast majority of shareholders are institutions. As of 2017, over 80% of CoreCivic's stock was held by institutional investors, compared to more than 93% of the GEO Group's stock. Though the portfolio of institutional investors differed slightly across the two companies, the firms shared the top two institutional shareholders: Vanguard Group, an investment company, and Blackrock, Inc., a hedge fund. Among the hundreds of other investors are included a multitude of investment banks like Northern Trust Corporation, multinational banks like Wells Fargo, and even public retirement funds from at least a dozen states,[6] including, ironically, one state that has statutorily outlawed private prisons: New York.

These institutions hold most of the stock in the two currently existing private prison firms, and it is safe to say a fair amount of the individual investors in the firms are employees. While the largest investors in both CoreCivic and the GEO Group hold millions of shares, the board of directors and executive officers routinely hold thousands, sometimes hundreds of thousands, of shares themselves. This provides employees an incentive to grow the business, thereby raising the stock price and resulting in more money for the workers.

Taken together, the institutional and individual investors of private prison firms determine each company's stock price. Though there is some evidence that these two groups behave differently in their investment behavior,[7] I will largely focus on the attitudes of large institutions as these actors are the over-whelming shareholders in these firms.

Institutional investors have a fairly lengthy history with these companies as the four companies included in this analysis have been publicly traded for multiple decades. CoreCivic has been publicly traded since October 1, 1986; GEO Group since July 27, 1994; Correctional Services Corporation (CSC) from February 1, 1994 to November 7, 2005; and Cornell Companies from October 3, 1996 to August 13, 2010. The GEO Group acquired both CSC and Cornell Companies in 2005 and 2010, respectively; and both GEO Group and CoreCivic have acquired smaller, nontraded private prison companies since the 1980s. Figure 5.2 highlights the bid stock price of all four firms over the time period 1986 to 2016.

The data for this figure comes from the Center for Research in Security Prices (CRSP) and represents bid price, the daily maximum price an investor is willing to pay for a share in each private prison company. The CRSP data

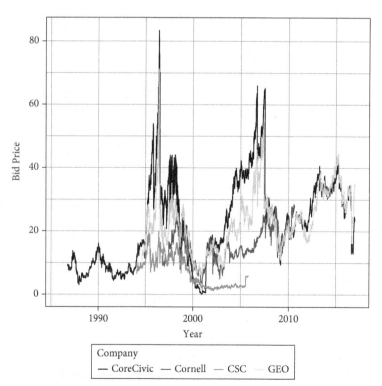

Figure 5.2 Bid price of private prison firms' stocks, 1986 to 2016.

encompasses a variety of stock market characteristics, including the volume of shares traded any given day, the price of the shares, and value-weighted returns, among other variables. This data source will also be used to construct the variables used in the analyses in this section.

All four companies have varying stock prices, but the broad patterns across the time period are consistent: a growing value of the firms' stocks as more private prisons are opened and the businesses grow, in the late 1990s and the first decade of the 2000s. After both CSC and Cornell are acquired by the GEO Group, the market for the private prison industry grows equally for both GEO and CoreCivic—their stock prices are nearly identical beginning in 2010, and that mirroring pattern remained even six years later. It appears that, at least in the aggregate, shifts in one company's stock are mirrored nearly exactly by shifts in the other's stock. This suggests that broad market forces affect the stock performance of the entire industry more so than an individual firm's changes in financial fortune.

Stock Market Volatility

Assessing the effect of events, prison or jail court orders in this context, on stock prices is a challenging estimation. The aim of the argument is to assess the effect of one event on the stock performance of these firms; but there can be multiple events not only per year but per month, and the events are common to all firms (i.e., a successful lawsuit in California may affect the business of all private prison firms, not just those firms that operate in that state). To accommodate multiple events that affect multiple firms, I utilize an empirical approach typically chosen by scholars in marketing, finance, and economics: an event study analysis. An event study analysis is a useful tool for scholars seeking to understand the immediate effect of an event. It is difficult to measure how an event affects an outcome like public policy regarding private prisons, for example, because there is no clear and unequivocal measure of what that policymaking would look like. It is therefore nearly impossible to isolate the precise effect of one unique event on policymaking without acknowledging the theoretically endless other factors that could determine changes in that policy. Furthermore, the time period of the effect is entirely unclear. The advantage of analyzing how an event affects an outcome like stock prices is that I can isolate the immediate effect of the event on a rapidly changing outcome like stock prices (Campbell, Lo, and MacKinlay, 1996, chap. 4). Intuitively, this approach relies on the assumption that investors take into account events relevant to the businesses they are invested in and respond accordingly, via the buying or selling of stock (Fama et al., 1969).

An event study analyzes how an event, the announcement of a prison or jail court order, immediately affects stock prices. This approach is not novel as scholars both within and outside political science have used this approach to examine the effects of a variety of events. Applications within economics and finance include: the effect of the announcement of Timothy Geithner as Treasury secretary on the stock prices of firms that he had a prior connection with (Acemoglu et al., 2016), the announcement of a celebrity endorser on firm stock prices (Agrawal and Kamakura, 1995), and the effects of protests on stock prices (King and Soule, 2007). Studies utilizing this approach in political science are relatively more scarce but include the following events and their corresponding effect on stock prices: terrorist attacks (Chen and Siems, 2004), the nomination of a politically connected board member (Goldman, Rocholl, and So, 2009), the election of candidates the firm gave campaign contributions to (Fowler, Garro, and Spenkuch, 2020), the news release of reports of ill health of H. Muhammad Suharto on firms connected to him (Fisman, 2001), the effect of Senator James Jeffords switching from Republican to Independent and tipping the Senate to Democrats (Jayachandran, 2006), how oil and gas companies' stocks respond to key procedural votes in Congress (Gilligan and Krehbiel, 1988), the sudden death of Senator Henry Jackson on prices of firms affected by his committee leadership (Roberts, 1990), and the effect of terrorism in Basque Country in Spain on businesses in that area (Abadie and Gardeazabal, 2003). This approach is thus a useful and commonplace one in a variety of literatures to identify the effect of one event on firms' stock prices.

Though we seek to understand the effect of particular events on stock prices, scholars do not use the raw stock prices as the variable of interest. Stock prices fluctuate wildly across any time period, so utilizing the raw returns may reflect market-wide changes in investor behavior rather than the precise effect of the event. Therefore, like the studies mentioned in the previous paragraph, I use the raw stock returns to calculate cumulative abnormal returns (CARs), an approach that adjusts firm stock prices around the event for both the past performance of that firm's stock prices and the behavior of the entire stock market. I calculate CARs using the market model, which relates the performance of the private prison company's stock to the performance of the entire stock market (Fama et al., 1969). The advantage of this particular method of estimating CARs is that it reduces variance in the estimates by accounting for common, market-wide shifts in financial performance (Campbell, Lo, and MacKinlay, 1996, chap. 4).

Intuitively, this approach provides a numerical estimation for how "abnormal" a stock price is on day t when an event occurs, taking into account past stock market behavior. With that intuition in mind, there are a few methodological steps for calculating this variable, the first of which is to calculate the daily abnormal returns (ARs), which I will sum to calculate the CARs:

$$AR_{i,t} = R_{i,t} - \left[\widehat{\alpha_i} + \hat{\beta}_i R_{m,t} \right] \qquad (5.1)$$

This equation calculates the daily abnormal return for firm i, $AR_{i,t}$, by taking the actual return on that day, $R_{i,t}$, and subtracting $(\hat{\alpha}_i + \hat{\beta}_i R_{m,t})$, where $R_{m,t}$ is the return on the market for the event day t.[8] This is calculated for each day over the event window, which is chosen by the analyst. For my purposes, I try a variety of windows: CAR[–1,1], CAR[–2,2], CAR[–5,5], CAR[–10,10], and CAR[–30,30] as I am agnostic at the outset about whether the effect of the event, the court order, will take 1, 2, 5, 10, or 30 days to materialize in firms' stock performance. $\hat{\alpha}_i$ and $\hat{\beta}_i$ are calculated using the following equation:

$$R_{i,t} = \alpha_i + \beta_i R_{m,t} + \epsilon_{it} \qquad (5.2)$$

As before, $R_{i,t}$ is the actual daily return for each company's stock, and $R_{m,t}$ is the daily return of the stock market. The estimated values of both α_i and β_i from this equation are then plugged back into Equation 5.1 to calculate the daily annual return for firm i.

This equation is estimated using market- and firm-specific stock returns 250 to 30 trading days before the event, following the literature (Acemoglu et al., 2016; Fowler, Garro, and Spenkuch, 2020). This window allows me to estimate what the "normal" returns of these companies look like over the last 220 days. For a successful lawsuit decided in November, for example, the firm's normal return would be determined by the stock's prices from approximately March to October of that same year. Finally, these values are plugged into Equation 5.1 and subsequently summed to calculate the CAR.

$$CAR\left[t_1, t_2\right]_i = \sum_{t=t_1}^{t_2} AR_{i,t} \qquad (5.3)$$

$CAR[t_1, t_2]_i$ represents the cumulative abnormal return for firm i from time t_1 to time t_2. In the following analyses, I utilize a variety of different specifications for this variable: CAR[−1,1], CAR[−2,2], CAR[−5,5], CAR[−10,10], and CAR[−30,30]. Equation 5.3 forms the basis for the calculation of the dependent variables included in my analysis, effectively measuring the normalized change in the returns for firm i after a particular event, a successful lawsuit.

Political Events

Thus far, the description of the procedure used to estimate the CARs has been relatively general about the "event" that occurs. Here, the announcement of a successful prison or jail court order comprises the event in my data. As in Chapter 4, I rely on the Civil Rights Clearinghouse (CRC) as a source of information on successful prison and jail condition cases that resulted in substantive policy or operational change within correctional facilities. These cases are filed in the federal district courts, where the majority of prisoners' rights cases are heard, and include cases in every state save Alaska, Minnesota, North Dakota, and West Virginia. These successful cases were the ones in which a court order was issued to mandate the government operating the correctional facility to take some kind of action. Some of the orders are specific, placing specific caps on inmate population, whereas others are more general and merely order the state or county operating the prison or jail to develop clear standards in response to a prisoner lawsuit. Either way, these orders mandate some action by the government responsible for the correctional facility and generally require them to develop clear guidelines about inmate care and behavior.

To find the precise dates of these orders, I combed through the CRC database and the legal records through Westlaw to find the exact date a judge handed down the court order in each case. Though there were often preliminary settlements prior to the final settlement or court order, I chose the date of the *final, court- approved order* as the date of the event as this is the final action the judge undertakes in the original case[9] and acts as the final settlement of the court case. In total, there were 442 such court orders between 1986 and 2016.

These dates represent important events for the local and state governments under court order, but why do we expect private prison companies to be similarly affected by these judicial decisions? The theory laid out in Chapter 3 suggests that private companies rely on lawsuits as a signal of the government's correctional vulnerability, lobbying states with more lawsuits to privatize their prisons. On the other hand, successful lawsuits, like the ones in the CRC database, should discourage private prison firms and their investors because the orders indicate that the government is professionalizing, limiting the incentive to privatize to reduce accountability. The government bureaucratizes and adapts to the court order, effectively eliminating the need for private prison firms to step in. I argue that investors pay attention to these events as important signals of the strength of the industry and predict that they will sell more stock after a successful court order.

I estimate CARs for each firm around each lawsuit. According to the dates each firm has been publicly traded then, that means that CoreCivic CARs are matched with lawsuit data from 1986 to the present, GEO Group from 1994 to the present, CSC from 1994 to 2005, and Cornell Companies from 1996 to 2010. I assume all court orders affect all companies, so each court order can be theoretically matched with stock data from all four companies if those companies were all publicly traded at that point. The reason for this inclusion is that successful prisoners' litigation can fundamentally alter the character of a state's corrections system, via the implementation of new rules and procedures. Any company, whether it be CoreCivic, GEO Group, CSC, or Cornell Companies, is then subject to those rules.

Event Study Methodology

Following the common practice of papers that use event study methodology (e.g., Abadie and Gardeazabal, 2003; King and Soule, 2007), the empirical strategy of this chapter is twofold. First, I estimate the average CAR across all firms in response to the successful lawsuit. Second, I use an ordinary least squares (OLS) model which incorporates various aspects of the successful lawsuits to estimate which facets of the court orders are the most consequential for the behavior of the firms' stock prices.

The first approach is largely descriptive, and it estimates the average effect of the lawsuit on CARs in the aggregate, across all firms. This allows me to identify the overall average CAR after an event occurs, regardless of firm or other characteristics. I will also subset the data to find the average CARs across firms to see if one company is more affected by the lawsuit announcement than others. I estimate this relationship by regressing the CARs[10] on an intercept and cluster the standard errors by company.

However, there may be reason to think this approach is not wholly appropriate: notably, it assumes that the effect of the court orders is uniform across multiple subsets of the data. To account for this, I next estimate a series of OLS regressions that add an indicator for the sum of private facilities that exist in the state that experience a successful lawsuit. This variable comes from the original data set collected as part of this project, described more fully in Chapter 2, and represents a facility-year database of private prisons since 1986. The data set used for these analyses is therefore a company–lawsuit pair, with the stock prices of particular companies matched with the number of private facilities that company operates within the state where the lawsuit was handed down. Equivalently, I use Equation 5.4, where i indicates the firm and t indicates the day the court order was announced.

$$\mathrm{CAR}\left[t_1, t_2\right]_i = \alpha_i + \beta_1 \left(\mathrm{SumFacilities}\right) + \epsilon_{i,t} \qquad (5.4)$$

In Equation 5.4, α_i is a set of company fixed effects (I add year fixed effects to a specification in the Appendix, and the results are consistent). The effect of interest is the coefficient β_1, which represents the effect of the sum of private facilities in the state and the year the lawsuit took place on the company's stock price. I calculate *Sum Facilities* by aggregating the private prison facility data set to the state-year level, so this variable represents the number of private correctional institutions operated by each company that exist within a state (whether they be operated by local, state, or federal authorities). That means that states like New York that do not contract with private prison firms for state inmates but do have a federal private immigration facility have a positive value for this variable, whereas states like Alaska that contract with private prison companies but exclusively ship inmates to out-of-state private facilities do not. The reason for this differentiation lies in the nature of these lawsuits. Because these are prisoner lawsuits filed in federal court, the outcome of the case acts as a useful signal for state governments about district court judges' attitudes toward inmate lawsuits. A positive outcome for an inmate in a local jail in Arizona, for example, may give pause to state prison officials as that case sets the precedent for favorable treatment of prisoners in that district. So, regardless of the jurisdiction of the facility, I assume that states take signals from successful lawsuits within the district courts in their state to roughly estimate how amenable those judges could hypothetically be to lawsuits brought by prisoners within the state's jurisdiction.

Approximately one-third of the successful lawsuits occur in states with at least one private facility, and about 20% of the states in the sample have more than one operating private correctional institution at the time of the court order announcement. The sum ranges from 0 to 20 (the GEO Group operated 20 facilities in Texas in 2007). Finally, I cluster errors by company to account for variation across firms in stock performance.

Results

Armed with the two empirical strategies, we can speak to the effect of an announcement of a successful lawsuit on the stock performance of firms. First, what is the average effect of these court orders?

Average CARs and Lawsuits

This section takes a simple approach and merely calculates the average cumulative abnormal returns across all firms to analyze the effect of a lawsuit on stock prices. I also subset the sample to assess whether the effect of lawsuits differs across firms in Table 5.1, columns 2–5.

5.1 shows the average CAR[−5, 5] first for all firms pooled together (column 1), then subset into the different companies (columns 2–5). None of the specifications are significant, indicating that the announcement of a settlement for a successful lawsuit does not affect the overall performance of the private prison companies, to either pooled together or subset separately. This null finding is in fact compatible with the expectations of Hypothesis 1: not all lawsuits are consequential to the business operations of these companies either in the aggregate or separately, .

Do these results differ if you choose a different window around the event? I also calculated CAR[−2,2], CAR[−5,5], CAR[−10,10], and CAR[−30,30] as

Table 5.1 Average CAR[-5,5] Across and Within Firms After a Successful Lawsuit

	CAR[-5,5]				
	All Firms	CoreCivic	GEO Group	CSC	Cornell
	(1)	(2)	(3)	(4)	(5)
Constant	0.002	0.004	−0.007	0.014	0.002
	(0.004)	(0.006)	(0.005)	(0.011)	(0.006)
N	1,120	458	314	143	205
R^2	0.000	−0.000	0.000	0.000	0.000
Adjusted R^2	0.000	−0.000	0.000	0.000	0.000
Residual SE	0.115	0.136	0.086	0.132	0.086
	(df = 1,119)	(df = 457)	(df = 313)	(df = 142)	(df = 204)

Standard errors (SEs) clustered by company in column 1.
df, degrees of freedom.

alternative dependent variables for Table 5.1, the results of which are in the Appendix. Only one specification—the CAR[-10,10] for the GEO Group subset—is significant and negative. Surprisingly, the pooled results for all firms for the CAR[-1,1] and CAR[-2,2] subsets are significant and *positive*, indicating that potentially the negative effect of the lawsuit announcement may only be felt with a longer time period, once investors are able to assess how it might affect their business. Otherwise, the null effect is robust to a variety of different event windows.

CARs in States with Private Facilities and Lawsuits

Hypothesis 2 suggests that lawsuits, in the aggregate, ought not to influence stock returns. Instead, I expect investors of these firms to only be concerned with the successful lawsuits in the states the companies are already operating in. I next consider this possibility in Table 5.2.

Columns 1–5 of this table represent the varying event windows for the CARs, but the result is broadly consistent around all of them. In states with growing numbers of private facilities, the announcement of a successful lawsuit decreases the stock performance of private prison firms, particularly for one- and 10-day windows around the event. These significant coefficients translate into a fairly significant financial outcome for these companies: for

Table 5.2 Average CAR After a Successful Lawsuit in States with Increasing Numbers of Private Prisons

	CAR[-1,1]	CAR[-2,2]	CAR[-5,5]	CAR[-10,10]	CAR[-30,30]
	(1)	(2)	(3)	(4)	(5)
Sum private facilities	-0.0004**	-0.0003	-0.001	-0.002*	-0.005
	(0.0001)	(0.0002)	(0.001)	(0.001)	(0.002)
N	1,120	1,120	1,120	1,120	1,120
R^2	0.001	0.001	0.004	0.007	0.007
Adjusted R^2	-0.003	-0.003	0.0002	0.004	0.003
Residual SE (df = 1,115)	0.058	0.079	0.115	0.148	0.253

$^*p < .1; ^{**}p < .05.$

All standard errors (SEs) clustered by company.

df, degrees of freedom.

each increase in the number of private facilities in a state, the announcement of a successful lawsuit results in 0.04% lower abnormal returns for firms in a one-day window around the event. For the 10-day windows, the effect gets larger, with abnormal returns falling by 0.2%. Though it is difficult to pin down the exact monetary influence of those values, these coefficients represent roughly one-fourths and one times the value of the mean for each of the variables, CAR[-1,1] and CAR[-10,10], respectively (the effect size for the CAR[-10,10] variable is approximately equal to the mean of that variable). Therefore, there is a significant and negative effect of the announcement of an additional lawsuit in the states that are contracting with more private facilities.

It is interesting to note the variation in the significance and magnitude of the dependent variables as the event window grows. This could be attributable to a lag in investors' understanding of the court order. The stock drops significantly initially simply in response to the order, then investors react 10 days later after the consequences of the lawsuit are made clear, either by company reports to investors about the litigation, individual investor research into the event, or news media surrounding it. This could also explain why in the unconditional model for some of the event windows, the results are positive initially and null afterward, indicating that the effects of the lawsuit may take a few days to be fully understood by investors. The independent variable in

Table 5.2 is the sum of private facilities in a given state-year. However, does the presence of *any* private facility matter? In the Appendix, I simplify this variable to a dummy variable, which is listed as a 1 when a state that has a successful lawsuit has any positive number of private facilities and 0 when there are none. The results from the identical regression as the one shown in Table 5.2 are in the Appendix, and none are significant. A state that has any private facilities and a successful lawsuit has no significant effect on the stock prices of private prison firms. This result suggests that the mechanism is driven primarily by *increases* in states' usage of private prisons, not the sheer presence of them. That is, investors are particularly concerned about the states with the most business and not necessarily the states that only have one private facility and do not provide much revenue to the firm. This is intuitive from the firms' perspectives: as one example, 6–12% of CoreCivic's revenue in the years 2014–2016 came only from the state of California (CoreCivic, 2016). If California were to experience a court order with deleterious consequences for that state's usage of private prisons (see the following section), that would likely affect the future of CoreCivic more significantly than a lawsuit in Montana, for example, as that state only had one contract with CoreCivic.

Taken together, the results from Tables 5.1 and 5.2 support this chapter's hypotheses. There is no unequivocal effect of a successful lawsuit on the stock returns of private prison firms, either in the aggregate or separated by firm. However, when I add an indicator for the sum of private facilities in the state, it becomes clear that investors are particularly concerned about lawsuits in states with existing private facilities, likely because those legal orders have the highest likelihood of affecting the business of private prison firms. Additionally, it seems that these negative effects increase as the event window grows. This implication suggests that investors need time to assess how a particular court order will affect the business of the firm and ultimately realize that the court order bodes poorly for the future of private prison firms.

Successful Lawsuits Prompt Company Caution

Though Table 5.2 presents suggestive evidence of the negative influence of announced court orders on company stock prices in those states that have growing numbers of private facilities, does this result translate into variation in company behavior? Substantively, this phenomenon is evident from the companies' perspectives illustrated by one significant California case. In

2011, the Supreme Court handed down a historical decision regarding the extent of overcrowding in California's prison system. Writing for the majority[11] in *Brown v. Plata* (2011), Justice Anthony Kennedy asserted,

> Just as a prisoner may starve if not fed, he or she may suffer or die if not provided adequate medical care. A prison that deprives prisoners of basic sustenance, including adequate medical care, is incompatible with the concept of human dignity and has no place in civilized society.

This blockbuster case was the product of two decades of litigation surrounding the unconstitutionality of mental health care and general medical services in California's prisons (e.g., Simon, 2014). After the state dragged its heels in imposing real, procedural change in response to earlier court cases, a three-judge district court panel met to decide whether to limit the state's prison population. The panel ordered California to reduce its prison overcrowding to 137.5% of the correctional facilities' design capacity, as those facilities were regularly operating at 200–300% of design capacity (Simon, 2014, chaps. 5 and 6). The Supreme Court's affirmation of this order, that the judiciary has the right and responsibility to impose such an order, reinvigorated the calls for reform within California's criminal legal system. Not only was the case momentous for its scope and effect on one of the largest prison systems in the United States but it highlights the profound effect inmate litigation has on both the operation and character of correctional systems.

This case was resolved in 2011 when the Supreme Court affirmed the three-judge district court panel's decision to impose a strict occupancy limit of 137.5% of a facility's rated design capacity, to counteract the horrific levels of prison and jail overcrowding (Simon, 2014, chap. 6). After this decision was handed down, the two largest private prison companies in the country, CoreCivic and GEO Group, indicated to their shareholders that this decision may negatively affect the future of their business (see Chapter 3). CoreCivic's report for fiscal year 2011 reads, "in an effort to meet the Federal court ruling, the fiscal year 2012 budget of the state of California calls for a significant reallocation of responsibilities from state government to local jurisdictions. . . . The return of the California inmates to the state of California would have a *significant adverse impact on our financial position,* results of operations, and cash flows" (Corrections Corporation of America,

2012, emphasis added). The GEO Group's annual report for shareholders in fiscal year 2012 is similarly negative: California "discontinued contracts with Community Correctional Facilities which housed low level state offenders across the state . . . a material decrease in occupancy levels at one or more of our facilities could have a *material adverse effect on our revenues and profitability*, and consequently, on our financial condition and results of operations" (GEO Group, 2012, emphasis added).

I argue that this negative attitude of private prison companies to *Brown v. Plata* is not unique but is instead indicative of a broader unease about the effect of successful lawsuits on finances. As states professionalize and adapt to the demands of the court order, not only do they have less demand for the beds offered by private companies but it is also unnecessary for them to rely on private companies to pick up the slack when a successful order mandates clear action on behalf of the state corrections systems.

This chapter aimed to flesh out the dynamics described in Chapters 3 and 4 from the perspective of private prison firms. That is, how, if at all, are the financial outcomes of the businesses dependent on political factors? I focus here specifically on prison or jail court orders as the events that give investors pause about the future financial outlook for private carceral firms. I leverage approaches commonly taken in economics and finance to ask, how do the stock prices of private prison firms change in response to the announcement of successful court orders? I find that, on aggregate, investors are not particularly concerned with these judicial decrees. Rather, as Table 5.2 and the Appendix materials suggest, investors are responding to the lawsuits particularly in those states that are the most consequential for private prison firms' business.

These results have a few important implications. First, they provide encouraging evidence that the dynamics described theoretically in Chapter 3 and empirically in Chapter 4 exist from the perspective of private prison companies. Investors and executives from these companies pay attention to the legal status of correctional facilities and the court orders handed down against them. It is not just state governments that are responding to successful lawsuits, as shown in Chapter 4, but the companies themselves that are similarly vulnerable to shifts in judicial attention and favor. Second, though the growth of private prisons since the 1980s has touched nearly all regions of the country, only court orders in those states that are increasing business opportunities for firms are consequential for their stock performance. It is not enough for states to have merely one or more private facilities, but those states must have swelling numbers of them to attract investor attention. This is intuitive from institutional investors' perspectives as it limits their attention to the most important areas for the future of their business. These investors are likely much more concerned about their business prospects in Texas or California, states with up to 20 private facilities, than they are about those in Alabama or Idaho, states with only one facility at any point since the 1980s.

If, as this chapter suggests, investors are responsive to shifts in the political (and particularly legal) environment, what are the consequences for the behavior of these firms in relation to politics? It is difficult to imagine that a company that is so deeply financially affected by political outcomes does not try to influence politics to limit those negative shocks from affecting their business. What actions, if any, are these companies taking to ensure their continued business with the government? How can we see those connections happening? These sorts of questions raise many normative concerns about the appropriate nature of privatization for prisons and jails but are also dependent on the nature of the private prisons themselves. If the conditions are more deplorable than those of public correctional institutions, then these questions about accountability are more urgent than ever.

6

Captive Market

... you have a uniquely disempowered and literally captive market that's affected when costs are cut and corners are cut. Privatization of services in sort of the outside world may have its own problems, but at least if you don't like the care you're getting at private hospital A, you can take your business elsewhere. You can go to private hospital B. The prisoner can't say, "Wow, this private prison is really terrible. I think I'm going to go down the road to this public prison or this other private prison and see if it's better there."

—Advocacy director interview, 2020

In 1983, Thomas W. Beasley, Doctor R. Crants, and T. Don Hutto founded the Corrections Corporation of America (now CoreCivic). Beasley, a former chair of the Tennessee Republican Party, and Crants, a businessman, joined forces with Hutto, a former state Department of Corrections director, to form the first modern private prison company, now valued at nearly $2 billion. Beasley emphasized that the business model for CoreCivic was no different from that of other industries: "You just sell it like you were selling cars, or real estate, or hamburgers" (Schlosser, 1998). Though Beasley and other entrepreneurs who work for CoreCivic or other for-profit corrections companies downplay the human consequences of their business model, their impact is far from small. In 2016, nearly 18% of federal prisoners and approximately 9% of state prisoners were housed in private facilities, and nearly 130,000 people were held in facilities operated not by any governmental entity but by for-profit companies (and this number does not include those held in immigration detention facilities pending adjudication [Carson, 2018]). And though this number is small compared to the vast population held in government-operated prisons or jails, it nevertheless represents a sea change in the character of state corrections systems since the 1980s.

The massive growth of this policy has not escaped scholarly attention, though thus far the research has focused on common explanations of privatization—like partisanship, economics, unionization, or campaign contributions—or the question of whether private prisons are worse than public ones on a variety of metrics (e.g., Blakely and Bumphus, 2005; Burkhardt and Jones, 2016; Kim and Price, 2014; Nicholson-Crotty, 2004; Perrone and Pratt, 2003; Price and Riccucci, 2005; Schneider, 1999; Selman and Leighton, 2010; Spivak and Sharp, 2008). Though these are all important questions to investigate, this book emphasizes the key incentives for states to reduce accountability via privatization, an important overlooked driver of carceral privatization. And certainly, the implications of these incentives are normatively troubling. Though public prisons are not bastions of inmate health, the privatization of prisons adds layers of bureaucracy that make it even more difficult to hold public (or private) officials accountable for the very real horrors that occur within prisons. We cannot afford to turn away from these horrors and must acknowledge the humanity of those incarcerated in prisons and jails across the country. And, perhaps most importantly, we must assign blame to the appropriate institution that is responsible for the health and well-being of prisoners: as one advocacy director argues, "we want to keep everyone's eyes, the judges, the public, everyone, their eye on the fact that it is the *government agency* who is the legal custodian of the prisoner" (emphasis added).

"You Send a Check and Send a Prisoner"

Though there is variation in states' experiences with prison privatization, the bureaucratic and contracting process is fairly consistent across states. Chapter 2 explored key utilitarian questions at the heart of prison privatization, like how did states privatize? And what are the steps involved in privatizing a prison? I also introduced the original data set I collected, a significant contribution to this literature as scholars can now study private prisons across time and space, for all 50 states since the 1980s. I read thousands of pages of Securities and Exchange Commission reports to painstakingly create a record of every private facility operated by a publicly traded company from 1986 to 2016 (introduced in Gunderson, 2020c). I considered the dominant theories of privatization and suggested that they alone are not sufficient to explain either the adoption or growth of prison privatization since the 1980s. If these explanations, the ones commonly cited by journalistic and scholarly accounts of this policy, do not explain the rise of prison privatization, what does?

Chapter 3 introduced a theoretical framework to explain the rise of state prison privatization and emphasized the growth of inmate lawsuits as the major contributing factor to the expansion of this policy. I argue that the growth of inmate lawsuits prompts states to privatize: more prisoner lawsuits, regardless of outcome, makes it more likely a state will turn to private prison operators. These states face ever-increasing numbers of inmates entering prisons and jails each year but do not have the ability to negotiate with the legislature or the public at large to provide funds for new prison construction. States are incentivized to privatize to transfer political and legal accountability for these lawsuits away from themselves to private companies. The other theoretical prediction from Chapter 3 considers successful lawsuits and argues that the rare victorious lawsuits will be *negatively* associated with prison privatization. Successful lawsuits prompt substantive legal and procedural change within state prisons and thus make privatization unappealing as a means to avoid accountability. States have no incentive to privatize as successful legal orders already mandate substantive changes within prisons. These two dynamics place inmate lawsuits squarely at the heart of states' decision-making regarding prison privatization.

Chapter 4 then tested my arguments using the original data set introduced in Chapter 2. I find support for my central claim, that more lawsuits overall are associated with more private prisoners, and tentative evidence of my secondary claim, that successful lawsuits are associated with fewer prisoners in private facilities. These results are largely robust to a variety of alternative specifications and dependent variables, highlighting the role of inmate litigation in the growth of private prisons since the 1980s. I situate these findings in real-world contexts by providing examples of both ways governments shirk when privatizing—building liability clauses into contracts and enabling legislation—and of successful lawsuits that promoted correctional reform and not prison privatization, to the chagrin of these for-profit companies.

Finally, Chapter 5 considered how private companies respond to some of the mechanics theorized in Chapter 3. Specifically, how do for-profit correctional companies, and their investors, respond to the announcement of successful lawsuits? I used event study methodology and found that private prison companies' stocks are lower after the announcement of successful lawsuits in states with active private prison contracts, highlighting the negative effect of inmate legal victories on the likelihood of states privatizing. Investors are particularly savvy at recognizing threats to business from successful court orders and respond accordingly, by selling more private prison stock.

This book paints a complicated picture of the means by which states have privatized their prisons since the 1980s, one of the most controversial developments in the criminal legal system. It emphasizes the key incentive of accountability in the decision to privatize, though there are additional lessons from carceral privatization that are relevant to the future of not only prison privatization but the politics of the criminal legal system more broadly: first, that the question of whether public or private prisons are worse ought not to be at the center of debates on privatization; second, that the rights revolution for incarcerated people in public and private prisons is a promise yet unfulfilled; third, that privatization of prisons is just one (and not the most common) form of privatization in our prison systems; and fourth, that privatization is merely a symptom, and not a cause, of the massive expansion of the carceral state over the last few decades.

"It's Like Comparing Atrocity to Atrocity"

Much of the empirical work on prison privatization seeks to understand whether those institutions are worse or better than public prisons on a variety of metrics, from cost to judicial intervention to recidivism, among many other considerations (Blakely and Bumphus, 2005; Burkhardt and Jones, 2016; Perrone and Pratt, 2003; Spivak and Sharp, 2008). Though these evaluations are important from a public policy perspective, I argue that this focus is misguided for reform efforts and lends too much deference to the public operation of these facilities.

First, I suggest that the question of whether public or private prisons are worse is irrelevant from the perspective of criminal legal reform. It is not the case that public prisons are models of inmate well-being, much to the contrary. Rather than focusing on this comparison, it is important to evaluate the performance of *all* carceral institutions, public and private, and state-, locally, or federally operated. Regardless of the character of corrections systems, we ought to be evaluating these institutions similarly and without regard for their bureaucracy, emphasizing the question of which institution is better disregards the fact that *neither* are rehabilitating or reforming those locked up within them: mass atrocities occur within both. As one advocacy director emphasized, "it's like comparing atrocity to atrocity" in trying to define and explain the differences between public and private prisons. Another interviewee remarked, "I'd say conditions are worse when the privates are involved, but the curves overlap substantially . . . I certainly would not say that every private prison is worse than every public prison. There are some truly awful public prisons out there."

Second, when considering the "evils" of the private prison market, I argue that the role of the state in the privatization process is too often neglected. As some of the qualitative evidence from Chapter 3 suggests, public officials demean private prison companies for their prison conditions without acknowledging that *those atrocities would not have happened if the government did not contract with the companies in the first place.* The decision to privatize is a partnership, from the private companies seeking out business or submitting proposals to operate facilities to the state government expressly asking firms to operate and manage these facilities. Each assault or murder within private facilities ought to be considered the fault of the government as well—and though they try to sidestep this accountability (as I argue primarily here), we must not lose focus on who is responsible for these atrocities. The blame is shared by public and private entities in this cooperative relationship.

Finally, questioning the differences, or lack thereof, between public and private prisons assumes that there is a threshold at which we would accept private prisons. That is, if private prisons perform better at particular metrics, we would then privatize accordingly. The question ought not to be whether public or private prisons are better but rather whether profit should play a part in public *or* private prisons. Broad divestment strategies, pursued by student activists at universities, state pension funds, and even major banks, are the beginning of a conversation about stemming the influence of profits in prisons (Eisen, 2018, chap. 6). One legislator who pursued divestment in her district mentioned that the "domino effect that we had . . . it was more like Jenga" once they voted to divest from private prison companies. She lamented that the structure of these contracts meant that the government could not divest easily, that it could not pursue a step-by-step strategy but instead needed to divest quickly without adequate time to explore options for what would happen to those housed in private facilities. So, while divestment is a sound strategy to pursue, it must be accompanied by policy changes that facilitate that divestment without chaos ensuing within correctional facilities. We ought to go even further than divestment from these private prison companies, however, to the many industries and companies that engage in profit-seeking activities within prisons. We must consider not what level of privatization we are comfortable with in our correctional system more generally but rather how to root out profit motives in correctional administration in the public sector as well as the private sector.

"As Long as They're Functioning, That's Fine"

The rights revolution of the mid-twentieth century sought to expand civil liberties through the courts (e.g., Epp, 1998). And while this effort included representatives from a broad swathe of marginalized groups, like people of color or women, perhaps one of the most direct beneficiaries has been incarcerated people. As I detail in Chapter 3, prisoners used the judiciary to challenge their conditions of confinement and secure rights previously denied to them. One of the implications of this book, however, is that the movement to provide these legal rights may have prompted states to privatize, a policy choice that may (or may not) have resulted in worse outcomes for the incarcerated (Blakely and Bumphus, 2005; Burkhardt and Jones, 2016; Perrone and Pratt, 2003; Spivak and Sharp, 2008). How do we evaluate the movement in this light, and what comes next?

The rights revolution has made great strides in providing legal rights to inmates, but it is a promise unfulfilled as of yet. Public and private prisons alike suffer from a neglect from policymakers and the public. As one state legislator remarked, "I just don't think you traditionally get enough people engaged to have a meaningful debate on it. And I think that's why the system sort of stagnates in a lot of ways. It's a neglect. And it's not even . . . I don't even really see it necessarily as a malicious neglect. It's more like sort of, 'It's just not really a priority. There are other priorities so as long as they're functioning, that's fine.'" That same state legislator lamented that the condition of his state's correctional facilities would not be in the top 10, or even top 40, of the most important issues that the state government was concerned with. I argue that this neglect is significant and illustrative of a broader "malign neglect" of incarcerated people and their rights (or lack thereof) while in prison or jail (Tonry, 1995). Indeed, as I have argued elsewhere (Gunderson, 2021a), this malign neglect is not confined to policymaking but includes a greater ignorance or outright dismissal of the importance or study of legal rights of incarcerated people by scholars who study the courts.

Legal rights act as one of the foundations of American democracy, and those rights ought not to be conditional on criminal justice contact. Prisoners still face significant hurdles when bringing lawsuits in federal courts and face wide skepticism about their quality from policymakers, scholars, and the public (e.g., Calavita and Jenness, 2015). Indeed, as one advocacy director mentioned, bringing any lawsuits against correctional systems or private companies alike is "so resource-intensive and so difficult . . . David against Goliath" that they must be extraordinarily picky about which cases to take. "unless we see a pattern and practice that we can kind of look at that would impact many people," that advocacy group does not have the resources to take on these costly cases. This means that claims of legitimate concern are falling through the cracks as there are not enough legal representatives to argue these cases well. Incarcerated people in public and private prisons alike suffer from a lack of representation. In this way, the rights revolution is a promise yet unfulfilled for those incarcerated. And whether those inmates are in public or private prisons, the fight continues to provide them with adequate representation and treatment in our legal system. Legitimate democratic governance requires that even state punishment and confinement adheres to basic human rights and principles of democratic accountability.

"They Are Always Going to Have a Place"

Chapter 2 detailed the extensive history of profit in American carceral institutions to highlight that though the modern private prison industry is unique in its character, it is by no means the first involvement of private enterprise in the administration of justice and punishment in America. Indeed, most of the interviewees I spoke to emphasized the ever-changing involvement of the private sector in correctional administration. These companies are "always looking for the next iteration" of private enterprise in corrections and are "there to plant seeds" in conversations around criminal legal reform and change. As one participant suggested, private firms ask, "where is the next trend going, and how can [I] make money off that?" Existing private prison companies have diversified into industries like community corrections as these firms consider the "emergent needs" of government partners (as one interviewee suggested). Another interviewee discussed their profit motives succinctly: "if they thought they could make more money making widgets than running prisons, they'd go make widgets."

The evolving nature of private enterprise in corrections has spread far beyond the management and operation of carceral facilities, as is the focus in this book. Private companies, including a subsidiary of CoreCivic, provide private prisoner transport ("You route the prisoner like a package, but miss a single deadline, and you lose money" [Hager and Santo, 2016]), private probation ("Once you get on probation, especially, it's one fee after another and if you can't pay then you go to jail, and then once you're in jail and then you get out, you have more court fees, and then more fees, and more, and more, and more. It never ends, and that's why some people would just rather go to jail and just deal with it that way" [Human Rights Watch, 2018]), private healthcare (private company Corizon is "not providing medical care known to be necessary and just generally exalting the profit motive over the provision of medical care" [Jenkins, 2017]), and private technology and video calls (one estimate finds those with incarcerated loved ones spend an average of $63 per month on video calls only [Lewis and Lockwood, 2019]), among dozens of other industries. One estimate finds that at least 4,100 corporations, from data and information services, food and commissary, and personnel service, are profiting from the partial privatization of services within prisons (Worth Rises, 2020). Though private companies like CoreCivic and GEO Group often bear the brunt of critiques of private interests in prisons, there are thousands of other companies that profit from this system as well (including Aramark, CenturyLink, Bank of America, 3M, and Amazon [Worth Rises, 2020]). One state bureaucrat mentioned industry conferences as a primary way private companies sell their products to correctional professionals: "You'll see vendors that are there selling that stuff, all the way down to this is the newest walkie talkie. And you want all of your guards to have it . . . government officials that are charged with running the systems are constantly bombarded by the private correctional industry on every imaginable front." The myopic focus on private prisons instead of the vast privatization in the criminal justice system obscures a broader conversation about the role of profit in public *and* private prisons alike. As we begin to discuss divestment as a broad policy choice for private prisons (Eisen, 2018, chap. 6), we must similarly focus those conversations on the many industries and companies that profit off incarcerated bodies in public prisons as well. One state bureaucrat summarized this perspective: "incarceration pays no matter if you're operating in a private or a public based operation."

There are therefore two related implications for the future of private prisons: first, at least for the largest firms (like CoreCivic and GEO Group), those companies will evolve to meet the changing needs of their government partners and, second, the specific focus on those firms that operate and manage private prisons ignores the thousands of other companies that profit directly off the semi-privatization of the corrections industry. It is unlikely that private enterprise will disappear from the corrections landscape, even as conversations emerge around the elimination of the private operation of corrections facilities. They will simply rebrand and re-emerge as private partners for governments' changing carceral needs: diversifying in anticipation and direct response to Joe Biden's presidential victory, for example, and turning to community supervision and even general real estate (Lartey, 2020).

"Metastasis of the Larger Cancer of Mass Incarceration"

In the 2020 Democratic presidential primary, one of the most consistent policy positions among the candidates was a critique of governments' use of private prisons and a pledge to ban them once the candidate became president (Park and Lartey, 2020). Shortly after becoming president, Joe Biden lived up to this promise and ordered the Justice Department to end its use of private prisons. Despite this attention—and the vilification of private prison firms in the media (Burkhardt, 2014)—this focus is too myopic. Eliminating private prisons would not result in criminal legal reform, nor would it even make much of a dent: of the over 1.5 million prisoners the United States had in 2016, only 130,000 of those were held in private facilities (Carson, 2018). And though the Justice Department may end the use of private prisons, this does not include federal immigration facilities, a significant oversight considering that 81% of detained people were in facilities owned and/or operated by private companies in January 2020 (Human Rights Watch, 2020). A re-evaluation of the appropriate role of profit in the American carceral system must move beyond the relatively small impact of the Justice Department announcement to federal immigration facilities, local jail facilities, and state facilities, the focus of this book.

This is not to suggest that privatization is an unimportant concern in the conversations around criminal legal reform (it certainly is and especially considering the dozens of industries involved in the privatization of corrections) but that relying on the elimination of private prisons as a panacea for criminal legal reform is not accurate. Interviewees affiliated with advocacy groups, in particular, emphasized that "this is not just about private prisons . . . this is so much bigger than private prisons." We need to broaden our understanding of privatization in corrections to include the many industries and companies that profit off of people entangled in the criminal justice system.

And while eliminating or reforming the nature of profit in the American carceral state is a part of criminal legal reform, it is but one plank. More generally, reform efforts ought to consider prisoners as *people*, to recognize their humanity, and to place the responsibility for their care and safety firmly at the feet of the government. Holding these officials accountable for the horrors that occur within prisons shines the appropriate spotlight on why people are locked up and what happens once we close the prison doors. American private prisoners are a captive market but captive to whom and for what purpose? We must not forget that the government is ultimately responsible for corrections policy and that any meaningful criminal legal reform is transparent about the complicity of government in the confinement, supervision, and punishment of millions.

Qualitative Data

This project draws on dozens of interviews with private prison officials, state politicians and bureaucrats, and nonprofit and advocacy groups (approved by both the Emory University and Louisiana State University Institutional Review Boards). I began by contacting state bureaucrats and legislators from several states who used, use, or were considering using private prisons; public-facing private prison companies; and advocacy groups and researchers involved in private prisons or litigation of those currently incarcerated. I conducted two waves of interviews—first, as a Ph.D. student in 2019 and then as an assistant professor a year later, in 2020. I first sent letters to the potential participants, followed by an email, then a phone call. Because the decision to privatize prisons is a controversial one, I guaranteed confidentiality to my participants, that no quotes would be attributable to that person directly and that their responses would be attributable to a random five-digit number, known only to me. Throughout the book, the participants are referenced as current or former state legislators, state bureaucrats, advocacy directors or researchers, private prison company representatives, or simply informants or interviewees. I also requested permission to record the interviews electronically, which most allowed but some did not. I took physical notes regardless of whether the interview was recorded or not.

In my first wave, I cast a wide net and contacted 121 individuals beginning in March 2019 and only completed six interviews—though nearly half of the larger sample was comprised of dozens of private prison company executives and employees, and often those companies would appoint one person to speak with me out of the potential 20–40 I contacted. In May 2020, I contacted 45 individuals, a different sample of state representatives, advocacy groups, and private prison representatives, and ultimately conducted 18 additional interviews. These interviews ranged in length from 14 minutes to over an hour; were largely conducted over the phone or via Zoom; and were semi-structured, roughly following a list of questions I developed but with some flexibility to explore themes, events, or concepts the participants brought up themselves that I had not yet thought of. Some responded by email to my listed questions in lieu of an in-person interview. In total, I conducted 24 interviews, which helped to flesh out the concepts and themes of the book. The state legislators or bureaucrats come from a variety of states: Hawaii, Tennessee, Louisiana, Texas, Colorado, Florida, Colorado, Alabama, and Georgia. These states represent the ones that use or were considering the use of private prisons currently or at some point in the last few decades.

Quantitative Data

Data Collection Description

All variables were gleaned directly from 10-K reports filed by private prison companies. This data set includes private facilities operated by both the federal and state governments, along with county jails. I do not include community corrections facilities (residential facilities) operated by these companies. I do include juvenile facilities if the purpose is listed as correctional (i.e., they are incarcerated) but do not include those juvenile facilities that are simply treatment centers. Importantly, this choice deviates from the Bureau of Justice Statistics' (BJS) variable of the number of inmates in private facilities as the BJS number includes inmates housed in privately operated correctional facilities including any privately operated halfway houses, treatment facilities, hospitals, or other special facilities and excludes inmates housed in any publicly operated facility, even if under contract. BJS data also does not include prisoners under federal jurisdiction. This data set covers the private jail or prison facilities, at either the local, state, or federal level, in each state-year.

The following indicates the coverage of the data.

Securities and Exchange Commission 10-Ks available

- Corrections Corporation of America (CCA; now CoreCivic): 1986–Present
- Cornell Companies: 1997–2010
  - Cornell acquired by GEO Group in 2010
- Correctional Services Corporation (CSC; also known as Esmor Correctional Corporation): 1998–2005
  - CSC acquired by GEO Group in 2005
- GEO Group (formerly Wackenhut Corrections): 1996–2016
  - 10-Ks available for Wackenhut prior to 1996, but there is no capacity data, only location data available.

Data Availability

- CCA
  - Facility names and capacity: 1986–Present
  - The Securities and Exchange Commission (SEC) data contains the locations of the facilities. Though the early 10-Ks do not list the names of those facilities, I used their later properties to label the facilities with their probable names.
  - Primary customer explicitly listed: 1996–Present
- Cornell Companies
  - Names of facilities, capacity, and primary customer: 1996–2009
- CSC, as with CCA and Cornell Companies
  - CSC (also known as Esmor Correctional Corporation)
  - Names of facilities, capacity, and primary customer: 1997–2004
- GEO Group (formerly Wackenhut Corrections)
  - Facility names: 1989–Present
  - Like CCA, the SEC data for Wackenhut only contained the locations of the facilities they operated. Using the names and locations of the properties they operate at later dates, I labeled the properties with their probable names.
  - Capacity: 1996–Present
  - Primary customer explicitly listed: 1996–Present

Missing Data

- CCA 10-K for fiscal year ending 1993
- CSC 10-K for fiscal years ending 1994–1997

I Inputted the Following Information

- CCA 1993 is inputted from the CCA 1992 variables
- Wackenhut 1991 is inputted from Wackenhut 1990
- Because so many years are missing from CSC, I simply omitted the years I was missing.

Note: For Cornell Companies and the CSC, I only listed the Adult Secure Services Facilities: Residential Facilities, not community corrections facilities.

Note: The data for CCA in 1999 is spotty given its conversion to Prison Realty Trust, an attempt to change the company into a real estate investment trust. The data in that year lists capacity and other variables as normal but does not list the primary customer of the facility. As such, I inputted the primary customer according to previous and future years. If the facility had one operator in 1998 and 2000, I inputted that operator for 1999 as well. If the facility was opened in 1999, I listed the 2000 operator as the primary customer for 1999. If the facility does not exist past 2000, I listed the 1998 customer for 1999. If there was disagreement in the customers in 1998 and 2000, I only listed the customers that were in both years. If there was complete disagreement in the customers in 1998 and 2000, I left the primary customer blank. If the facility listed no customer for 1998 but one for 2000, I listed the customer from 2000 for the 1999 value.

Finally, some facilities CCA owned and operated in both 1998 and 2001 are missing for some reason in the 1999 filing. Because it is highly unlikely the operation of the facility changed back and forth from some other private contractor or the state in a span of one year, I inputted the 1998 data for 1999, providing the design capacity number was the same.

Chapter 4

Hypothesis 1

Ordinary Least Squares Models
Alternative Independent Variables

One of the concerns with Hypothesis 1 could be the choice of the dependent variable. Is this effect driven by big lawsuits (i.e., those that are successful; see Hypothesis 2) or small lawsuits, those that do not result in any substantive change within prisons?

The Federal Judicial Center (FJC) data does not show consistent information on whether the prisoner (the plaintiff) is victorious. Therefore, it is not possible to create a variable that is just the number of victorious inmate lawsuits. However, there is a relatively straightforward way of roughly estimating this quantity: analyzing the number of days (or years) from the initial filing of the lawsuit to the eventual adjudication of the dispute. Most successful prisoner lawsuits are extremely long litigation processes, like the blockbuster Florida prisoner rights case *Costello v. Wainwright*, which originated in 1973 and lasted until the state was fully in compliance with the court orders in 1993 (Schoenfeld, 2010). The long duration of these processes is driven by negotiations over court orders and the monitoring and checking of states' compliance with these orders. Therefore, we can reasonably proxy for the success of a court order via the length of the litigation, the difference in days (or years) from the initial filing date to the adjudication date. Figure A.1 shows this difference, in years, for the data set.

Not surprisingly, the vast majority of cases are adjudicated quickly. The mean length is 0.72 of a year (about 264 days), with the maximum year to completion at more than 23 years (more than 8,400 days). More than 75% of the cases are completed within one year of the filing date and are likely failures for the inmates bringing them.

I use this information to calculate two alternative independent variables, *Sum Small Cases* and *Sum Large Cases*. I rely on the Schlanger (2015) definition that 88% of prisoner lawsuit cases are failures and create a sum of cases above and below that cutpoint: *Sum Small Cases* represents the 88% of cases with the shortest length to termination (in years, with a mean of about 157 days), and *Sum Large Cases* represents the remaining 12% with the longest length to termination (in years, with a mean of more than 2.8 years). I estimate the ordinary least squares (OLS) model using these alternative variables in Tables A.1 and A.2.

From these tables, this effect seems to be driven by the small lawsuits, those that are adjudicated quickly and are likely failures (or those that do not prompt comprehensive change to the state prison system). This helps to provide further evidence for Hypothesis 1, specifically the argument that all lawsuits are consequential in the decision to privatize—even, and especially, those that are small and unsuccessful.

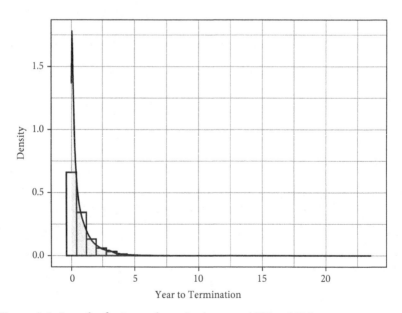

Figure A.1 Length of prisoner lawsuits, in years, 1986 to 2016.

Table A.1 Hypothesis 1: Prisoner Lawsuits and Private Prisons, Small Lawsuits Only

	Private Design Capacity		Proportion in Private Facilities		Sum State Private Facilities	
	(1)	(2)	(3)	(4)	(5)	(6)
Sum small lawsuits		1.617***		0.00003***		0.002***
		(0.359)		(0.00001)		(0.0005)
Republican legislature	−29.151	136.991	−0.006	−0.003	−0.417**	−0.243
	(281.499)	(268.246)	(0.013)	(0.013)	(0.198)	(0.167)
Republican governor	118.295	140.832	0.018*	0.019*	−0.052	−0.028
	(143.788)	(131.824)	(0.010)	(0.010)	(0.117)	(0.099)
Unified Republican gov't	238.898	152.022	−0.005	−0.007	0.218	0.127
	(330.027)	(332.770)	(0.016)	(0.015)	(0.211)	(0.192)
Budget gap per capita	13.003	5.616	−0.015**	−0.015**	0.038	0.030
	(89.918)	(83.390)	(0.007)	(0.007)	(0.057)	(0.050)
No. unionized corrections officers (1000s)	298.209*	200.839	−0.003	−0.005**	0.346*	0.245*
	(173.056)	(140.367)	(0.002)	(0.002)	(0.180)	(0.137)
Incarceration rate	7.566***	7.725***	0.0001	0.0001	0.008***	0.008***
	(2.786)	(2.357)	(0.0001)	(0.0001)	(0.003)	(0.002)
Violent crime rate	−3.887**	−3.503**	0.0001	0.0001	−0.002*	−0.002*
	(1.852)	(1.633)	(0.0001)	(0.0001)	(0.001)	(0.001)
N	1,417	1,417	1,417	1,417	1,417	1,417
R^2	0.734	0.755	0.565	0.570	0.841	0.859
Adjusted R^2	0.718	0.739	0.538	0.543	0.831	0.850
Residual SE	1,245.408 (df = 1,333)	1,196.517 (df = 1,332)	0.064 (df = 1,333)	0.064 (df = 1,332)	1.061 (df = 1,333)	0.997 (df = 1,332)

$^*p < .1;$ $^{**}p < .05;$ $^{***}p < .01.$

Standard errors (SEs) clustered by state.

df, degrees of freedom.

Table A.2 Hypothesis 1: Prisoner Lawsuits and Private Prisons, Big Lawsuits Only

	Private Design Capacity		Proportion in Private Facilities		Sum State Private Facilities	
	(1)	(2)	(3)	(4)	(5)	(6)
Sum big lawsuits		4.861		0.0001		0.001
		(4.251)		(0.0001)		(0.002)
Republican legislature	−29.151	90.139	−0.006	−0.005	−0.417**	−0.388**
	(281.499)	(294.506)	(0.013)	(0.013)	(0.198)	(0.192)
Republican governor	118.295	119.033	0.018*	0.018*	−0.052	−0.052
	(143.788)	(155.307)	(0.010)	(0.010)	(0.117)	(0.118)
Unified Republican gov't	238.898	210.138	−0.005	−0.005	0.218	0.211
	(330.027)	(355.372)	(0.016)	(0.016)	(0.211)	(0.210)
Budget gap per capita	13.003	5.388	−0.015**	−0.015**	0.038	0.036
	(89.918)	(85.004)	(0.007)	(0.007)	(0.057)	(0.055)
No. unionized corrections officers (1000s)	298.209*	216.739	−0.003	−0.004*	0.346*	0.326*
	(173.056)	(164.179)	(0.002)	(0.002)	(0.180)	(0.165)
Incarceration rate	7.566***	7.704***	0.0001	0.0001	0.008***	0.008***
	(2.786)	(2.527)	(0.0001)	(0.0001)	(0.003)	(0.003)
Violent crime rate	−3.887**	−3.417**	0.0001	0.0001	−0.002*	−0.002*
	(1.852)	(1.586)	(0.0001)	(0.0001)	(0.001)	(0.001)
N	1,417	1,417	1,417	1,417	1,417	1,417
R^2	0.734	0.743	0.565	0.566	0.841	0.841
Adjusted R^2	0.718	0.726	0.538	0.538	0.831	0.831
Residual SE	1,245.408 (df = 1,333)	1,226.077 (df = 1,332)	0.064 (df = 1,333)	0.064 (df = 1,332)	1.061 (df = 1,333)	1.060 (df = 1,332)

*$p < .1$; **$p < .05$; ***$p < .01$.

Standard errors (SEs) clustered by state.

df, degrees of freedom.

Next, though inmates in federal and local private facilities are excluded from the calculation of private design capacity, it is not straightforward to exclude lawsuits filed by inmates in federal facilities or local jails. The FJC data does not include information on where the inmate is filing the lawsuit from, so it is impossible to tell from the aggregate data whether the inmate is filing a lawsuit against a federal, state, or local entity. There is a way to proxy that, however, using the 1995 Census of State and Federal Adult Correctional Facilities from the BJS.

This data set includes all correctional facilities in the country in each state (including federal facilities), along with the rated capacity of those facilities. From this, it is straightforward to calculate the *percent of all inmates within a state that are housed in federal facilities* as of 1995. Because I do not expect this quantity to change much from year to year,[1] I use this calculation to then multiply the state-year estimates of the sum of all lawsuits, to proxy for the number of lawsuits filed by state inmates:

$$(100 - \text{percent in federal}) \text{ total lawsuits } (1)$$

While this is not a perfect estimate, it provides a rough proxy of the number of lawsuits filed solely by state inmates, assuming that federal and state inmates file at similar rates within each state. I use this variable in place of sum lawsuits, as seen in Table A.3. The results are consistent with those reported in Chapter 4.

Adding Control Variables

Table A.4 adds several variables to the OLS specification in the main text. First, I collected information on the operational capacity of state corrections systems in each year to calculate an additional variable, *Percent Overcrowded*. This measure represents the percent of the state's operational capacity that is taken up by the then-current prison population (i.e., I divided the state's prison population in that year by operational capacity and multiplied by 100). Related to that, I also collected a variable called *Deaths in Custody*, the number of inmates who died in that state-year. Both of these measures represent real strains to the corrections system and could prompt a state to privatize (above and beyond the stress of inmate litigation). Second, though the partisanship variables represent the Democratic–Republican difference, most privatization efforts were bipartisan ones. I would ideally include a measure of neoliberalism to represent this, but to my knowledge, there is no consistent source of this data for all states across all years. However, I collected additional data from Caughey and Warshaw (2018) to provide a measure of *Economic Policy Liberalism* in that state-year. This measure estimates economic policy liberalism (for policies like social welfare, taxation, labor, and the environment) using a Bayesian factor-analytic model for mixed data (Caughey and Warshaw, 2018). This effectively provides a measure of the liberalism of the state policies (and presumably the views of that state's leaders) that is not expressly linked to the partisanship of its leaders. Finally, what about firm behavior? I also included the *Sum of Campaign Contributions* given to candidates running for state office in each state-year from the "private prisons and correctional facilities" industry, collected from Follow the Money.[2] Unfortunately, this data is only collected consistently from 2000 on, so this variable is included in only some specifications.

Table A.3 Hypothesis 1: Prisoner Lawsuits and Private Prisons, State Lawsuits Only

	Private Design Capacity		Proportion in Private Facilities		Sum State Private Facilities	
	(1)	(2)	(3)	(4)	(5)	(6)
Sum state-only lawsuits		1.634***		0.00003***		0.002***
		(0.443)		(0.00001)		(0.0005)
Republican legislature	−29.151	164.346	−0.006	−0.002	−0.417**	−0.236
	(281.499)	(275.437)	(0.013)	(0.013)	(0.198)	(0.172)
Republican governor	118.295	137.655	0.018*	0.018*	−0.052	−0.034
	(143.788)	(136.326)	(0.010)	(0.010)	(0.117)	(0.103)
Unified Republican gov't	238.898	149.562	−0.005	−0.006	0.218	0.134
	(330.027)	(342.978)	(0.016)	(0.015)	(0.211)	(0.194)
Budget gap per capita	13.003	3.222	−0.015**	−0.015**	0.038	0.029
	(89.918)	(82.407)	(0.007)	(0.007)	(0.057)	(0.049)
No. unionized corrections officers (1000s)	298.209*	178.597	−0.003	−0.005**	0.346*	0.235*
	(173.056)	(139.056)	(0.002)	(0.002)	(0.180)	(0.138)
Incarceration rate	7.566***	7.784***	0.0001	0.0001	0.008***	0.008***
	(2.786)	(2.297)	(0.0001)	(0.0001)	(0.003)	(0.002)
Violent crime rate	−3.887**	−3.374**	0.0001	0.0001	−0.002*	−0.002*
	(1.852)	(1.584)	(0.0001)	(0.0001)	(0.001)	(0.001)
N	1,417	1,417	1,417	1,417	1,417	1,417
R^2	0.734	0.757	0.565	0.570	0.841	0.857
Adjusted R^2	0.718	0.741	0.538	0.543	0.831	0.848
Residual SE	1,245.408 (df = 1,333)	1,192.416 (df = 1,332)	0.064 (df = 1,333)	0.064 (df = 1,332)	1.061 (df = 1,333)	1.006 (df = 1,332)

*$p < .1$; **$p < .05$; ***$p < .01$.
Standard errors (SEs) clustered by state.

Table A.4 Hypothesis 1: Prisoner Lawsuits and Private Prisons, Adding Control Variables

	Private Design Capacity		Proportion in Private Facilities		Sum State Private Facilities	
	(1)	(2)	(3)	(4)	(5)	(6)
Sum lawsuits	1.280***	1.719**	0.00002*	0.00002*	0.001***	0.001*
	(0.422)	(0.728)	(0.00001)	(0.00001)	(0.0004)	(0.0005)
Republican legislature	180.001	200.521	−0.005	0.008	−0.225	−0.096
	(343.979)	(253.176)	(0.014)	(0.009)	(0.192)	(0.154)
Republican governor	237.840*	353.283*	0.020	0.021*	0.027	−0.010
	(131.678)	(195.532)	(0.013)	(0.011)	(0.102)	(0.111)
Budget gap per capita	−85.635	−12.347	−0.019***	−0.008	0.002	0.045
	(69.944)	(84.585)	(0.007)	(0.007)	(0.050)	(0.044)
No. unionized corrections officers (1000s)	139.319	274.224	−0.003	0.002	0.198*	0.141
	(125.652)	(183.368)	(0.002)	(0.002)	(0.118)	(0.310)
Incarceration rate	6.026***	4.111	0.0001	0.0002	0.007***	0.011**
	(1.724)	(3.823)	(0.0001)	(0.0001)	(0.002)	(0.005)
Violent crime rate	−2.841**	−4.336*	0.0001	−0.0001	−0.002*	−0.001
	(1.262)	(2.446)	(0.0001)	(0.0001)	(0.001)	(0.001)
Percent overcrowded	0.612	6.607	0.0004	0.0004	−0.006	−0.006*
	(5.125)	(5.221)	(0.0003)	(0.0003)	(0.004)	(0.004)
Deaths in custody	9.592*	−6.914	−0.0001	−0.0001	0.009***	−0.004
	(5.428)	(7.275)	(0.0001)	(0.0001)	(0.003)	(0.004)
Economic policy liberalism	−528.739	−417.846	−0.012	0.040**	−0.217	0.173
	(350.671)	(514.081)	(0.022)	(0.020)	(0.276)	(0.276)
Sum contributions		0.008***		0.00000*		0.00000
		(0.003)		(0.00000)		(0.00000)
Unified Republican gov't	−47.697	−325.640	−0.008	−0.024*	0.061	0.153
	(380.506)	(287.231)	(0.018)	(0.012)	(0.185)	(0.166)
N	1,107	573	1,107	573	1,107	573
R^2	0.794	0.881	0.579	0.783	0.880	0.917
Adjusted R^2	0.777	0.864	0.545	0.752	0.870	0.906
Residual SE	1,146.520 (df = 1,023)	1,081.255 (df = 502)	0.067 (df = 1,023)	0.056 (df = 502)	1.005 (df = 1,023)	0.927 (df = 502)

*$p < .1$; **$p < .05$; ***$p < .01$.

Standard errors (SEs) clustered by state.

df, degrees of freedom.

The results are clear and consistent with those in Chapter 4 and indicate that the sum of prisoner lawsuits is a significant predictor of all three dependent variables.

Lagged Dependent Variable Model
Table A.5 adds a lagged dependent variable to the OLS estimation of Hypothesis 1. The sum of lawsuits variable remains significant and positive.

Table A.5 Hypothesis 1: Prisoner Lawsuits and Private Prisons, Lagged Dependent Variable Model

	Private Design Capacity	Proportion in Private Facilities	Sum State Private Facilities
	(1)	(2)	(3)
Sum lawsuits	1.408***	0.00002***	0.001***
	(0.306)	(0.00001)	(0.0005)
Republican legislature	−33.224	−0.003	−0.263
	(199.876)	(0.010)	(0.158)
Republican governor	50.925	0.007	−0.050
	(106.358)	(0.007)	(0.092)
Unified Republican gov't	59.951	−0.003	0.069
	(234.269)	(0.011)	(0.158)
Budget gap per capita	−4.129	−0.013**	0.034
	(70.071)	(0.006)	(0.044)
No. unionized corrections officers (1000s)	94.649	−0.004**	0.191*
	(71.675)	(0.002)	(0.101)
Incarceration rate	4.410***	0.0001	0.007***
	(1.519)	(0.0001)	(0.002)
Violent crime rate	−1.976**	0.00004	−0.001
	(0.889)	(0.00003)	(0.001)
Lagged DV: DC	0.453***		
	(0.064)		
Lagged DV: proportion		0.367***	
		(0.083)	
Lagged DV: facilities			0.203***
			(0.044)
N	1,417	1,417	1,416
R^2	0.829	0.638	0.870
Adjusted R^2	0.818	0.614	0.862
Residual SE	999.151 (df=1,331)	0.059 (df = 1,331)	0.959 (df = 1,330)

$^*p < .1$; $^{**}p < .05$; $^{***}p < .01$.
Standard errors (SEs) clustered by state.
DV, dependent variable; DC, design capacity; df, degrees of freedom.

All Private Facilities as Dependent Variable

In Chapter 4, I use the sum of state-only private facilities, to reflect state decision-making around private prisons. I revisit that decision here and include *all* private facilities in a state as the dependent variable (Table A.6). These facilities can hold state inmates, local (city or county) inmates, or federal inmates or immigrant detainees. The results are consistent.

Table A.6 Hypothesis 1: Prisoner Lawsuits and Private Prisons, All Private Facilities

	Private Design Capacity		Proportion in Private Facilities		Sum All Private Facilities	
	(1)	(2)	(3)	(4)	(5)	(6)
Sum lawsuits		1.503***		0.00003***		0.002***
		(0.406)		(0.00001)		(0.0004)
Republican legislature	−29.151	162.236	−0.006	−0.002	−0.444	−0.220
	(281.499)	(272.620)	(0.013)	(0.013)	(0.355)	(0.344)
Republican governor	118.295	139.480	0.018*	0.018*	−0.198	−0.173
	(143.788)	(136.696)	(0.010)	(0.010)	(0.194)	(0.179)
Unified Republican gov't	238.898	149.217	−0.005	−0.007	0.800*	0.695
	(330.027)	(342.027)	(0.016)	(0.015)	(0.454)	(0.467)
Budget gap per capita	13.003	3.779	−0.015**	−0.015**	0.052	0.041
	(89.918)	(82.612)	(0.007)	(0.007)	(0.071)	(0.067)
No. unionized corrections officers (1000s)	298.209*	182.470	−0.003	−0.005**	0.822***	0.687**
	(173.056)	(139.107)	(0.002)	(0.002)	(0.279)	(0.258)
Incarceration rate	7.566***	7.756***	0.0001	0.0001	0.010***	0.010***
	(2.786)	(2.309)	(0.0001)	(0.0001)	(0.004)	(0.003)
Violent crime rate	−3.887**	−3.385**	0.0001	0.0001	−0.006***	−0.005***
	(1.852)	(1.594)	(0.0001)	(0.0001)	(0.002)	(0.002)
N	1,417	1,417	1,417	1,417	1,417	1,417
R^2	0.734	0.756	0.565	0.570	0.882	0.890
Adjusted R^2	0.718	0.741	0.538	0.543	0.875	0.883
Residual SE	1,245.408 (df=1,333)	1,193.720 (df=1,332)	0.064 (df=1,333)	0.064 (df=1,332)	1.639 (df=1,333)	1.586 (df=1,332)

*$p < .1$; **$p < .05$; ***$p < .01$.

Standard errors (SEs) clustered by state.

df, degrees of freedom.

Logged Sum of Lawsuits
See Table A.7.

Differential Weighting of Capacity
One may be concerned about the way I constructed the design capacity variable. Regarding facilities with multiple customers, I merely averaged the design capacity between the

Table A.7 Hypothesis 1: Prisoner Lawsuits and Private Prisons, Logged Lawsuits

	Private Design Capacity		Proportion in Private Facilities		Sum All Private Facilities	
	(1)	(2)	(3)	(4)	(5)	(6)
Log sum lawsuits		322.268		0.001		0.501**
		(206.382)		(0.009)		(0.227)
Republican legislature	−29.151	−0.405	−0.006	−0.006	−0.444	−0.399
	(281.499)	(268.218)	(0.013)	(0.013)	(0.355)	(0.335)
Republican governor	118.295	120.877	0.018*	0.018*	−0.198	−0.194
	(143.788)	(144.936)	(0.010)	(0.010)	(0.194)	(0.194)
Unified Republican gov't	238.898	214.166	−0.005	−0.005	0.800*	0.761*
	(330.027)	(326.889)	(0.016)	(0.015)	(0.454)	(0.448)
Budget gap per capita	13.003	8.166	−0.015**	−0.015**	0.052	0.045
	(89.918)	(85.575)	(0.007)	(0.007)	(0.071)	(0.068)
No. unionized corrections officers (1000s)	298.209*	288.613*	−0.003	−0.003	0.822***	0.807***
	(173.056)	(168.646)	(0.002)	(0.002)	(0.279)	(0.275)
Incarceration rate	7.566***	7.452***	0.0001	0.0001	0.010***	0.010***
	(2.786)	(2.761)	(0.0001)	(0.0001)	(0.004)	(0.004)
Violent crime rate	−3.887**	−3.797**	0.0001	0.0001	−0.006***	−0.006***
	(1.852)	(1.817)	(0.0001)	(0.0001)	(0.002)	(0.002)
N	1,417	1,417	1,417	1,417	1,417	1,417
R^2	0.734	0.736	0.565	0.565	0.882	0.884
Adjusted R^2	0.718	0.720	0.538	0.538	0.875	0.876
Residual SE	1,245.408 (df = 1,333)	1,241.025 (df = 1,332)	0.064 (df = 1,333)	0.064 (df = 1,332)	1.639 (df = 1,333)	1.631 (df = 1,332)

*$p < .1$; **$p < .05$; ***$p < .01$.

Standard errors (SEs) clustered by state.
df, degrees of freedom.

customers. However, it is possible that this is not an accurate depiction of the distribution of inmates across jurisdictions. North Lake Correctional Facility, the facility I referenced in Chapter 4, has Vermont and Washington as its customers, but it is likely Vermont houses fewer inmates overall than Washington does, simply because the prison population of the former is smaller than that of the latter. To counteract this, I weighted the capacity variable via the following strategy: I found the total number of inmates under federal, state, or jail (i.e., local) jurisdiction for each year. Then, if a facility had multiple customers, I multiplied the total capacity by this share[3] to get a more realistic representation of what proportion of the facility each jurisdiction would hold. If there were multiple customers of the same level (i.e., two cities or two states), I used a similar weighting scheme with their total prison or jail populations. I then recalculated *Private Design Capacity* and *Proportion in Private Facilities* according to this measure. The substantive results do not change as a result of this alternative operationalization of the dependent variable (Table A.8).

Table A.8 Hypothesis 1: Prisoner Lawsuits and Private Prisons, Differential Weighting

	Weighted Private Design Capacity		Weighted Proportion in Private Facilities		Sum State Private Facilities	
	(1)	(2)	(3)	(4)	(5)	(6)
Sum lawsuits		1.529***		0.00003***		0.001***
		(0.398)		(0.00001)		(0.0004)
Republican legislature	−28.422	166.182	−0.005	−0.001	−0.417**	−0.235
	(284.651)	(275.097)	(0.014)	(0.014)	(0.198)	(0.169)
Republican governor	117.467	139.008	0.018	0.018	−0.052	−0.032
	(142.616)	(135.197)	(0.011)	(0.011)	(0.117)	(0.103)
Unified Republican gov't	226.042	134.854	−0.004	−0.006	0.218	0.133
	(325.632)	(335.424)	(0.016)	(0.016)	(0.211)	(0.193)
Budget gap per capita	8.539	−0.840	−0.015*	−0.015*	0.038	0.029
	(94.505)	(86.714)	(0.008)	(0.008)	(0.057)	(0.050)
No. unionized corrections officers (1000s)	300.629*	182.944	−0.003	−0.005**	0.346*	0.236*
	(175.088)	(139.940)	(0.002)	(0.002)	(0.180)	(0.137)
Incarceration rate	7.584***	7.778***	0.0001	0.0001	0.008***	0.008***
	(2.796)	(2.311)	(0.0001)	(0.0001)	(0.003)	(0.002)
Violent crime rate	−3.862**	−3.351**	0.0001	0.0001*	−0.002*	−0.002*
	(1.855)	(1.594)	(0.00005)	(0.00004)	(0.001)	(0.001)
N	1,417	1,417	1,417	1,417	1,417	1,417

(*continued*)

Table A.8 Continued

	Weighted Private Design Capacity		Weighted Proportion in Private Facilities		Sum State Private Facilities	
	(1)	(2)	(3)	(4)	(5)	(6)
R^2	0.737	0.759	0.585	0.590	0.841	0.857
Adjusted R^2	0.721	0.744	0.559	0.564	0.831	0.848
Residual SE	1,251.330 (df = 1,333)	1,198.102 (df = 1,332)	0.063 (df = 1,333)	0.063 (df = 1,332)	1.061 (df = 1,333)	1.006 (df = 1,332)

$^*p < .1; ^{**}p < .05; ^{***}p < .01.$

Standard errors (SEs) clustered by state.

df, degrees of freedom.

Instrumental Variable Models

All Private Facilities as Dependent Variable

In Chapter 4, I use the sum of state-only private facilities, to reflect state decision-making around private prisons. I revisit that decision here and include *all* private facilities in a state as the dependent variable. These facilities can hold state inmates, local (city or county) inmates, or federal inmates or immigrant detainees. The results are consistent (Table A.9).

Logged Sum of Lawsuits

See Tables A10–A12.

Table A.9 The Effect of Terminated Prisoner Lawsuits on Lagged Number of All Private Facilities

	Lagged Sum Facilities	Sum Lawsuits	Lagged Sum Facilities
	OLS	First Stage IV	IV
	(1)	(2)	(3)
Sum lawsuits	0.004***		0.006***
	(0.001)		(0.002)
Weight per judge serving		1.075**	
		(0.441)	
Constant	–0.906***	–511.281***	–0.516**
	(0.292)	(180.162)	(0.226)
N	1,501	1,400	1,400
R^2	0.554	0.362	0.486
Adjusted R^2	0.541	0.345	0.472
Residual SE	3.061 (df = 1,459)	519.587 (df = 1,361)	3.207 (df = 1,361)

$^{**}p < .05; ^{***}p < .01.$

Standard errors (SEs) clustered by circuit. F statistic is 19.32.

IV, instrumental variable; df, degrees of freedom.

Table A.10 The Effect of Terminated Prisoner Lawsuits on Lagged Private Design Capacity, Logged Lawsuits

	Lagged Private DC	Log Sum Lawsuits	Lagged Private DC
	OLS	First Stage IV	IV
	(1)	(2)	(3)
Log sum lawsuits	475.835**		742.383**
	(215.512)		(373.372)
Weight per judge serving		0.003**	
		(0.001)	
Constant	−2,656.725***	2.535***	−3,558.473**
	(1,015.999)	(0.417)	(1,576.840)
N	1,501	1,400	1,400
R^2	0.374	0.491	0.363
Adjusted R^2	0.356	0.477	0.345
Residual SE	1,837.139 (df = 1,459)	1.001 (df = 1,361)	1,810.508 (df = 1,361)

$^{**}p < .05;\ ^{***}p < .01.$

Standard errors (SEs) clustered by circuit. F statistic is 21.35.

IV, instrumental variable; DC, design capacity; df, degrees of freedom.

Table A.11 The Effect of Terminated Prisoner Lawsuits on Lagged Proportion of Inmates in Private Facilities, Logged Lawsuits

	Lagged Proportion in Private	Log Sum Lawsuits	Lagged Proportion in Private
	OLS	First Stage IV	IV
	(1)	(2)	(3)
Log sum lawsuits	−0.014		−0.007
	(0.009)		(0.020)
Weight per judge serving		0.003**	
		(0.001)	
Constant	0.007	2.535***	−0.016
	(0.029)	(0.417)	(0.073)
N	1,500	1,400	1,400
R^2	0.250	0.491	0.252
Adjusted R^2	0.230	0.477	0.231
Residual SE	0.081 (df = 1,459)	1.001 (df = 1,361)	0.079 (df = 1,361)

$^{**}p < .05;\ ^{***}p < .01.$

Standard errors (SEs) clustered by circuit. F statistic is 21.35.
IV, instrumental variable; df, degrees of freedom.

Table A.12 The Effect of Terminated Prisoner Lawsuits on Lagged Number of State Facilities, Logged Lawsuits

	Lagged Sum State Facilities	Log Sum Lawsuits	Lagged Sum State Facilities
	OLS	First Stage IV	IV
	(1)	(2)	(3)
Log sum lawsuits	0.546**		1.158*
	(0.256)		(0.600)
Weight per judge serving		0.003**	
		(0.001)	
Constant	−2.809**	2.535***	−4.992**
	(1.187)	(0.417)	(2.409)
N	1,550	1,400	1,400
R^2	0.400	0.491	0.345
Adjusted R^2	0.383	0.477	0.327
Residual SE	1.948 (df = 1,508)	1.001 (df = 1,361)	2.074 (df = 1,361)

$^*p < .1; ^{**}p < .05; ^{***}p < .01.$

Standard errors (SEs) clustered by circuit. F statistic is 21.35.

IV, instrumental variable; df, degrees of freedom.

Differential Weighting of Capacity
See Tables A13 and A14.

Hypothesis 2

OLS Models

Adding Control Variables
Table A.15 adds several variables to the OLS specification in the main text for Hypothesis 2. The results remain insignificant with the inclusion of these control variables.

Lagged Dependent Variable Model
Table A.16 adds a lagged dependent variable to the OLS estimation of Hypothesis 2. The coefficient on the court orders variable is insignificant.

All Private Facilities as Dependent Variable
In Chapter 4, I use the sum of state-only private facilities to reflect state decision-making around private prisons. I revisit that decision here and include *all* private facilities in a state as the dependent variable. These facilities can hold state inmates, local (city or county) inmates, or federal inmates or immigrant detainees. The results are consistent (Table A.17).

Table A.13 The Effect of Terminated Prisoner Lawsuits on Lagged Private Design Capacity, Differential Weighting

	Lagged Weighted Private DC	Sum Lawsuits	Lagged Weighted Private DC
	OLS	First Stage IV	IV
	(1)	(2)	(3)
Sum lawsuits	1.786***		2.177***
	(0.508)		(0.787)
Weight per judge serving		1.075**	
		(0.441)	
Constant	−696.179***	−511.281***	−600.264***
	(194.726)	(180.162)	(149.777)
N	1,501	1,400	1,400
R^2	0.501	0.362	0.497
Adjusted R^2	0.487	0.345	0.483
Residual SE	1,656.610 (df = 1,459)	519.587 (df = 1,361)	1,626.141 (df = 1,361)

**$p < .05$; ***$p < .01$.

Standard errors (SEs) clustered by circuit. F statistic is 19.32.

IV, instrumental variable; df, degrees of freedom.

Table A.14 The Effect of Terminated Prisoner Lawsuits on Lagged Proportion of Inmates in Private Facilities, Differential Weighting

	Lagged Weighted Proportion in Private	Sum Lawsuits	Lagged Weighted Proportion in Private
	OLS	First Stage IV	IV
	(1)	(2)	(3)
Sum lawsuits	−0.00001*		−0.00001
	(0.00001)		(0.0001)
Weight per judge serving		1.075**	
		(0.441)	
Constant	−0.045***	−511.281***	−0.044***
	(0.013)	(180.162)	(0.016)
N	1,500	1,400	1,400
R^2	0.238	0.362	0.241
Adjusted R^2	0.217	0.345	0.220
Residual SE	0.082 (df = 1,459)	519.587 (df = 1,361)	0.082 (df = 1,361)

*$p < .1$; **$p < .05$; ***$p < .01$.

Standard errors (SEs) clustered by circuit. F statistic is 19.32.

IV, instrumental variable; df, degrees of freedom.

Table A.15 Hypothesis 2: Successful Prisoner Lawsuits and Private Prisons, Adding Control Variables

	Private Design Capacity		Proportion in Private Facilities		Sum State Private Facilities	
	(1)	(2)	(3)	(4)	(5)	(6)
Court order began	191.249	215.014	0.004	−0.001	0.126	−0.062
	(123.633)	(180.072)	(0.005)	(0.006)	(0.088)	(0.121)
Republican legislature	22.334	200.112	−0.008	0.008	−0.397*	−0.088
	(344.095)	(259.063)	(0.014)	(0.009)	(0.226)	(0.162)
Republican governor	219.161	320.799	0.020	0.021*	0.008	−0.015
	(139.405)	(193.870)	(0.013)	(0.011)	(0.119)	(0.112)
Budget gap per capita	−86.754	−16.620	−0.019***	−0.009	−0.001	0.038
	(68.169)	(89.156)	(0.007)	(0.007)	(0.056)	(0.047)
No. unionized corrections officers (1000s)	240.188	326.217	−0.001	0.002	0.308*	0.166
	(161.178)	(219.520)	(0.002)	(0.002)	(0.159)	(0.330)
Incarceration rate	5.897***	5.797	0.0001	0.0002	0.007**	0.012**
	(1.982)	(3.653)	(0.0001)	(0.0001)	(0.003)	(0.006)
Violent crime rate	−3.163**	−5.674*	0.0001	−0.0001	−0.002*	−0.002
	(1.440)	(2.957)	(0.0001)	(0.0001)	(0.001)	(0.001)
Percent overcrowded	0.766	7.143	0.0004	0.0004	−0.006	−0.006
	(5.483)	(5.624)	(0.0003)	(0.0003)	(0.004)	(0.004)
Deaths in custody	9.758	−7.960	−0.0001	−0.0001	0.009**	−0.004
	(5.950)	(7.649)	(0.0001)	(0.0001)	(0.004)	(0.004)
Economic policy liberalism	−593.931	−423.371	−0.013	0.041**	−0.287	0.179
	(387.919)	(522.100)	(0.022)	(0.019)	(0.336)	(0.280)
Sum contributions		0.010***		0.00000*		0.00000
		(0.003)		(0.00000)		(0.00000)
Unified Republican gov't	22.463	−287.388	−0.007	−0.023*	0.142	0.176
	(355.084)	(301.629)	(0.018)	(0.012)	(0.198)	(0.169)
N	1,107	573	1,107	573	1,107	573
R^2	0.779	0.869	0.577	0.781	0.866	0.914
Adjusted R^2	0.761	0.851	0.543	0.751	0.855	0.902
Residual SE	1,187.068 (df = 1,023)	1,133.458 (df = 502)	0.067 (df = 1,023)	0.056 (df = 502)	1.061 (df = 1,023)	0.945 (df = 502)

*$p < .1$; **$p < .05$; ***$p < .01$.

Standard errors (SEs) clustered by state.

df, degrees of freedom.

Table A.16 Hypothesis 2: Successful Prisoner Lawsuits and Private Prisons, Lagged Dependent Variable Model

	Private Design Capacity	Proportion in Private Facilities	Sum State Private Facilities
	(1)	(2)	(3)
Court order began	109.354	0.005	0.066
	(76.284)	(0.004)	(0.071)
Republican legislature	−218.254	−0.006	−0.443**
	(204.744)	(0.010)	(0.189)
Republican governor	29.758	0.007	−0.071
	(111.284)	(0.007)	(0.106)
Unified Republican gov't	138.513	−0.001	0.149
	(221.536)	(0.011)	(0.168)
Budget gap per capita	6.471	−0.013**	0.044
	(80.583)	(0.006)	(0.053)
No. unionized corrections officers (1000s)	201.800*	−0.002	0.297**
	(106.693)	(0.002)	(0.147)
Incarceration rate	4.196**	0.0001	0.007***
	(1.986)	(0.0001)	(0.002)
Violent crime rate	−2.436**	0.00003	−0.002**
	(1.081)	(0.00003)	(0.001)
Lagged DV: DC	0.461***		
	(0.072)		
Lagged DV: proportion		0.371***	
		(0.083)	
Lagged DV: facilities			0.208***
			(0.052)
N	1,417	1,417	1,416
R^2	0.810	0.635	0.855
Adjusted R^2	0.798	0.611	0.845
Residual SE	1,052.727 (df = 1,331)	0.059 (df = 1,331)	1.014 (df = 1,330)

*$p < .1$; **$p < .05$; ***$p < .01$.

Standard errors (SEs) clustered by state.

DV, dependent variable; DC, design capacity; df, degrees of freedom.

Table A.17 Hypothesis 2: Successful Prison Lawsuits and Private Prisons, All Private Facilities

	Private Design Capacity		Proportion in Private Facilities		Sum All Private Facilities	
	(1)	(2)	(3)	(4)	(5)	(6)
Court order began		117.987		0.004		−0.018
		(109.456)		(0.004)		(0.157)
Republican legislature	−29.151	−31.918	−0.006	−0.006	−0.444	−0.443
	(281.499)	(281.308)	(0.013)	(0.013)	(0.355)	(0.356)
Republican governor	118.295	118.497	0.018*	0.018*	−0.198	−0.198
	(143.788)	(143.575)	(0.010)	(0.010)	(0.194)	(0.194)
Unified Republican gov't	238.898	234.785	−0.005	−0.005	0.800*	0.800*
	(330.027)	(328.090)	(0.016)	(0.016)	(0.454)	(0.455)
Budget gap per capita	13.003	15.275	−0.015**	−0.015**	0.052	0.052
	(89.918)	(91.745)	(0.007)	(0.007)	(0.071)	(0.071)
No. unionized corrections officers (1000s)	298.209*	298.606*	−0.003	−0.003	0.822***	0.822***
	(173.056)	(172.940)	(0.002)	(0.002)	(0.279)	(0.279)
Incarceration rate	7.566***	7.589***	0.0001	0.0001	0.010***	0.010***
	(2.786)	(2.779)	(0.0001)	(0.0001)	(0.004)	(0.004)
Violent crime rate	−3.887**	−3.902**	0.0001	0.0001	−0.006***	−0.006***
	(1.852)	(1.853)	(0.0001)	(0.0001)	(0.002)	(0.002)
N	1,417	1,417	1,417	1,417	1,417	1,417
R^2	0.734	0.735	0.565	0.565	0.882	0.882
Adjusted R^2	0.718	0.718	0.538	0.538	0.875	0.875
Residual SE	1,245.408 (df = 1,333)	1,245.087 (df = 1,332)	0.064 (df = 1,333)	0.064 (df = 1,332)	1.639 (df = 1,333)	1.640 (df = 1,332)

$^*p < .1$; $^{**}p < .05$; $^{***}p < .01$.

Standard errors (SEs) clustered by state.

df, degrees of freedom.

Differential Weighting of Capacity

See Table A.18.

Table A.18 Hypothesis 2: Successful Prison Lawsuits and Private Prisons, Differential Weighting

	Weighted Private Design Capacity		Weighted Proportion in Private Facilities		Sum State Private Facilities	
	(1)	(2)	(3)	(4)	(5)	(6)
Court order began		122.103		0.005		0.105
		(109.451)		(0.004)		(0.081)
Republican legislature	−28.422	−31.285	−0.005	−0.005	−0.417**	−0.419**
	(284.651)	(284.328)	(0.014)	(0.014)	(0.198)	(0.196)
Republican governor	117.467	117.676	0.018	0.018	−0.052	−0.052
	(142.616)	(142.403)	(0.011)	(0.011)	(0.117)	(0.117)
Unified Republican gov't	226.042	221.786	−0.004	−0.004	0.218	0.214
	(325.632)	(323.621)	(0.016)	(0.016)	(0.211)	(0.209)
Budget gap per capita	8.539	10.891	−0.015*	−0.015*	0.038	0.040
	(94.505)	(96.409)	(0.008)	(0.008)	(0.057)	(0.058)
No. unionized corrections officers (1000s)	300.629*	301.041*	−0.003	−0.003	0.346*	0.346*
	(175.088)	(174.968)	(0.002)	(0.002)	(0.180)	(0.180)
Incarceration rate	7.584***	7.609***	0.0001	0.0001	0.008***	0.008***
	(2.796)	(2.788)	(0.0001)	(0.0001)	(0.003)	(0.003)
Violent Crime rate	−3.862**	−3.877**	0.0001	0.0001	−0.002*	−0.002**
	(1.855)	(1.856)	(0.00005)	(0.00005)	(0.001)	(0.001)
N	1,417	1,417	1,417	1,417	1,417	1,417
R^2	0.737	0.737	0.585	0.585	0.841	0.841
Adjusted R^2	0.721	0.721	0.559	0.559	0.831	0.831
Residual SE	1,251.330 (df = 1,333)	1,250.958 (df = 1,332)	0.063 (df = 1,333)	0.063 (df = 1,332)	1.061 (df = 1,333)	1.060 (df = 1,332)

*p < .1; **p < .05; ***p < .01.

Standard errors (SEs) clustered by state.

df, degrees of freedom.

Instrumental Variable Models

All Private Facilities as Dependent Variable

In Chapter 4, I use the sum of state-only private facilities, to reflect state decision-making around private prisons. I revisit that decision here and include *all* private facilities in a state as the dependent variable. These facilities can hold state inmates, local (city or county) inmates, or federal inmates or immigrant detainees. The results are consistent (Table A.19).

Table A.19 The Effect of Court Orders Begun on Lagged Number of All Private Facilities

	Lagged Sum Facilities	Court Order Began	Lagged Sum Facilities
	OLS	First Stage IV	IV
	(1)	(2)	(3)
Court order began	66.595*		201.932
	(35.809)		(389.035)
Proportion prior prosecutor		0.530**	
		(0.217)	
Constant	285.356***	0.235***	256.286***
	(12.854)	(0.050)	(79.376)
N	1,426	1,426	1,426
R^2	0.268	0.085	0.212
Adjusted R^2	0.248	0.060	0.190
Residual SE (df = 1,386)	195.633	0.398	203.029

*$p < .1$; **$p < .05$; ***$p < .01$.

Standard errors (SEs) clustered by circuit. F statistic is 19.69.

IV, instrumental variable; df, degrees of freedom.

Differential Weighting of Capacity

See Tables A20–A21.

Chapter 5

Stocks Data

This chapter uses information from the Center for Research in Security Prices, which contains daily information on the stock performance of individual firms. I consider the four publicly traded private prison companies described in Chapter 2 and use the identifying information below. PERMNOs are permanent ID numbers of a given security and PERMCOs are identifying ID numbers for companies (one PERMCO, one company, can have multiple PERMNOs).

- CoreCivic: PERMNOs are 10716 and 85234; PERMCOs are 8613 and 32025 (tickers are CCAX; CXC; CCA; CXW)

Table A.20 The Effect of Court Orders Begun on Lagged Private Design Capacity, Differential Weighting

	Lagged Weighted Private DC	Court Order Began	Lagged Weighted Private DC
	OLS	First Stage IV	IV
	(1)	(2)	(3)
Court order began	328.541		−1,558.125
	(305.175)		(3,981.608)
Proportion prior prosecutor		0.506**	
		(0.210)	
Constant	−1,008.552***	0.181***	−703.033
	(313.495)	(0.052)	(696.158)
N	1,550	1,550	1,550
R^2	0.325	0.084	0.220
Adjusted R^2	0.307	0.060	0.198
Residual SE (df = 1,508)	1,900.631	0.396	2,043.876

**$p < .05$; ***$p < .01$.
Standard errors (SEs) clustered by circuit. F statistic is 19.61.
IV, instrumental variable; df, degrees of freedom.

Table A.21 The Effect of Court Orders Begun on Lagged Proportion of Inmates in Private Facilities, Differential Weighting

	Lagged Weighted Proportion in Private	Court Order Began	Lagged Weighted Proportion in Private
	OLS	First Stage IV	IV
	(1)	(2)	(3)
Court order began	−0.013		−0.174
	(0.011)		(0.196)
Proportion prior prosecutor		0.511**	
		(0.211)	
Constant	−0.039***	0.181***	−0.013
	(0.012)	(0.052)	(0.036)
N	1,548	1,548	1,548
R^2	0.235	0.085	−0.240
Adjusted R^2	0.215	0.060	−0.274
Residual SE (df = 1,506)	0.081	0.395	0.104

**$p < .05$; ***$p < .01$.
Standard errors (SEs) clustered by circuit. F statistic is 19.98.
IV, instrumental variable; df, degrees of freedom.

- GEO Group: PERMNO is 80774; PERMCO is 13225 (tickers are GEO, GGI, WCCCX, WHC)
- Cornell Companies: PERMNO is 84023; PERMCO is 31760 (ticker is CRN)
- CSC: PERMNO is 80242; PERMCO is 12817 (tickers are ESRM; CSCQ)

Average Cumulative Abnormal Returns and Lawsuits: Different Dependent Variables

In Chapter 5, the main specifications use the cumulative abnormal return (CAR) [−5,5], a five-day spread around the lawsuit event as the dependent variables. Here, I revisit that decision and use the other dependent variables calculated: CAR[−1,1], CAR[−2,2], CAR[−10,10], and CAR[−30,30] (Tables A.22–A.25).

Table A.22 Average CAR[−1,1] Across and Within Firms After a Successful Lawsuit

CAR[−1,1]					
	All Firms	CoreCivic	GEO Group	CSC	Cornell
	(1)	(2)	(3)	(4)	(5)
Constant	0.002**	0.003	0.002	−0.001	0.0003
	(0.001)	(0.003)	(0.003)	(0.006)	(0.003)
N	1,120	458	314	143	205
R^2	0.000	0.000	−0.000	0.000	0.000
Adjusted R^2	0.000	0.000	−0.000	0.000	0.000
Residual SE	0.057	0.062	0.048	0.073	0.046
	(df = 1,119)	(df = 457)	(df = 313)	(df = 142)	(df = 204)

**p < .05.
Standard errors (SEs) clustered by company in column 1.
df, degrees of freedom.

Table A.23 Average CAR[−2,2] Across and Within Firms After a Successful Lawsuit

CAR[−2,2]					
	All Firms	CoreCivic	GEO Group	CSC	Cornell
	(1)	(2)	(3)	(4)	(5)
Constant	0.003**	0.005	0.001	−0.0005	0.003
	(0.001)	(0.004)	(0.003)	(0.009)	(0.004)
N	1,120	458	314	143	205
R^2	0.000	−0.000	0.000	0.000	0.000
Adjusted R^2	0.000	−0.000	0.000	0.000	0.000
Residual SE	0.078	0.087	0.061	0.104	0.060
	(df = 1,119)	(df = 457)	(df = 313)	(df = 142)	(df = 204)

**p < .05.
Standard errors (SEs) clustered by company in column 1.
df, degrees of freedom.

Table A.24 Average CAR[−10,10] Across and Within Firms After a Successful Lawsuit

	CAR[−10,10]				
	All Firms	CoreCivic	GEO Group	CSC	Cornell
	(1)	(2)	(3)	(4)	(5)
Constant	−0.002	−0.002	−0.015**	0.003	0.017*
	(0.006)	(0.007)	(0.007)	(0.013)	(0.010)
N	1,120	458	314	143	205
R^2	0.000	0.000	0.000	0.000	0.000
Adjusted R^2	0.000	0.000	0.000	0.000	0.000
Residual SE	0.148 (df = 1,119)	0.155 (df = 457)	0.131 (df = 313)	0.157 (df = 142)	0.148 (df = 204)

$^*p < .1$; $^{**}p < .05$
Standard errors (SEs) clustered by company in column 1.
df, degrees of freedom.

Table A.25 Average CAR[−30,30] Across and Within Firms After a Successful Lawsuit

	CAR[−30,30]				
	All Firms	CoreCivic	GEO Group	CSC	Cornell
	(1)	(2)	(3)	(4)	(5)
Constant	0.0001	−0.003	−0.013	−0.008	0.033*
	(0.008)	(0.012)	(0.014)	(0.020)	(0.019)
N	1,120	458	314	143	205
R^2	0.000	−0.000	0.000	0.000	0.000
Adjusted R^2	0.000	−0.000	0.000	0.000	0.000
Residual SE	0.254 (df = 1,119)	0.259 (df = 457)	0.243 (df = 313)	0.235 (df = 142)	0.269 (df = 204)

$^*p < .1$.
Standard errors (SEs) clustered by company in column 1.
df, degrees of freedom.

CARs in States with any Private Facilities
See Table A.26.

Adding Year Fixed Effects
See Table A.27.

Table A.26 Average CAR After a Successful Lawsuit in States with Any Private Prisons

	CAR[−1,1]	CAR[−2,2]	CAR[−5,5]	CAR[−10,10]	CAR[−30,30]
	(1)	(2)	(3)	(4)	(5)
Private facility exists	0.001	0.00004	−0.006	−0.012	−0.017
	(0.002)	(0.003)	(0.008)	(0.013)	(0.019)
N	1,120	1,120	1,120	1,120	1,120
R^2	0.001	0.001	0.004	0.007	0.005
Adjusted R^2	−0.003	−0.003	0.001	0.003	0.001
Residual SE (df = 1,115)	0.058	0.079	0.115	0.148	0.253

All standard errors (SEs) clustered by company.
df, degrees of freedom.

Table A.27 Average CARs After a Successful Lawsuit in States with Increasing Numbers of Private Prisons, Plus Year Fixed Effects

	CAR[−1,1]	CAR[−2,2]	CAR[−5,5]	CAR[−10,10]	CAR[−30,30]
	(1)	(2)	(3)	(4)	(5)
Sum private facilities	−0.0002	−0.0001	−0.001	−0.002[***]	−0.003
	(0.0001)	(0.0003)	(0.0003)	(0.0004)	(0.002)
N	1,120	1,120	1,120	1,120	1,120
R^2	0.026	0.025	0.029	0.064	0.145
Adjusted R^2	−0.004	−0.004	−0.0001	0.035	0.119
Residual SE (df = 1086)	0.058	0.079	0.115	0.145	0.238

[***]$p < .01$.
All standard errors (SEs) clustered by company.
df, degrees of freedom.

Notes

Chapter 1

1. See http://www.cca.com/about/cca-history/.
2. While no states had passed prohibitory legislation regarding private prisons in 1988, two states (Illinois in 1991 and New York in 1997) since adopted statutes expressly prohibiting the privatization of correctional facilities (Quinlan, Thomas, and Gautreaux, 2004).
3. Alaska, Arizona, Arkansas, California, Colorado, Connecticut, Florida, Idaho, Indiana, Kentucky, Louisiana, Michigan, Mississippi, Montana, Nebraska, Nevada, New Hampshire, New Mexico, North Carolina, Ohio, Oklahoma, Tennessee, Texas, Utah, Virginia, West Virginia, Wisconsin, and Wyoming (Quinlan, Thomas, and Gautreaux, 2004).
4. In the 1990s in particular, some private companies built facilities "on spec" without securing a government partner for them, a gamble that was a profitable one (McDonald and Patten, 2003). This approach is not common today.
5. There are many ways to refer to the complex institutions that comprise the carceral state, from police to courts to jails and prisons. This book references this system as the criminal legal system, though others may call it the criminal justice system, the criminal punishment system, or the criminal system (Mayeux, 2018).

Chapter 2

1. There were a few name changes for these companies over the last few decades: CoreCivic is formerly the Corrections Corporation of America, the GEO Group is formerly Wackenhut Corrections Corporation, and Correctional Services Corporation was formerly Esmor Correctional Corporation.
2. This choice deviates from the BJS variable because the BJS figure also includes inmates in privately operated halfway houses, treatment facilities, or hospitals. My data only reflects those privately incarcerated in prisons or jails.
3. Formally, Illinois Statutes Chapter 730, Act 140 and New York Correction Law Statute 72 expressly prohibit privatization (Quinlan, Thomas, and Gautreaux, 2004).

Chapter 3

1. Though this was the primary approach in the early twentieth century, the term "hands-off" doctrine was only coined in 1961. The term is first used in a document prepared for the Federal Bureau of Prisons and was adopted shortly thereafter into the academic lexicon about these lawsuits ("Beyond the Ken of the Courts," 1963).

2. This act, enacted after the ratification of the Thirteenth and Fourteenth Amendments, primarily sought to tamper the violence committed by the Ku Klux Klan and sought to eliminate remaining abusive practices after the adoption of these constitutional amendments, specifically by eliminating civil rights violations "under color of state law" in Section 1983 of Title 42 (Dowd, 1984). Though this act later provides the constitutional basis of the multitude of prisoners' rights litigation, that provision remained dormant in inmate litigation for nearly a century until this decision.

3. As of 2014, Black Americans were incarcerated at a rate more than five times that of whites, while Hispanic Americans were incarcerated at 1.4 times the white incarceration rate (Nellis, 2016). That same year, at least 1 in 20 adult Black men were incarcerated in 11 states.

4. Senator Ted Kennedy was the main driver behind the Sentencing Reform Act of 1984, which established the US Sentencing Commission, instituted mandatory minimums for dozens of offenses, and abolished federal parole (Stith and Koh, 1993).

5. Indeed, Supreme Court Justice William Rehnquist dissented in a 1978 case, *Hutto v. Finney*, which approved of the remedial actions the lower court had mandated in Arkansas prisons, writing "I fear that the Court has allowed itself to be moved beyond the well-established bounds limiting the exercise of remedial authority by the federal district courts" (Feeley and Rubin, 2000, 45).

6. In the five years after the Arkansas decision, entire corrections systems were declared unconstitutional in whole or in part in five states: Mississippi, Oklahoma, Florida, Louisiana, and Alabama (Feeley and Rubin, 2000, 39).

7. For example, Maine's ballot had a bond measure in 1991 for $5.5 million to construct, purchase, and renovate correctional facilities that only received 35.4% of the vote.

8. And California was one of the first states to privatize in the 1980s.

9. The question wordings are as follows: "Which one of the following would you most like to see lead the effort to address the problem of prison overcrowding in your state? State legislators, the governor, or judges?" The second question: "Now I'm going to ask you about some specific issues and problems for state government to address. . . . The issue is prison overcrowding. Changes in state laws have led to more people being sentenced to prison for longer terms. This has made it more difficult for states to control spending for prisons while also protecting the public, successfully rehabilitating those convicted of crimes, and providing acceptable living conditions for prisoners. How much, if anything, have you personally seen, heard or read about the problem of prison overcrowding in your state . . . a lot, some, only a little, or nothing at all?"

10. Note that private corrections officers do not receive qualified immunity as public corrections guards do, making them relatively easier to sue than their public counterparts (Volokh, 2013).

11. It is possible private companies will then simply absorb the litigation costs into their contract. While this is possible, contractors remain solely financially responsible for litigation within these facilities that is prompted by deliberate and misleading reports to the state government (Raher, 2010).

12. Interestingly, the new state corrections commissioner at the time was Terrell Don Hutto, one of the co-founders of CoreCivic (Selman and Leighton, 2010, 56–58).

13. In a more colorful comment, Alabama Governor George Wallace remarked "thugs and federal judges" had "just about taken over society" (Yackle, 1989, 105).

14. Judge Justice also sought out the advice of Judge Johnson, who presided over the expansive order in *Pugh v. Locke* in Alabama in the 1970s (Justice, 1990).

15. Court orders may force states to spend more on corrections, specifically on capital outlays, or the construction of new facilities and the like (Taggart, 1989).

Chapter 4

1. Formally, this data set includes cases with the Nature of Suit codes of either 540 (Prisoner Petitions: Mandamus and Other), 550 (Prisoner Petitions: Civil Rights), or 555 (Prisoner Petitions: Prison Conditions). It does not include those cases filed under Nature of Suit code 440 (Civil Rights: Other Civil Rights), which may also include important prisoner litigation (Schlanger, 2003). Because not all of those cases involve prisoners and because identifying those applying to inmates would require individual research into each case, I only focused on those cases that were explicitly included in the "Prisoner Petition" category as identified by the US courts.

2. This does not include cases filed in the District of Columbia, Puerto Rico, Guam, the Northern Mariana Islands, the Virgin Islands, or the Canal Zone.

3. Moreover, the PLRA stipulates that defendants (in my case, state governments) unhappy with court orders that are more than two years old can seek immediate termination of those orders. Additionally, defendants have a period of 30–90 days after the immediate termination proceedings have initiated during which the court order is not in effect, thus giving a time advantage to those governments (Schlanger, 2006).

4. See http://clearinghouse.net.

5. I include "Jail Conditions" cases in my analysis because states did and continue to hold state inmates in local jails to ease overcrowding issues (Carson, 2018). Therefore, court orders against local jails can also burden state governments.

6. Cases in which the plaintiffs were not successful or that did not result in an injunction are mostly also not included. The only exception is the inclusion of jail and prison strip search class actions (see the CRC website for more information).

7. The difficulty is exacerbated further because there is no consistent database on specific filings in state courts, so this data collection effort would likely involve scouring individual states' electronic or physical legal records.

8. Weir v. Nix, filed in the Southern District of Iowa 1991; McDonald v. Armontrout, filed in the Western District of Missouri in 1985; Hallett v. Payne, filed in the Western District of Washington in 1993, respectively.

9. ACLU of New Mexico v. Board of County Commissioners of Valencia County, filed in 1997 in the District of New Mexico; Perry v. Fair, filed in 1989 in the District of Massachusetts; Cruz v. County of Fresno, filed in 1993 in the Eastern District of California; Woodson v. Sully, filed in 1985 in the District of Kansas, respectively.

10. See the Appendix for the inclusion of campaign contributions. Because of data limitations (it is only available for roughly half of my data), I do not present it alongside the main results.

11. See the Appendix materials for the sum of all private facilities in each state-year (inclusive of state, federal, and local correctional facilities).

12. See the Appendix for the logged sum of lawsuits as an alternative independent variable. The results are consistent.

13. Indeed, the Supreme Court ruled in Richardson v. McKnight (1997) that private prison guards do not possess qualified immunity and can thus be sued individually for civil rights abuses. Correctional officers in public facilities have qualified immunity, so "private prison inmates even (at least in this respect) get more favorable treatment by the federal courts" (Volokh, 2013).

14. Clerks in some district courts, like the Southern District of New York, literally spin a wooden wheel filled with index cards with judge names written on them and draw one name to randomly assign each case (Macfarlane, 2014).

15. The FJC defines case weights to account for the varying lengths of time different categories of cases take to adjudicate (Habel and Scott, 2014). See the Appendix for more details and alternative operationalizations of this variable.

16. Note, though, the results remain significant even when clustering by state.

17. See the Appendix for inclusion of population as a control.

18. Part of this problem is the availability of electronic data on the identification of judges.

Chapter 5

1. Information gathered from those companies' Securities and Exchange Commission reports. It is unclear how much of MTC's business was affected by this decision as the company does not publicly release revenue or customer information about its facilities, though only 2 of the 57 prisons it operated nationwide in 2016 appeared to be BOP facilities (information from MTC's website [Management and Training Corporation, 2016]).

2. The rest of the analysis only considers the publicly traded companies operating as of 2016, CoreCivic and GEO Group. Since MTC is not, I do not consider it here.

3. The companies' stock steadily fell during the latter half of the Trump presidency and fell with the announcement of Joe Biden's presidential victory. It appears, though, that the Yates memo was associated with a more severe stock drop than Election Day 2020 or when organizations began calling the election for Biden.

4. Indeed, about half of the variation in stock prices overall cannot be explained by macroeconomic shifts or major news events, meaning that decisions to purchase or sell stocks are explained at least half of the time by publicly unobservable choices or information held by investors (Cutler, Poterba, and Summers, 1989).

5. These figures are prior to the controversial involvement of these companies in Trump's family separation policy and the election of Joe Biden, both factors that negatively

influenced CoreCivic and GEO Group's stock prices (Pauly, 2020). Though it is still an open question whether and to what degree these companies will suffer under a Biden administration (e.g., Gunderson, 2020a), I nevertheless expect lawsuits to exert an effect on stock prices, even if a smaller effect than that caused by these larger political events.

6. Both CoreCivic and the GEO Group's investors as of 2017 included the public retirement funds for the states of California, New York, Alabama, Ohio, Texas, Arizona, Oregon, Michigan, New Mexico, Louisiana, Colorado, Kentucky, and Utah. The GEO Group also has investors from the state retirement systems in Florida and Pennsylvania. Since then, some funds from states like California have divested from these companies after much controversy (Venteicher, 2019).

7. For example, individual investors are more likely to respond to attention-grabbing events and buy stocks of firms that have media announcements or abnormally positive stock performance than institutional investors (Barber and Odean, 2008).

8. For this analysis, I use the value-weighted returns (including dividends) on all stock markets—NASDAQ, New York Stock Exchange, and the American Stock Exchange.

9. Often, these cases are immediately appealed by the government. I still use the date of the final settlement, not the appellate decision, because the initial ruling provides the clearest signal of the court's attitude toward the quality of operation at that particular facility.

10. Diagnostic tests indicate a high degree of heteroskedasticity in the variances in the dependent variable across firms, so comparing the means with a test like analysis of variance would not accurately account for the high degree of correlation between company and its associated standard errors.

11. See https://www.supremecourt.gov/opinions/10pdf/09-1233.pdf.

Appendix

1. And this series is conducted only twice in each decade, so there is not a consistent year-by-year estimate of this percentage.

2. See https://www.followthemoney.org/.

3. Therefore, I estimated the following equation:

$$\gamma_{ja,t,c} = \frac{\text{PrisonPop}_{ja,t}}{\text{PrisonPop}_{ja,t} + \text{PrisonPop}_{jb,t}} * \text{DesignCapacity}_{t,c}$$

Here, $\gamma_{ja,t,c}$ represents the design capacity of facility c for jurisdiction ja in time t, $PrisonPop_{ja,t}$ represents the prison population of jurisdiction a in time t, and $PrisonPop_{jb,t}$ represents the prison population of jurisdiction b in time t.

Bibliography

Abadie, A., and J. Gardeazabal. 2003. "The Economic Costs of Conflict: A Case Study of the Basque Country." *American Economic Review* 93, no. 1: 113–132.

Acemoglu, D., S. Johnson, A. Kermani, J. Kwak, and T. Mitton. 2016. "The Value of Connections in Turbulent Times: Evidence from the United States." *Journal of Financial Economics* 121, no. 2: 368–391.

Agrawal, J., and W. A. Kamakura. 1995. "The Economic Worth of Celebrity Endorsers: An Event Study Analysis." *Journal of Marketing* 59, no. 3: 56–62.

Alexander, M. 2010. *The New Jim Crow: Mass Incarceration in the Age of Colorblindness.* New York: New Press.

Anzia, S. F., and T. M. Moe. 2015. "Public Sector Unions and the Costs of Government." *Journal of Politics* 77, no. 1: 114–127.

Ashenfelter, O., T. Eisenberg, and S. J. Schwab. 1995. "Politics and the Judiciary: The Influence of Judicial Background on Case Outcomes." *Journal of Legal Studies* 24: 257–281.

Associated Press. 2013. "Inmate Lawsuits Cost California Taxpayers $200 Million Over Last 15 Years." February 11. https://www.dailybreeze.com/2013/02/11/inmate-lawsuits-cost-california-taxpayers-200-million-over-last-.

Austin, J., and G. Coventry. 2001. *Emerging Issues on Privatized Prisons.* Washington, DC: Bureau of Justice Assistance. https://www.ncjrs.gov/App/Publications/abstract.aspx?ID=181249.

Bales, W. D., L. E. Bedard, S. T. Quinn, D. T. Ensley, and G. P. Holley. 2005. "Recidivism of Public and Private State Prison Inmates in Florida." *Criminology & Public Policy* 4, no. 1: 57–82.

Barber, B. M., and T. Odean. 2008. "All That Glitters: The Effect of Attention and News on the Buying Behavior of Individual and Institutional Investors." *Review of Financial Studies* 21, no. 2: 785–818.

Barker, V. 2009. *The Politics of Punishment.* New York: Oxford University Press.

Bauer, S. 2019. *American Prison: A Reporter's Undercover Journey into the Business of Punishment.* New York: Penguin Books.

Bauer, Z., and J. M. Johnston. 2019. "Who Does It Better? Comparing Immigration Detention Facility Performance in an Intergovernmental and Intersectoral Context." *Public Administration Review* 80, no. 2: 244–258.

Beckett, K. 1999. *Making Crime Pay: Law and Order in Contemporary American Politics.* New York: Oxford University Press.

Berger, D. 2014. *Captive Nation: Black Prison Organizing in the Civil Rights Era.* Chapel Hill: University of North Carolina Press.

"Beyond the Ken of the Courts: A Critique of Judicial Refusal to Review the Complaints of Convicts." *Yale Law Journal* 1963; 72, no. 3: 506–558.

Blakely, C. R., and V. W. Bumphus. 2005. "An Analysis of Civil Suits Filed Against Private and Public Prisons: A Comparison of Title 42: Section 1983 Litigation." *Criminal Justice Policy Review* 16, no. 1: 74–87.

Blumstein, J. F., M. A. Cohen, and S. Seth. 2008. "Do Government Agencies Respond to Market Pressures? Evidence from Private Prisons." *Virginia Journal of Social Policy & the Law* 15, no. 3: 446–477.

Bonica, A., and M. Sen. 2017. "A Common-Space Scaling of the American Judiciary and Legal Profession." *Political Analysis* 25, no. 1: 114–121.

Boyd, C. L., L. Epstein, and A. D. Martin. 2010. "Untangling the Causal Effects of Sex on Judging." *American Journal of Political Science* 54, no. 2: 389–411.

Boylan, R. T., and N. Mocan. 2014. "Intended and Unintended Consequences of Prison Reform." *Journal of Law, Economics, and Organization* 30, no. 3: 558–586.

Brill, A. 2008. "Rights without Remedy: The Myth of State Court Accessibility After the Prison Litigation Reform Act." *Cardozo Law Review* 30: 645–682.

Brown v. Plata, 563 U.S. 493 (2011).

Brudney, J. L., S. Fernandez, J. Ryu, and D. Wright. 2005. "Exploring and Explaining Contracting Out: Patterns Among the American States." *Journal of Public Administration Research and Theory* 3: 393–419.

Burkhardt, B. C. 2014. "Private Prisons in Public Discourse: Measuring Moral Legitimacy." *Sociological Focus* 47, no. 4: 279–298.

Burkhardt, B. C. 2019. "Does the Public Sector Respond to Private Competition? An Analysis of Privatization and Prison Performance." *Journal of Crime and Justice* 42, no. 2: 201–220.

Burkhardt, B. C., and A. Jones. 2016. "Judicial Intervention into Prisons: Comparing Private and Public Prisons from 1990 to 2005." *Justice System Journal* 1: 39–52.

Butler, S. 1991. "Privatization for Public Purposes." In *Privatization and Its Alternatives*, edited by W. T. Gormley, 17–25. Madison: University of Wisconsin Press.

Calavita, K., and V. Jenness. 2015. *Appealing to Justice: Prisoner Grievances, Rights, and Carceral Logic*. Oakland: University of California Press.

Camp, S. D., and G. G. Gaes. 2002. "Growth and Quality of U.S. Private Prisons: Evidence from a National Survey." *Criminology & Public Policy* 1, no. 3: 427–450.

Campbell, J. Y., A. W. Lo, and A. C. MacKinlay. 1996. *The Econometrics of Financial Markets*. Princeton, NJ: Princeton University Press.

Cardarelli, A. P., and M. M. Finkelstein. 1974. "Correctional Administrators Assess the Adequacy and Impact of Prison Legal Services Programs in the United States." *Journal of Criminal Law and Criminology (1973–)* 65, no. 1: 91–102.

Carson, E. A. 2018. *Prisoners in 2016*. Washington, DC: Bureau of Justice Statistics. https://www.bjs.gov/content/pub/pdf/p16.pdf.

Caughey, D., and C. Warshaw. 2018. "Policy Preferences and Policy Change: Dynamic Responsiveness in the American States, 1936–2014." *American Political Science Review* 112, no. 2: 249–266.

Chase, R. T. 2015. "We Are not Slaves: Rethinking the Rise of Carceral States Through the Lens of the Prisoners' Rights Movement." *Journal of American History* 102, no. 1: 73–86.

Chen, A. H., and T. F. Siems. 2004. "The Effects of Terrorism on Global Capital Markets." *European Journal of Political Economy* 20, no. 2: 349–366.

Chilton, A. S., and M. K. Levy. 2015. "Challenging the Randomness of Panel Assignment in the Federal Courts of Appeals." *Cornell Law Review* 101: 1–56.

Cody, W. M., and A. D. Bennett. 1987. "The Privatization of Correctional Institutions: The Tennessee Experience." *Vanderbilt Law Review* 4: 829–849.

Collingwood, L., J. L. Morin, and S. O. El-Khatib. 2018. "Expanding Carceral Markets: Detention Facilities, ICE Contracts, and the Financial Interests of Punitive Immigration Policy." *Race and Social Problems* 10, no. 4: 275–292.

Conley, J. A. 1980. "Prisons, Production, and Profit: Reconsidering the Importance of Prison Industries." *Journal of Social History* 14, no. 2: 257–275.

CoreCivic. 2016. *CoreCivic Annual Report.* Brentwood, TN: CoreCivic.

Corrections Corporation of America. 1986. *CCA Annual Report.* Brentwood, TN: Corrections Corporation of America.

Corrections Corporation of America. 1987. *CCA Annual Report.* Brentwood, TN: Corrections Corporation of America.

Corrections Corporation of America. 1988. *CCA Annual Report.* Brentwood, TN: Corrections Corporation of America.

Corrections Corporation of America. 2012. *CCA Annual Report.* Brentwood, TN: Corrections Corporation of America.

Corrections Corporation of America. 2013. "Adding Value for Taxpayers." http://staging.cca.com/adding-value-for-taxpayers .

Culp, R. F. 2005. "The Rise and Stall of Prison Privatization: An Integration of Policy Analysis Perspectives." *Criminal Justice Policy Review* 16, no. 4: 412–442.

Cutler, D. M., J. M. Poterba, and L. H. Summers. 1989. "What Moves Stock Prices?" *Journal of Portfolio Management* 15, no. 3: 4–12.

Daley, D. 1996. "The Politics and Administration of Privatization: Efforts Among Local Governments." *Policy Studies Journal* 4: 629–631.

Davis, A. Y. 2000. "Masked Racism: Reflections on the Prison Industrial Complex [Article Reprinted from Colorlines]." *Indigenous Law Bulletin* 4, no. 27: 1–6.

de Tocqueville, A., and G. de Beaumont. 2014. *On the Penitentiary System in the United States, and Its Application in France.* London: White Press.

DiIulio, J. J., Jr. 1987. *Governing Prisons: A Comparative Study of Correctional Management.* New York: Free Press.

Dolovich, S. 2005. "State Punishment and Private Prisons." *Duke Law Journal* 3: 437–546.

Dowd, M. A. 1984. "Comparison of Section 1983 and Federal Habeas Corpus in State Prisoners' Litigation." *Notre Dame Law Review* 59: 1315–1338.

Eisen, L.-B. 2017. "Private Prisons Lock up Thousands of Americans with Almost no Oversight." *Time*, November 8. http://time.com/5013760/american-private-prisons-donald-trump/.

Eisen, L.-B. 2018. *Inside Private Prisons: An American Dilemma in the Age of Mass Incarceration.* New York: Columbia University Press.

Ekland-Olson, S., and S. J. Martin. 1988. "Organizational Compliance with Court Ordered Reform." *Law & Society Review* 22, no. 2: 359–383.

Enns, P. 2016. *Incarceration Nation: How the United States Became the Most Punitive Democracy in the World.* New York: Cambridge University Press.

Enns, P. K., and M. D. Ramirez. 2018. "Privatizing Punishment: Testing Theories of Public Support for Private Prison and Immigration Detention Facilities." *Criminology* 56, no. 3: 546–573.

Epp, C. R. 1998. *The Rights Revolution: Lawyers, Activists, and Supreme Courts in Comparative Perspective.* Chicago: University of Chicago Press.

Ethridge, P. A., and J. W. Marquart. 1993. "Private Prisons in Texas: The New Penology for Profit." *Justice Quarterly* 10, no. 1: 29–48.

Fama, E. F., L. Fisher, M. C. Jensen, and R. Roll. 1969. "The Adjustment of Stock Prices to New Information." *International Economic Review* 10, no. 1: 1–21.

Feeley, M. M. 1991. "The Privatization of Prisons in Historical Perspective." *Criminal Justice Research Bulletin* 6, no. 2: 1–10.

Feeley, M. M., and E. L. Rubin. 2000. *Judicial Policy Making and the Modern State: How the Courts Reformed America's Prisons.* Cambridge: Cambridge University Press.

Feeley, M. M., and V. Swearingen. 2004. "The Prison Conditions Cases and the Bureaucratization of American Corrections." *Pace Law Review* 24: 433–475.

Felber, G. 2019. *Those Who Know Don't Say: The Nation of Islam, the Black Freedom Movement, and the Carceral State*. Chapel Hill: University of North Carolina Press.

Ferris, J., and E. Graddy. 1986. "Contracting Out: For What? With Whom?" *Public Administration Review* 4: 332–344.

Fisman, R. 2001. "Estimating the Value of Political Connections." *American Economic Review* 91, no. 4: 1095–1102.

Fliter, J. 1996. "Another Look at the Judicial Power of the Purse: Courts, Corrections, and State Budgets in the 1980s." *Law Society Review* 30: 399–416.

"Law Aims to Reduce Prisoner Lawsuits; Top 10 Frivolous Lawsuits." *The Ledger*, April 28, 1996.

Forman, J. 2017. *Locking Up Our Own*. New York: Farrar, Straus and Giroux.

Fortner, M. 2015. *Black Silent Majority: The Rockefeller Drug Laws and the Politics of Punishment*. Cambridge, MA: Harvard University Press.

Fowler, A., H. Garro, and J. L. Spenkuch. 2020. "Quid Pro Quo? Corporate Returns to Campaign Contributions." *Journal of Politics* 82, no. 3: 844–858.

Frost, N. A., J. Trapassi, and S. Heinz. 2019. "Public Opinion and Correctional Privatization." *Criminology & Public Policy* 18, no. 2: 457–476.

Gallagher, D., and M. Edwards. 1997. "Prison Industries and the Private Sector." *Atlantic Economic Journal* 1: 91–98.

GEO Group. 2012. *GEO Group Annual Report*. Boca Raton, FL: GEO Group.

Gill, H. B. 1931. "The Prison Labor Problem." *Annals of the American Academy of Political and Social Science* 157, no. 1: 83–101.

Gilligan, T. W., and K. Krehbiel. 1988. "Complex Rules and Congressional Outcomes: An Event Study of Energy Tax Legislation." *Journal of Politics* 50, no. 3: 625–654.

Gilmore, R. W. 2007. *Golden Gulag: Prisons, Surplus, Crisis, and Opposition in Globalizing California*. Berkeley: University of California Press.

Gilmour, R. S., and L. S. Jensen. 1998. "Reinventing Government Accountability: Public Functions, Privatization, and the Meaning of 'State Action.'" *Public Administration Review* 58, no. 3: 247–258.

Goldfarb, R. L., and L. R. Singer. 1970. "Redressing Prisoners' Grievances." *George Washington Law Review* 39: 175–320.

Goldman, E., J. Rocholl, and J. So. 2009. "Do Politically Connected Boards Affect Firm Value?" *Review of Financial Studies* 22, no. 6: 2331–2360.

Gottschalk, M. 2006. *The Prison and the Gallows: The Politics of Mass Incarceration in America*. New York: Cambridge University Press.

Gottschalk, M. 2016. *Caught: The Prison State and the Lockdown of American Politics*. Princeton, NJ: Princeton University Press.

Greenberg, D. F., and V. West. 2001. "State Prison Populations and Their Growth, 1971–1991." *Criminology* 39, no. 3: 615–654.

Guetzkow, J., and E. Schoon. 2015. "If You Build It, They Will Fill It: The Consequences of Prison Overcrowding Litigation." *Law & Society Review* 49, no. 2: 401–432.

Gunderson, A. 2020a. "The Future of Federal Prison Privatization Is Bleak. . . or Is It?" *3Streams* (blog), December 11. https://medium.com/3streams/the-future-of-federal-prison-privatization-is-bleak-or-is-it-93cbc526d0ac.

Gunderson, A. 2020b. "Representation, Incorporation, and Corrections Spending: The Counterbalancing Effect of Black Political Incorporation." *Journal of Race, Ethnicity, and Politics*, 5, no. 3: 573–603.

Gunderson, A. 2020c. "Why Do States Privatize Their Prisons? The Unintended Consequences of Inmate Litigation." *Perspectives on Politics*, 1–18. doi:10.1017/S1537592720003485.

Gunderson, A. 2021a. "Ideology, Disadvantage, and Federal District Court Inmate Civil Rights Filings: The Troubling Effects of Pro Se Status." *Journal of Empirical Legal Studies*. https://doi.org/10.1111/jels.12290.

Gunderson, A. 2021b. "Who punishes more? partisanship, punitive policies, and the puzzle of democratic governors." *Political Research Quarterly*, 1–17.

Haas, K. C. 1977. "Judicial Politics and Correctional Reform: An Analysis of the Decline of the Hands-Off Doctrine." *Detroit College of Law Review* 1977: 795–831.

Habel, P., and K. Scott. 2014. "New Measures of Judges' Caseload for the Federal District Courts, 1964–2012." *Journal of Law and Courts* 2, no. 1: 153–170.

Hager, E., and A. Santo. 2016. "Inside the Deadly World of Private Prisoner Transport." *The Marshall Project*, July 6. https://www.themarshallproject.org/2016/07/06/inside-the-deadly-world-of-private-prisoner-transport.

Hall, M. 2010. "Randomness Reconsidered: Modeling Random Judicial Assignment in the U.S. Courts of Appeals." *Journal of Empirical Legal Studies* 7: 574–589.

Hallett, M. A. 2006. *Private Prisons in America: A Critical Race Perspective*. Urbana: University of Illinois Press.

Hanson, R. A., and H. W. Daley. 1995. *Challenging the Conditions of Prisons and Jails: A Report on Section 1983 Litigation*. Washington, DC: US Department of Justice, Office of Justice Programs, Bureau of Justice Statistics.

Harding, R. 1997. *Private Prisons and Public Accountability*. Piscataway, NJ: Transaction Publishers.

Harding, R. 2001. "Private Prisons." *Crime and Justice* 28: 265–346.

Harriman, L., and J. D. Straussman. 1983. "Do Judges Determine Budget Decisions? Federal Court Decisions in Prison Reform and State Spending for Corrections." *Public Administration Review* 43, no. 4: 343–351.

Hart, O., A. Shleifer, and R. W. Vishny, 1997. "The Proper Scope of Government: Theory and an Application to Prisons." *Quarterly Journal of Economics* 4: 1127–1161.

Haughwout, A. F., and C. J. Richardson. 1987. "Federal Grants to State and Local Governments in the 1980s." *Public Budgeting & Finance* 4: 12–23.

Hawkins, G. 1983. "Prison Labor and Prison Industries." *Crime and Justice* 5: 85–127.

Henig, J. R. 1989. "Privatization in the United States: Theory and Practice." *Political Science Quarterly* 4: 649–670.

Hinton, E. 2016. *From the War on Poverty to the War on Crime*. Cambridge, MA: Harvard University Press.

Hirsch, B. T., and D. A. Macpherson. 2003. "Union Membership and Coverage Database from the Current Population Survey: Note." *Industrial and Labor Relations Review* 2: 349–354.

Human Rights Watch. 2018. *"Set Up to Fail": The Impact of Offender-Funded Private Probation on the Poor*. New York: Human Rights Watch.

Human Rights Watch. 2020. *US: New Report Shines Spotlight on Abuses and Growth in Immigrant Detention under Trump*. New York: Human Rights Watch.

Inman, B. R. 2012. "Comparing Public and Private Prisons: The Trade-offs of Privatization." In *Prison Privatization: The Many Facets of a Controversial Industry*, edited by B. E. Price and J. C. Morris. Santa Barbara, CA: ABC-CLIO.

In the Public Interest. 2013. *How Lockup Quotas and "Low-Crime Taxes" Guarantee Profits for Private Prison Corporations*. Washington, DC: In the Public Interest. https://www.inthepublicinterest.org/wp-content/uploads/Criminal-Lockup-Quota-Report.pdf.

Jacobs, J. B. 1980. "The Prisoners' Rights Movement and Its Impacts, 1960–80." *Crime and Justice* 2: 429–470.

Jayachandran, S. 2006. "The Jeffords Effect." *Journal of Law & Economics* 49, no. 2: 397–425.

Jenkins, J. 2017. "On the Inside: The Chaos of Arizona Prison Healthcare." KJZZ, December 18. https://kjzz.org/content/572976/inside-chaos-arizona-prison-hea lth-care#start.

Jones, T., and T. Newburn. 2005. "Comparative Criminal Justice Policy-making in the United States and the United Kingdom." *British Journal of Criminology* 4: 58–80.

Joyce, P. G., and D. R. Mullins. 1991. "The Changing Fiscal Structure of the State and Local Public Sector: The Impact of Tax and Expenditure Limitations." *Public Administration Review* 3: 240–253.

Justice, W. W. 1990. "The Origins of Ruiz v. Estelle." *Stanford Law Review* 43, no. 1: 1–12.

Kaeble, D., and L. Glaze. 2016. *Correctional Populations in the United States in 2015*. Washington, DC: Bureau of Justice Statistics. https://www.bjs.gov/content/pub/pdf/ cpus15.pdf.

Kay, S. L. 1987. "The Implications of Prison Privatization on the Conduct of Prisoner Litigation Under 42 U.S.C. Section 1983." *Vanderbilt Law Review* 40: 867–888.

Kim, Y., and B. E. Price. 2014. "Revisiting Prison Privatization: An Examination of the Magnitude of Prison Privatization." *Administration & Society* 3: 255–275.

King, B. G., and S. A. Soule. 2007. "Social Movements as Extra-Institutional Entrepreneurs: The Effect of Protests on Stock Price Returns." *Administrative Science Quarterly* 52, no. 3: 413–442.

King, M. T. 2012. "A History of Private Prisons." In *Prison Privatization: The Many Facets of a Controversial Industry*, edited by B. E. Price and J. C. Morris, 1:9–17. Santa Barbara, CA: ABC-CLIO.

Laffont, J.-J., and J. Tirole. 1991. "Privatization and Incentives." *Journal of Law, Economics, & Organization* 7: 84–105.

Lartey, J. 2020. "Think Private Prison Companies Are Going Away Under Biden? They Have Other Plans." The Marshall Project, November 17. https:// www.themarshallproject.org/2020/11/17/think-private-prison-compan ies-are-going-away-under-biden-they-have-other-plans.

Leander, A. 2010. "The Paradoxical Impunity of Private Military Companies: Authority and the Limits to Legal Accountability." *Security Dialogue* 41, no. 5: 467–490.

Lerman, A. E. 2019. *Good Enough for Government Work: The Public Reputation Crisis in America (And What We Can Do to Fix It)*. Chicago: University of Chicago Press.

Levitt, S. D. 1996. "The Effect of Prison Population Size on Crime Rates: Evidence from Prison Overcrowding Litigation." *Quarterly Journal of Economics* 111, no. 2: 319–351.

Lewis, N., and B. Lockwood. 2019. "Can You Hear Me Now?" The Marshall Project, December 19. https://www.themarshallproject.org/2019/12/19/can-you-hear-me-now.

Lilly, J. R., and P. Knepper. 1993. "The Corrections–Commercial Complex." *Crime & Delinquency* 39, no. 2: 150–166.

Linowes, D. F. 1988. *Privatization: Toward More Effective Government*. Washington, DC: USAID. http://pdf.usaid.gov/pdf_docs/PNABB472.pdf.

Losier, T. 2013. " '. . . For Strictly Religious Reason[s]': Cooper v. Pate and the Origins of the Prisoners' Rights Movement." *Souls* 15: 19–38.

Macfarlane, K. A. 2014. "The Danger of Nonrandom Case Assignment: How the Southern District of New York's 'Related Cases' Rule Shaped Stop-and-Frisk Rulings." *Michigan Journal of Race and Law* 19: 199–246.

Makarios, M. D., and J. Maahs. 2012. "Is Private Time Quality Time? A National Private–Public Comparison of Prison Quality." *Prison Journal* 92, no. 3: 336–357.

Management and Training Corporation. 2016. "Making an Impact in People's Lives Since 1981." http://www.mtctrains.com/wp-content/uploads/2017/05/1pager_General.pdf.

Mancini, M. J. 1978. "Race, Economics, and the Abandonment of Convict Leasing." *Journal of Negro History* 63, no. 4: 339–352.

Mancini, M. J. 1996. *One Dies, Get Another: Convict Leasing in the American South, 1866–1928*. Columbia: University of South Carolina Press.

Mayeux, S. 2018. "The Idea of the Criminal Justice System." *American Journal of Criminal Law* 45: 55–94.

McDonald, D., E. Fournier, M. Russell-Einhourn, and S. Crawford. 1998. *Private Prisons in the United States: An Assessment of Current Practice*. https://www.privateprisonnews.org/media/publications/Private%20Prisons%20in%20the%20US%20-%20An%20Assessment%20of%20Current%20Practice%2C%20Abt%20McDonald%2C%201998.pdf.

McDonald, D., and C. Patten. 2003. *Governments' Management of Private Prisons*. Cambridge, MA: Abt Associates. https://www.ncjrs.gov/pdffiles1/nij/grants/203968.pdf.

McDonald, D. C. 1994. "Public Imprisonment by Private Means: The Reemergence of Private Prisons and Jails in the United States, the United Kingdom, and Australia." *British Journal of Criminology* 34: 29–48.

Minow, M. 2004. "Outsourcing Power: How Privatizing Military Efforts Challenges Accountability, Professionalism, Democracy." *Boston College Law Review* 46, no. 5: 989–1026.

Mumford, M., D. W. Schanzenbach, and R. Nunn. 2016. *The Economics of Private Prisons*. Brookings Institution. https://www.brookings.edu/research/the-economics-of-private-prisons/.

Murakawa, N. 2014. *The First Civil Right: How Liberals Built Prison America*. New York: Oxford University Press.

Myers, M. A. 1988. "Social Background and the Sentencing Behavior of Judges." *Criminology* 26: 649–676.

Naff, K. C. 1991. "Labor–Management Relations and Privatization: A Federal Perspective." *Public Administration Review* 1: 23–30.

National Center for State Courts. 2009. *National Center for State Courts Interbranch Relations Survey*. Washington, DC: Princeton Survey Research Associates International.

Neff, J., and A. Santo. 2019. "Corporate Confession: Gangs Ran This Private Prison." The Marshall Project, June 26. https://www.themarshallproject.org/2019/06/26/corporate-confession-gangs-ran-this-private-prison.

Nellis, A. 2016. "The Color of Justice: Racial and Ethnic Disparity in State Prisons." The Sentencing Project, June 14. http://www.sentencingproject.org/publications/color-of-justice-racial-and-ethnic-disparity-in-state-prisons/.

Nicholson-Crotty, S. 2004. "The Politics and Administration of Privatization: Contracting Out for Corrections Management in the United States." *Policy Studies Journal* 1: 41–57.

Ostrom, B. J., R. A. Hanson, and F. L. Cheesman. 2003. "Congress, Courts and Corrections: An Empirical Perspective on the Prison Litigation Reform Act." *Notre Dame Law Review* 78, no. 5: 1525–1560.

Page, J. 2011. *The Toughest Beat*. New York: Oxford University Press.

Park, K., and J. Lartey. 2020. "2020: The Democrats on Criminal Justice." The Marshall Project, April 8. https://www.themarshallproject.org/2019/10/10/2020-the-democrats-on-criminal-justice.

Patashnik, E. M. 2014. *Reforms at Risk: What Happens After Major Policy Changes Are Enacted.* Princeton, NJ: Princeton University Press.

Pauly, M. 2020. "Private Prison Stocks Drop as the Reality of Biden's Win Sinks In." *Mother Jones,* November 9.

Payne, A. A. 1997. "Does Inter-Judge Disparity Really Matter? An Analysis of the Effects of Sentencing Reforms in Three Federal District Courts." *International Review of Law and Economics* 17, no. 3: 337–366.

Perkinson, R. 2010. *Texas Tough: The Rise of America's Prison Empire.* London: Picador Books.

Perrone, D., and T. C. Pratt. 2003. "Comparing the Quality of Confinement and Cost-Effectiveness of Public versus Private Prisons: What We Know, Why We Do not Know More, and Where to Go from Here." *Prison Journal* 83: 301–322.

Piehl, A. M., and M. Schlanger. 2004. "Determinants of Civil Rights Filings in Federal District Court by Jail and Prison Inmates." *Journal of Empirical Legal Studies* 1, no. 1: 79–109.

Poterba, J. 1994. "State Responses to Fiscal Crises: The Effects of Budgetary Institutions and Politics." *Journal of Political Economy* 4: 799–821.

Preiser v. Rodriguez, 411 U.S. 475 (1973).

Price, B. E., and N. M. Riccucci. 2005. "Exploring the Determinants of Decisions to Privatize State Prisons." *American Review of Public Administration* 3: 223–235.

"Private Industry Won't Solve Woes of State Prisons." *Santa Fe New Mexican,* August 3, 1987.

Pugh v. Locke, 406 F. Supp. 318 (M.D. Ala. 1976).

Quinlan, J. M., C. W. Thomas, and S. Gautreaux. 2004. "The Privatization of Correctional Facilities." In *Privatizing Governmental Functions,* edited by D. Ballati. New York: Law Journal Press.

Raher, S. 2010. "The Business of Punishing: Impediments to Accountability in the Private Corrections Industry." *Richmond Journal of Law and the Public Interest* 8: 209–249.

Ramirez, M. D. 2021. "Understanding Public Blame Attributions when Private Contractors Are Responsible for Civilian Casualties." *Policy Sciences* 54: 21–40.

Robbins, I. P., and M. B. Buser. 1977. "Punitive Conditions of Prison Confinement: An Analysis of Pugh v. Locke and Federal Court Supervision of State Penal Administration Under the Eighth Amendment." *Stanford Law Review* 29, no. 5: 893–930.

Roberts, B. E. 1990. "A Dead Senator Tells No Lies: Seniority and the Distribution of Federal Benefits." *American Journal of Political Science* 34, no. 1: 31–58.

Rosenberg, G. N. 2008. *The Hollow Hope: Can Courts Bring About Social Change?* Chicago: University of Chicago Press.

Ruffin v. Commonwealth, 62 Va. 790, 21 Gratt. 790 (1871).

Savas, E. 1991. "It's Time to Privatize." *Fordham Urban Law Journal* 3: 781–794.

Savas, E. 2000. *Privatization and Public–Private Partnerships.* New York: Chatham House Publishers.

Schanzenbach, M. 2005. "Racial and Sex Disparities in Prison Sentences: The Effect of District-Level Judicial Demographics." *Journal of Legal Studies* 34, no. 1: 57–92.

Schlanger, M. 1999. "Beyond the Hero Judge: Institutional Reform Litigation as Litigation." *Michigan Law Review* 97: 1994–2036.

Schlanger, M. 2003. "Inmate Litigation." *Harvard Law Review* 116, no. 6: 1555–1706.

Schlanger, M. 2006. "Civil Rights Injunctions over Time: A Case Study of Jail and Prison Court Orders." *New York University Law Review* 2: 550–630.

Schlanger, M. 2015. "Trends in Prisoner Litigation, as the PLRA Enters Adulthood." *UC Irvine Law Review* 5: 153–178.

Schlosser, E. 1998. "The Prison–Industrial Complex." *Atlantic Monthly* 282, no. 6: 51–77.

Schneider, A. 1999. "Public–Private Partnerships in the U.S. Prison System." *American Behavioral Scientist* 1: 192–208.

Schoenfeld, H. 2010. "Mass Incarceration and the Paradox of Prison Conditions Litigation." *Law & Society Review* 44, no. 3–4: 731–768.

Schoenfeld, H. 2016. "A Research Agenda on Reform." *Annals of the American Academy of Political and Social Science* 664, no. 1: 155–174.

Schoenfeld, H. 2018. *Building the Prison State: Race and the Politics of Mass Incarceration.* Chicago: University of Chicago Press.

Seiter, R. P., and K. R. Kadela. 2003. "Prisoner Reentry: What Works, What Does not, and What Is Promising." *Crime & Delinquency* 49: 360–388.

Sellers, M. P. 1993. *The History and Politics of Private Prisons: A Comparative Analysis.* Teaneck, NJ: Fairleigh Dickinson University Press.

Selman, D., and P. Leighton. 2010. *Punishment for Sale: Private Prisons, Big Business, and the Incarceration Binge.* Lanham, MD: Rowman & Littlefield Publishers.

Simon, J. 2007. *Governing Through Crime: How the War on Crime Transformed American Democracy and Created a Culture of Fear.* Studies in Crime and Public Policy. New York: Oxford University Press.

Simon, J. 2014. *Mass Incarceration on Trial: A Remarkable Court Decision and the Future of Prisons in America.* New York: New Press.

Smith, K. B. 2004. "The Politics of Punishment: Evaluating Political Explanations of Incarceration Rates." *Journal of Politics* 66, no. 3: 925–938.

"Some Towns Looking for Part of Prison Business." *Daily Sitka Sentinel*, February 19, 1997.

Sovey, A. J., and D. P. Green. 2011. "Instrumental Variables Estimation in Political Science: A Readers' Guide." *American Journal of Political Science* 55, no. 1: 188–200.

Spivak, A. L., and S. F. Sharp. 2008. "Inmate Recidivism as a Measure of Private Prison Performance." *Crime & Delinquency* 54, no. 3: 482–508.

State of Hawaii Auditor. 2010. *Management Audit of the Department of Public Safety's Contracting for Prison Beds and Services.* Honolulu: State of Hawaii Auditor. http://files. hawaii.gov/auditor/Reports/2010/10-10.pdf.

Stevens, B. J. 1984. "Comparing Public- and Private-Sector Productive Efficiency: An Analysis of Eight Activities." *National Productivity Review* 4: 395–407.

Stith, K., and S. Y. Koh. 1993. "The Politics of Sentencing Reform: The Legislative History of the Federal Sentencing Guidelines." *Wake Forest Law Review* 28, no. 2: 223–290.

"Stopping Inmates' Silly Lawsuits." *Wisconsin State Journal*, December 29, 1998.

Sturm, S. P. 1994. "Lawyers at the Prison Gates: Organizational Structure and Corrections Advocacy." *University of Michigan Journal of Law Reform* 27: 1.

Taggart, W. A. 1989. "Redefining the Power of the Federal Judiciary: The Impact of Court-Ordered Prison Reform on State Expenditures for Corrections." *Law & Society Review* 23, no. 2: 241–271.

Tartaglia, M. 2014. "Private Prisons, Private Records." *Boston University Law Review* 94: 1689–1744.

Thomas, J. 1988. *Prisoner Litigation: The Paradox of the Jailhouse Lawyer.* Lanham, MD: Rowman & Littlefield.

Thompson, C. 2014. "Everything You Ever Wanted to Know About Private Prisons . . . Is None of Your Damn Business." The Marshall Project, December 18. https://www.the marshallproject.org/2014/12/18/everything-you-ever-wanted-to-know-about-priv ate-prisons.

Thompson, H. A. 2016. *Blood in the Water: The Attica Prison Uprising of 1971 and Its Legacy*. New York: Vintage Books.

Thompson, L., and R. C. Elling. 2002. "Mapping Patterns of Support for Privatization in the Mass Public: The Case of Michigan." *Public Administration Review* 4: 338–348.

Tonry, M. 1995. *Malign Neglect: Race, Crime, and Punishment in America*. New York: Oxford University Press.

US Congress House Committee on the Judiciary, Subcommittee on Courts, C. L. and the Administration of Justice. 1986. *Privatization of Corrections*. Serial Number 40. Washington, DC: US Government Printing Office.

US Department of Justice. 2016. Review of the Federal Bureau of Prisons' Monitoring of Contract Prisons." Washington, DC: Office of the Inspector General. https://oig.justice. gov/reports/2016/e1606.pdf.

Useem, B., and J. A. Goldstone. 2002. "Forging Social Order and Its Breakdown: Riot and Reform in U.S. Prisons." *American Sociological Review* 67, no. 4: 499–525.

Vaughn, M. S. 1993. "Listening to the Experts: A National Study of Correctional Administrators' Responses to Prison Overcrowding." *Criminal Justice Review* 18: 12–25.

Venteicher, W. 2019. "CalPERS Pulls Millions of Dollars out of Immigrant Detention Companies." *Sacramento Bee*. October 21.

Volokh, A. 2013. "The Modest Effect of Minneci v. Pollard on Inmate Litigants." *Akron Law Review* 46, no. 2: 287–329.

Wackenhut Corporation. 1990. *Wackenhut Corporation Annual Report*. Palm Beach Gardens, FL: Wackenhut Corporation.

Wacquant, L. 2009. *Punishing the Poor: The Neoliberal Government of Social Insecurity*. Durham, NC: Duke University Press.

Weaver, V. M. 2007. "Frontlash: Race and the Development of Punitive Crime Policy." *Studies in American Political Development* 21, no. 2: 230–265.

Weaver, V. M., and A. E. Lerman. 2010. "Political Consequences of the Carceral State." *American Political Science Review* 104, no. 4: 817–833.

White, A. A. 2001. "Rule of Law and the Limits of Sovereignty: The Private Prison in Jurisprudential Perspective." *American Criminal Law Review* 38: 111–146.

Williams, T. 2018. "Inside a Private Prison: Blood, Suicide and Poorly Paid Guards." *New York Times*. April 3.

Worth Rises. 2020. *The Prison Industry: Mapping Private Sector Players*. New York: Worth Rises.

Yackle, L. W. 1989. *Reform and Regret: The Story of Federal Judicial Involvement in the Alabama Prison System*. New York: Oxford University Press.

Yates, S. Q. 2016. "Memorandum for the Acting Director of the Federal Bureau of Prisons." https://www.justice.gov/archives/opa/file/886311/download.

Index

Michigan, University of, Law School, 83
Microsoft, prison labor, 21
military contracts, 14, 65, 67
mind control devices, 61
minimum-security facilities, 25
mining operations, 20
Minnesota, 42, 84, 119
Mississippi, 2, 42
Missouri, 40
mixing/sharing correctional
   facilities, 42, 46
monitoring
   compliance with court orders, 7, 8, 18,
      26, 65, 68, 70, 73–75, 103, 104
   electronic monitoring within the
      "carceral state," 18
moral concerns, 18, 89. *See also* profit
   opportunities and motives
moral hazard problems, 7
Moshannon Valley Correctional Center, 104
Mother Jones magazine, 25
moving prisoners to other states, 26, 31,
   37, 41, 42, 98
MTC (Management and Training
   Corporation), 2, 10, 108, 109
Muhammad, Elijah, 53
municipal/local facilities, 23, 40, 42, 69,
   132, 137
murders and assaults, 67, 108, 133
Muslim prisoner, 53

NAACP (National Association for
   Advancement of Colored People),
   56, 60, 72
Nation of Islam (NOI), 53–55
National Center for State Courts Inter-
   Branch Relations Survey, 65
National Conference on State
   Legislatures, 87
National Institute on Money in State
   Politics, 30
National Prison Project, ACLU, 56, 60,
   72, 104
Nebraska, 40
Neighborhood Legal Services Association,
   104
neoliberalism, 2, 30, 145
Nevada, 9, 40

new construction. *See* construction of
   facilities
New Mexico, 40, 67, 80, 98
New York, 40, 42, 54–56, 114, 121
New York City Legal Aid Society, 56
newspaper vilification of private prisons, 137
NOI (Nation of Islam), 54, 55
North Dakota, 84, 119
North Lake Correctional Facility, 86, 151
Northeast Ohio Correctional Center, 24
Northern Trust Corporation, 114
Number of Private Facilities-State Only
   variable, 86, 87, 94, 100

Obama administration, 108–111
Office of Inspector General (OIG)
   report, 108
Ohio, 24, 67
oil and gas companies, 117
Olympic Motel, 1
Open Secrets research organization, 30
operating rules. *See* standards and rules
Ordinary Least Squares (OLS) model, 86,
   90, 95–97, 101–103, 120, 121, 141–152,
   154–159
other states, shipping prisoners to, 26, 31,
   41, 42
Other Theories, explained, 86
out-of-state facilities, moving prisoners to,
   26, 31, 37, 41, 42, 98
overcrowding, 10, 40, 62, 65, 69–71, 74, 97,
   98, 104, 105, 112, 126
   caps on prisoner population, 85, 119
   occupancy guarantees, 7, 8
   total bed capacity, 86
oversight and monitoring, 7, 8, 18, 26, 65,
   68, 70, 73–75, 103, 104

pardons, 21
parole, 11, 18, 58, 62
partial privatization, 19, 136, 137
participation, certificates of, 69
partisanship as driving privatization, 2, 78,
   86–87, 90, 130
partnerships, 133, 137
penitentiary system, 51
Pennsylvania, 104
Percent Overcrowded variable, 145

PERMCOs and PERMNOs, explained, 160
plantations, prisoner leasing to, 9
PLRA (Prison Litigation Reform Act), 64,
    65, 80
police funding, 12, 18
police officers' unions, 29, 31, 89
politics
    conservative ideology, 13, 19, 28, 31, 62
    criminal justice policy, bipartisan
        nature of, 89
    effect on private companies' stock
        performance, 108–111
    elections, 30, 83, 109, 111, 117
    gubernatorial politics, 13
    incentive to privatize, partisanship as, 2,
        78, 87, 90, 130
    neoliberalism, 2, 30, 145
    See also Democratic Party; Republican
        Party
prison guards. See guards and other staff
Prison Industry Enhancement Act of
    1979, 21
Prison Litigation Reform Act, 64, 65, 80
Prison Realty Trust, 141
prisoner transport, 3, 136
prisoner work. See convict labor and
    convict-leasing systems
prisoners' rights movement, 49–77
    early "hands-off" doctrine, 52, 55
    longitudinal effect, 57
    rehabilitative aspect of incarceration,
        51, 52
    unintended consequences of, 15, 16, 77,
        79, 106, 134
Private Design Capacity variable, 86–88,
    91, 94, 100, 151
private prison, defined, 23
Private Prison Information Act, 33
pro se/jailhouse lawyers, 55, 60, 61
probation, 3, 11, 18, 62, 136
profiling of prisoners, 25
profit opportunities and motives, 8, 10,
    18–48
    "cherry-picking" of prisoners, 24, 25
    complexity of profit opportunities
        within criminal justice system, 138
    cost-savings requirements in
        contracts, 24

divestiture from private prison
    companies, 133–136
dueling interests of profit and
    accountability, 16, 17
lack of information on, 19
policy changes, 133–136
in public as well as private prisons, 133
punitive policies, growth in, 11
    See also costs/cost-cutting
Proportion Inmates in Private Facilities
    variable, 86–88, 91, 94, 100, 151
Proportion Prior Prosecutor variable, 99, 100
prosecutors becoming judges, 99–101
public finance underwriters, 69
public housing, 83
public opinion, 5, 65, 66
public records laws, 33
public retirement funds, 114
public works, prisoner leasing for, 9, 10, 20
Pugh v. Locke (1976), 71–73

qualitative data, 139

race. See Black Americans
railroad construction, 20
rape, 13
Reagan, Ronald, 19
real estate investment trusts, 141
recidivism, 58, 63, 132
recreation time, 85
rehabilitation of prisoners, 51, 52, 58, 133
release/return to community, 58, 62, 63, 72
religious accommodation in prisons, 53,
    57, 85
Republican Party, 12, 19, 28, 30, 31, 58, 86,
    87, 89, 117, 129
    partisanship as driving privatization, 2,
        78, 86, 87, 90, 130
    Trump administration, 109, 111
residential (community corrections)
    facilities, 35, 47, 58, 76, 114, 127,
        135, 140
responsibility evasion. See accountability
    and responsibility
RFPs (requests for proposal), 9, 10, 24
rights revolution. See prisoners' rights
    movement
riots, 67

road construction, prisoner leasing for, 9, 10, 20
Ruffin v. Commonwealth (1871), 51
Ruiz v. Estelle (1980), 71–73
rules of operation. *See* standards and rules

Safe Streets Act of 1968, 12
salaries/compensation of employees, 24, 25, 29
sanitation, 104, 105
Santa Fe New Mexican newspaper, 98
sawmill operations, 20
Schlanger, Margo, 83
Securities and Exchange Commission (SEC) reports, 35, 79, 139–141
semi-privatization, 19, 136, 137
sentencing
  assignment of judges, 93
  increased punitive policies, 28, 29, 32
  indeterminate, 58
  lobbying by private companies for tougher criminal sanctions, 32
  mandatory minimums, 12, 58
separation of powers issues, 52
Sessions, Jeff, 109–111
sexual violence, 13, 72
shared correctional facilities, 42, 46
shareholders. *See* investors in private companies
signatures forced without appropriate legal counsel, 33
slavery
  Black Americans, historical impact, 20, 21, 51
  indentured servitude (*see* labor/leasing of prisoners)
solitary confinement, 85
Southern Center for Human Rights, 60
Southern Poverty Law Center, 60
Spear v. Waihee (1984), 105
special masters, appointment of, 73–75
staffing. *See* guards and other staff
standards and rules of operation
  coherency of, 15
  federal standards, 26
  implementation following court orders, 26, 57, 71–75, 85, 119, 120, 131
  operations manuals, 33

State Correctional Institution in Pittsburgh (SCIP), 104
statutes permitting privatization, 6
stock performance in reaction to political events
  Obama administration, 108–111
  Trump administration, 109, 111
  volatility of stock market, 116–120
stock performance in reaction to prisoner lawsuits, 16, 109, 116–120, 131
  caution, 125–128
  Center for Research in Security Prices data, 160–162
  individual investors, 114
  institutional investors, 113–115
  lag in investors' understanding of court orders, 124, 125
  "normal" stock returns, 118
  politics, effect of, 108–111, 114–120
  raw stock prices, 117
  volatility of stock market, 116–120
stockholders. *See* investors in private companies
substance abuse treatment, 58
successful lawsuits by prisoners, 62, 63, 67, 71–76, 85, 99–105, 107–128, 141, 154
  behavior of private companies following successful lawsuits, 125–128
  blockbuster cases, 83, 84, 103, 126
  collation of prisoners' claims, 104
  instrumental variables (IV) analysis, 160
  likelihood of privatization, 76
  Ordinary Least Squares (OLS) Models, 154–159
  responses by private companies, 107–128
  See also court orders against states
sugar plantations, 20
Suharto, H. Muhammad, 117
Sum Facilities, 121
Sum Large Cases, 142
Sum Lawsuits, 87, 95
Sum Lawsuits Terminated, 86, 93, 94, 145
Sum Small Cases, 142
sunshine laws, 27, 32

tax exempt municipal bonds, 69
taxpayer benefits, 70